W9-ANV-811

Poetic Traditions of the English Renaissance

Poetic Traditions of the English Renaissance

EDITED BY
Maynard Mack
AND
George deForest Lord

YALE UNIVERSITY PRESS
NEW HAVEN AND LONDON

Designed by Sally Harris
and set in Garamond type by
The Composing Room of Michigan, Inc.
Printed in the United States of America by
Vail-Ballou Press, Binghamton, New York.

Library of Congress Cataloging in Publication Data

Main entry under title:
Poetic traditions of the English Renaissance.
 Bibliography: p.
 Includes index.
  1. English poetry—Early modern, 1500–1700—
History and criticism—Addresses, essays, lectures.
2. Martz, Louis Lohr. I. Mack, Maynard, 1909–
II. Lord, George deForest, 1919–
PR533.P63   820'.9'003   82-1941
ISBN 0-300-02785-0   AACR2
10 9 8 7 6 5 4 3 2 1

Ἐὰν ᾖς φιλομαθής, ἔσει πολυμαθής

Contents

Preface

The essays brought together in this volume reflect many facets of Louis Martz's long concern with poetic traditions of the English Renaissance. The glory of that period shines through the quantity, variety, and matchless quality of its art, which Louis has explored with insight and virtuosity. All of us are indebted in so many ways to his example and achievements that to recite them would be tedious. These contributions will serve to celebrate his widespread and deep influence.

M. M.

G. deF. L.

JOHN GLADSON GARDNER

Northwest Passage

Epistle to a Professor of Seventeenth-Century English Literature
now in London Studying Paradise Lost

So here I am, back after thirty years,
Clothed and clean, taking my former place
Half-way down the table on your right
Prepared after a night of watching for
You to call my turn and lead the room
Into another listening as the smoke
Curls to the plastered sky from a dozen pipes.

This is my home, my dogs lie by my chair
As I read to you: and your other friends
Stretch out their legs and follow where I lead:
That pleasant land appearing in our eyes
That you, more fortunate than I, resolved
To build your life within (though you too knew
The pain and fright) with just three years of search.

I had not known that you would keep my chair
So long—and yet there is no aging here:
Trolleys give place to buses beyond the bottle
Glass of casement windows made for show
Not vision and we listened unaware
Of time out there on College Street descending
Though once you rose to switch on lights for reading.

Now it is your turn in the course to stand
Beside that altar, sprinkling the incense on
That little immemorial fire and come

Into the angel's presence who will strike
You for a season dumb until that time
There in the London streets your tongue is freed
To babble of green trees reserved for you.

We only seeming loungers wait until
That moment when you name again the Child
Within that wood so we may shout for turns
To get into your act and indicate
How we too see those features standing forth
From the surrounding city as its cars
Carry the tradesmen to suburban homes.

But shall you not need listeners in that fog?
Even in our time Pip and Sherlock found
Heart's Hall only when they took on board
Magwitch and Watson for their chase down Thames
And saw shapes clear that had been words till then
And there on the river's tide laid hold their man.

What do you seek there that you could not find
At home? Old books, the Ur-text of the Thing
Itself? Do their museums compound a group
Of readers that link meditation with
Those hooded eyes that woke each morning with
The day's vocation standing at bed's head?

It may be so. And yet I'd have you trust
Your own companionable Gabriel more
Than borrow spirits past. What you have been
To me I'd be to you as you take up
Your vigil in the ruined chapel: there
You may be told that you are all alone
And only feel the Bogie in your hair.

And is there perhaps Northwest a passage to
Paradise? Must Paradise return
To the muses' cases every night

And you go home to fish and chips again?
I whom you started on that voyage write
To tell you it is found, only return
To take your chair above that board

There where the smoke curls up, where laughter sings,
Where we have all we ever wanted—friends
At our side and poems in our hands
And there in the place below the salt, the foot,
That ghost of every Christmas present since
One's first bicycle or first island treasure,
The unseen Gabriel promised to us then!

Love from your unseen friend, my David,

                                        Jonathan

A. BARTLETT GIAMATTI

Hippolytus among the Exiles:
The Romance of Early Humanism

Exile was a central and abiding preoccupation of Petrarch's life, as it would be for that cultural epoch, the Renaissance, that he seems to initiate. In his fragmentary autobiographical piece, the *Letter to Posterity*, written near the end of his life, Petrarch says:

> My parents were worthy people, of Florentine origin, middling well-off, indeed, to confess the truth, on the edge of poverty. As they were expelled from their home city, I was born in exile in Arezzo, in the 1304th year of Christ's era, at dawn on a Monday, the 20th of July.[1]

Or again, in the prefatory epistle to his *Familiares,* or *Letters on Familiar Affairs* (that massive epic of the self in twenty-four books, comprising 350 letters written between 1325 and 1366), Petrarch tells his closest friend, the Belgian musician Lodewyck Heyliger, whom he called "Socrates," "Compare my wanderings with those of Ulysses; if we were equal in name and fame, it would be known that he traveled no longer or farther than I. He was a mature man when he left his hometown; though nothing lasts long at any age, everything runs very fast in old age. But I was conceived in exile and born in exile."[2] "Ego in exilio genitus, in exilio natus sum." "Ego ... sum"—his deepest concern: "genitus," "natus"—the life of man: and through it, balancing and ordering the terse, pregnant span of the sentence, and the life, the dominant chord—"in exilio," "in exilio." This is January 1350.

I wish to acknowledge the help of Mr. Stephen Cushman, without whose scholarship and diligence this essay could not have been prepared for publication. Rarely have I had such a congenial collaborator.

I

Petrarch's whole existence, his sense of himself, would be determined by his obsession with origin and exile; by his conviction that he was displaced and marginal. Unlike Ulysses, who wandered but came home, he, Petrarch, was never at home save in books. Only in books, and in words, did he feel at peace and at rest, only then not moving, as he says in the broken last sentence of his *Letter to Posterity,* "like a sick man, to be rid of distress by shifting position."[3] Petrarch's odyssey, his endless exile, depended—as his courtship of Laura depended—on not achieving what he said he desired. His sense of identity depended on being displaced, for only in perpetual exile could Petrarch gain the necessary perspective on himself truly to determine, or create, who he was. Only by being eccentric, could he center, or gather in and collect, his self.[4] Exile was essential to his view of himself, and it was, as we will see, essential in varying ways to his culture's view of itself. Both Petrarch, the individual, and humanism, the dominant elite culture of Europe for the next three centuries, had to assert exile, whether from secular antiquity and its ethics or Scriptural Paradise and its bliss, in order to refashion, or revive, or give rebirth to, or regain, what had once been purer, holier, or simply more whole.

For the Renaissance, integration of self and culture meant seeing Origin or the Original as distant and lost, so that one could imitate and emulate and thus make oneself a new copy or assert a genuine revision. A seminal tension in Renaissance culture, as in individuals like Petrarch, stems from the conviction that, on the one hand, origins so distant were also for the first time clearly perceived after the darkness, but that, on the other hand, what was recreated on that clear model would never be truly authentic. The Renaissance, for all its assertive, expansive, cultural imperialism—its revival of the past, its new texts, institutions and perceptions—would never completely shake the sense that what it made was removed, not quite worthy of the original; if not second-rate, at least secondhand, just as beneath the oft-repeated boast of each people that their land had been colonized by a hero from Troy—Italy by Aeneas, France by Francus, Portugal by the sons of Lusus, Britain by Brutus—there would be the constant awareness that Europe was founded by the losers, that the European people were colonists who, for all their glory, were exiled from the Homeland, that in the Westering of culture, much had been gained but something had also been lost.

But this is to anticipate the sixteenth century, the end of the Renaissance, and we are at the beginning, in the fourteenth, and my point is simple: exile is the precondition to identity.[5] So Petrarch, never truly at home, always refuses to return. In March 1315, Giovanni Boccaccio carries to Padua a letter to Petrarch from the governors of Florence promising restitution of his patrimony and a chair at their new university. Petrarch writes two letters of refusal—one, to Zanobi da Strada (*Ep. Met.* 3.8) in early 1351, saying he must bear his exile with equanimity; the other, to the Priors and People of Florence (*Fam.*, 11.5) of April 1351, thanking them but saying the Pope had called him to Avignon. He needed his exile. And we get even better insight into why he needed it in two letters (*Fam.* 2.3–4) to an otherwise unknown correspondent, Severo Appenninicola, letters of consolation for the other's fate. Since the letters are long, I shall summarize.

The letter to Appenninicola begins with an etymology of "exilium," a derivation not remarkable in itself but interesting because the etymologizing habit, the philological cast of mind, is, of course, typical of the whole humanist effort to uncover and reconstitute meaning by returning to origins. Whether through single words or whole bodies of texts, philology reaffirms the humanist's exile from true meaning as he struggles to overcome it. We shall return to this philological impulse. Then Petrarch goes on to say that exile resides in one's attitude when one is outside one's homeland; if one feels beaten, one is an exile; if one goes with dignity, one is a traveler. Exile consists of an attitude; the attitude is the fear of loss—loss of riches, fame, life. Exile is therefore an error in judgement, and anyone can make this error. But, and Petrarch adopts the perspective of his correspondent,

> if you firmly believe that whoever is absent from his native land is without question an exile, where are those who are not exiles? For what man, unless he were lazy and soft, has not departed from his

home and his native land several times either because he was desirous of seeing new things, or of learning, or of enlightening his mind, or was concerned about his health, or was desirous of increasing his wealth, or because of the demands or wars, or at the command of his state, of his master, of his parents?[6]

But Petrarch explains—and this is the heart of the matter—one can be forced into exile, but not forced to despair of returning:

> We have seen men sent into exile who, before they had arrived at their destination, were called back to the homeland because of the unbearable grief of the citizens. Others, after a long time, returned with so much honor. . . . No one was committed to such a horrible place that he was not allowed to raise his eyes; no one viewed the loss of his belongings as so deplorable that he was unable to hope for better things.[7]

Let us pause here, for it strikes me that there is more at issue than simply a moralizing injunction to be optimistic. Petrarch, in his meditation on exile, is saying not that one will, or even should, come home, but that the hope of returning is ever alive—indeed, that the hope of returning home is as strong as the force that sends one away in the first place. The man who would not go home always had to believe he could. Indeed, much as life—for Petrarch—was an endless marginality, so also was it sustained, precisely because of that marginality, by the belief that one might become central. Petrarch's need to believe he was displaced was the only way he could believe in genuine return, revival, recall.

This perspective is what we may call the Romance of Early Humanism—the secondary culture's deep belief that, despite distance and loss, it might become primary; the conviction that, through effort and emulation, the copy might become an original, the removed might restore the beginning, the exile might—through purposeful wandering—become a point, or recapture the point, of origin. Petrarch tells his friend to imitate the virtue of those ancients in exile, so that he may not despair that what has been done so often cannot be done again. And as he goes on, he seems to be saying: as we imitate the virtue of the ancients, we become virtuous; as we become virtuous, we are at home; we are at home because we are at one with the ancients, and they are our home. So he writes in 1359 to his beloved Socrates: "Homeland is for a man in any niche in the universe; only by impatience can he make himself believe [he is] in exile."[8]

He is groping for a definition; to call this a "theory" of exile is to make it sound too systematic, too abstract. He is working out, constantly, his attitudes toward exile, always fixing his intuitions in the balanced periods of his prose, his style both affirming his distance from the ancients and seeking, by imitation, to bridge that gulf. For it was finally the ancients, not Florence, or friends, or Tuscany, that Petrarch felt most exiled from, and because he expressed this perspective so powerfully, Renaissance culture, after him, would imitate him—both in his sense of exile and his efforts to return.

Petrarch's radical solitude stemmed from what we would call his sense of history. "He would have liked," says Peter Burke, "to have lived in Augustan Rome. For him, the period before the conversion of Constantine (the *aetas antiqua*) was an age of light; the *aetas nova*, the modern age which succeeded it, was an age of darkness. This was the reversal of the traditional Christian distinction."[9] Others, like Flavio Biondo, after him would speak of a "media aetas" between antiquity and the present; and still later others, like Vasari, would speak of the present as a "rebirth."[10] But the essential perspective on the ancients as distinct, distant, and the home we had left was established by Petrarch and his language of exile.

His efforts to find his true self in their selves is expressed in everything he wrote but never more clearly, or poignantly, than in the last ten letters of the last book, the twenty-fourth, of his *Familiares*—written between 1345 and 1360 to the great figures of Antiquity. These letters, two to Cicero, one each to Seneca, Varro, Quintilian, Livy, Pollio, and then, building to the summit of poets and receding in time, to Horace, Virgil and Homer, are meditations on his distance from them, his desire to be with them. They are exercises in exile: fruitless efforts to go home that at the same time allow Petrarch to create himself. We need only look at one of these letters, keeping in mind what exile means for Petrarch, to see where the course of Renaissance humanism would run for some time to come. This is the fifth letter in the series, to Quintilian.

Petrarch wrote to Quintilian on December 7, 1350, the very day when, passing through Florence on his way to Rome, he was given an incomplete manuscript of Quintilian's *Institutes* by a young scholar named Lapo di Castiglionchio. Deeply moved, Petrarch wrote a lovely letter, finally praising Quintilian himself for being a great man, but saying, "greater than you, your highest merit lay in your ability to ground and to mold great men."[11] Shape others as he may, however, it is Quintilian's own shape that concerns Petrarch most and that draws his attention in the opening lines: "Your book, called *Institutes of Oratory*, has come to my hands, but alas how mangled and mutilated. I recognize therein the hand of time—the destroyer of all things."[12] Then, after saying how he admires Quintilian, Petrarch returns to his figure again: "I saw the dismembered limbs of a beautiful body and admiration mingled with grief seized me."[13]

This language for the imcomplete book is crucial for what humanism would come to mean: the text is a beautiful body, a "corpus" whose limbs are scattered, a body mutilated and mangled. Petrarch uses the words *discerptus*, from *discerpere*, ("to mutilate") and *lacer,* meaning mangled, lacerated. The words have their own enormous resonances. *Discerptus* for instance, is the word Virgil uses in the *Fourth Georgic* (l. 522) to describe the mutilated Orpheus; *lacer* occurs in *Aeneid* 6.495 to describe how Deiphobus appeared to Aeneas in the underworld; and it is used again in *Aeneid* 9.491 to describe Euryalus, he who fell as a purple flower cut by the plow. Potent words, and images, for anyone steeped—as Petrarch was—in Virgil. But I would suggest that beneath the image of the book as mutilated body, beneath Deiphobus and Euryalus and even Orpheus, another Virgilian passage is buried so deep that Petrarch does not seem to know it, though others, imitating him, would almost instinctively bring it to the surface. This is *Aeneid* 7.765–73, describing the death of Hippolytus and his resurrection at the hands of Aesculapius:

For they tell how that Hippolytus, when he fell by a Stepmother's
craft,
and slaked his father's vengeance in blood,
ripped apart by terrified horses, came again to the starry firmament,
and heaven's upper air, recalled by the Healer's
herbs and the love of Diana. Then the Father
omnipotent, angry that any mortal should rise
from the nether shades to the light of life,
hurled with his thunder beneath the Stygian waves
the finder of such healing-craft, him Apollo-born.[14]

Virgil goes on to say that Hippolytus, now named Virbius, was
taken to live out his life in Italy, and that his son, also Virbius, now
rode another chariot to join the army of Turnus.[15] I suggest this
passage, in conjunction with Petrarch's images of Quintilian mutilated, for two reasons. Here again, as with Deiphobus, Euryalus,
and Orpheus, we are dealing with the story of a lacerated body, and
this time with the story of one who came back, one who was
"revocatus," says Virgil, as Petrarch's exiled ancients were sometimes recalled, "to the starry firmament and heaven's upper air."
Jove was angry that one should go from "the nether shades to the
light of life," but Hippolytus did it—then to find a home in Italy.
His healer was punished with exile to Hell, but the shredded Hippolytus came home again, whole.

I suggest that in the story of Hippolytus and Aesculapius we
have a version of what I have been calling the Romance of Early
Humanism—the sense that return or rebirth or restoration of origin
and original form is possible, a hope that not only sustained but
necessitated Petrarch's sense of exile. I suggest that in the mutilated
body of Hippolytus, mangled like those other Virgilian heroes but
older than all save Orpheus, Petrarch might see a figure for the
shapes of all those ancients, now known only in fragmentary texts,
in mangled corpora, whom he desired to see whole, and be with—if
not one of. And I suggest, lest you think I lack the courage of my
aberrations, that in Aesculapius, the healer who could not be cured,
the victim of his own powers, the scion of Apollo to whom the light

was denied, Petrarch might see figured the humanist's power to restore—texts, bodies, traditions—and also his inability to experience the integrity, the wholeness, thus wrought.[16] A humanist might see the endless dialectic of his own dilemma—always being exiled so that he might find himself, always bringing the curative balm of ancient ethics to his culture, yet himself shifting like a sick man in distress.

II

I cannot prove that the Virgilian story of Hippolytus and Aesculapius is the link that binds Petrarch's sense of his and his culture's exile to his desire to integrate himself by restoring the fragments of the past; but I do know that Humanists would use a language alluding to exile, fragmented bodies, and Aesculapius shortly after Petrarch, in ways that would have been impossible, I think, without him. And I know it is possible once again to affirm that if Petrarch did not create all the formulations humanism would use for itself, he did at least define the fundamental issues to which those formulations would respond—and those were the issues of how one saw oneself, particularly in relation to the ethical wisdom of the ancient world, and what that relationship meant for the modern individual and his society—indeed, what it meant to be modern at all.

At the end of his letter to Quintilian, Petrarch says: "I ardently desire to find you entire; and if you are anywhere in such condition, pray do not hide from me any longer. Vale."[17] This humanist-physician was forever barred from reassembling that Hippolytus, and thus barred from restoring his own wounds, from ending his exile from his homeland in ancient culture, because Lapo di Castiglionchio had given him only a partial manuscript. But Quintilian was "totus," "entire"; was—as Petrarch had prophetically hoped earlier in the letter—"resting intact in someone's library."[18] He was resting, to be precise, in his entire twelve-book body in the tower of the monastery at St. Gall, outside Constance. And there he

was found, and revived, in June or July of 1416, one afternoon, by
Poggio Bracciolini and two friends.

   With Poggio, the second phase of our inquiry, and the second
generation of Italian humanism, can be said to begin. Poggio
(1380–1459), native of Arezzo, student of Salutati, who had studied with Petrarch, served the papacy as apostolic secretary for fifty
years, would be chancellor of Florence at the end of his life, learned,
acerb, shrewd, was one of the great discoverers of lost manuscripts
in the Renaissance. Some of his greatest finds came when he was
attending the Council of Constance in 1416.[19] There he and his
friends made four sallies to search for pagan texts while the Church
was convulsed in disputes. On the second trip, in the tower of St.
Gall, Poggio found books 1–4 of the *Argonautica* of Valerius Flac-
cus, commentary on five orations of Cicero, and all of Quintilian.
Like America, Quintilian whole had been known to others since
Petrarch; but like Columbus, Poggio gets credit for the find because
he knew how to publicize the discovery. Poggio immediately wrote
his learned friend and fellow bibliophile, Niccolò de Niccolis in
Florence, and the letter circulated. On September 15, 1416, a
former and future chancellor of Florence, Leonardo Bruni, having
read of Poggio's finds, wrote him from Florence in ecstatic terms:

> Just as Camillus was called a second founder of Rome after Romulus,
> who established the city, while Camillus restored it after it was lost,
> so you will deservedly be called the second author of all the works
> which were once lost and now returned to us by your integrity and
> diligence.[20]

Here the references to being the "second founder," "second author,"
carry the pride and pleasure of rediscovery, and not—as they would
have earlier, and might later—a note of melancholy at being derivative of that which remained just beyond reach. Here, the pride and
confidence of early humanism asserts itself; and why not? The promise of a return to former glory, and indeed a surpassing new glory,
seemed at hand. Bruni then turns to specific concerns:

> For Quintilian, who used to be mangled and in pieces, will recover all
> his parts through you. I have seen the headings of the chapters; he is

whole, while we used to have only the middle section and that incomplete.[21]

And then he addresses Quintilian directly:

> Oh wondrous treasure! Oh unexpected joy! Shall I see you, Marcus Fabius, whole and undamaged, and how much will you mean to me now? For I loved you even when you were cruelly deprived of your mouth, of your mouth and both your hands, when you were "spoiled of your nose and shorten'd of your ears;" still I loved you for your grace.[22]

The language of mutilation and wholeness is reminiscent of the figures of Petrarch. Yet it derives more immediately from Poggio. For Poggio doubtless used to Niccolò de Niccolis the same language he uses on December 15, 1416 when he writes from Constance to Guarino da Verona. First he extols language to Guarino in classic humanist fashion as that which alone

> we use to express the power of our mind and which separates us from the other beings. And so we must be deeply grateful to the pioneers in the other liberal arts and especially those who by their concern and efforts have given us rules for speaking and a pattern of perfection. They have made it possible for us to excel other men in the ability in which all men excel beasts.[23]

This celebration of rhetoric and the power of speech as the formative energy in human affairs—what Petrarch had praised in his letter—leads naturally to the greatest rhetorician and trainer of Orators, Quintilian. He alone—even without Cicero—could have taught us all we needed to know of oratory. But among us Italians, says Poggio, "Quintilian was to be had only in such a mangled and mutilated state (the fault of the times, I think), that neither the figure nor the face of the man was to be distinguished in him."[24] So far, in the adjectives and the allusion to time, Poggio says immediately, "So far you have seen the man only thus,"[25] and cites *Aeneid* 6.495–97:

> his whole frame mangled
> His face cruelly torn, his face and either hand,
> His ears wrenched from despoiled brows, and
> His nostrils lopped by a shameful wound.[26]

This is the Virgilian passage about Deiphobus, one of those passages latent in Petrarch's use of the word "lacer." Thus, beneath the imagery of fragments—applied to Quintilian—we get an actual instance—in the Virgilian reminiscences—of the way humanists would handle and reintegrate fragments for their own purposes. We have humanist texts talking about reassembling Quintilian on one level, and the same texts fragmenting and reintegrating Virgil on another level—enacting what they talk about. Again, we see the process of aggression and accommodation towards antiquity that we saw in the notion of exile—a constant longing for origins that serves to allow the humanist the distance to make himself over into something like an original.

Poggio is the master of this method. After the illusion to Deiphobus mangled, he tells how he found the actual Quintilian text, now figured as a man in prison: he speaks of the squalor of his jail, the cruelty of his jailers, and describes Quintilian "with ragged beard, with hair matted with blood,"[27] this time alluding to *Aeneid* 2.277, where the figure of Hector appears to Aeneas in a dream before the sack of Troy.

All of these mangled Virgilian heroes, Hector, Deiphobus, Euryalus, tend to link the massive weight and authority of the *Aeneid* to the humanist enterprise, and tend to imply that the humanist enterprise, like the *Aeneid* itself, is a celebration of the way limbs, or a people dispersed, like the Trojans, may be brought home—home to Italy where, like Hippolytus, they live out their lives whole, healthy, and secure. The progress in the *Aeneid* of Aeneas himself, from exiled individual to restored institution, becomes another analogue to the Romance of Early Humanism, the hope for restoration: restoration of humanists to the ancients, of ancient texts to Italy.

Indeed, this much Poggio implies in a passage separating the two Virgilian allusions: we should congratulate ourselves, he says, that "he [Quintilian] has now been restored to us in his original appearance and grandeur, whole and in perfect condition."[28] The thrust is still to find origins, but where Petrarch wanted to go back across distance to Rome, Poggio will bring Romans across the distance to home:

For if Marcus Tullius rejoiced so fervently when Marcus Marcellus was returned from exile, and that at a time when Rome had a great many able and outstanding men like Marcellus both at home and abroad, what should men do now in learned circles, and especially men who devote themselves to oratory, when the one and only light of the Roman name, except for whom there was no one but Cicero and he likewise cut to pieces and scattered, has through our efforts been called back not only from exile but from almost complete destruction?[29]

For the exiled Petrarch, return was only a hope; for Poggio, the return of the exiled ancients is a fact. In this reversal of the basic image, we sense the massive confidence acquired by humanism in two generations: they now know the tide flows toward them; they know they are Aesculapiuses who can restore lacerated heroes, and bring them to Italian woods, and incorporate the potent ethical virtues of those heroes into their civic institutions. Poggio has no doubt the fragments are whole, their exile is over.

Nor does another of his correspondents—the last we will consider—have any doubts. Indeed, that writer—Francesco Barbaro, a distinguished Venetian humanist—congratulates Poggio on his discoveries in terms that bring to the full light of consciousness the images I have mentioned. Barbaro writes to Poggio on July 6, 1417—about a year after the whole series of discoveries. He praises the apostolic secretary for "releasing the monuments of literature from darkness into light"[30]—the imagery for history is beginning to acquire the Dark Ages / New Dawn antithesis so familiar, alas, to us. Then:

> You and your helpful companion Bartholomeus have endowed Tertullian with life, and M. Fabius Quintilian, Q. Asconius Pedianus, Lucretius, Silius Italicus, Marcellinus, Manilius the astronomer, Lucius Septimus, Valerius Flaccus; you have revived the grammarians Caprus, Eutychius, and Probus, and many others who had suffered a like fate, or you have brought them back to Latium from a long absence.[31]

The metaphors are of resuscitation and return from exile, and the result is that all the Gods are home.

Then Barbaro praises Poggio by reminding him of Lycurgus,

who "was the first to bring back whole to Greece from Asia the work of Homer scattered in bits in various places"[32] and this, by now, traditional language of fragments—following on the image of exile—leads Barbaro to the figure that I believe has been present by implication ever since Petrarch first looked upon the mutilated corpus of Quintilian:

> We accept Aesculapius as belonging among the gods because he called back Hippolytus, as well as others from the underworld, when he had reached the day fixed as the last of his life, and thus allowed him [Hippolytus] to die only some years later. If peoples, nations, and provinces have dedicated shrines to him, what might I think ought to be done for you, if that custom had not already been forgotten? You have revived so many illustrious men and such wise men, who were dead for eternity, through whose minds and teachings not only we but our descendants will be able to live well and honorably.[33]

Now not a single text but a series of texts, not one mangled Hippolytus but a Pantheon of Hippolyti, have been revived and brought home. (Barbaro adds to the myth the idea that Aesculapius refashioned not only Hippolytus but "others" as well, to accommodate his paradigm to the actual series of books discovered by Poggio.) And from this act of restoration, this successful ending to the Romance of Early Humanism, Barbaro draws the proper humanistic conclusion: this act is not only glorious in itself, but, and this has been implicit in the figure of Aesculapius all along, the curative and healing powers of the restored bodies of work will pass into the new culture, to subsequent generations. This view of ancient virtue, once whole, now infused, is the essence of the humanist vision. It was adumbrated in Petrarch's exile who imitated the virtue of the ancient heroes, and thus found a home; it rings out in a glorious period as Barbaro, finishing another figure of praise for Poggio—the commander who has liberated those beseiged—says that "there must be no doubt that culture and mental training which are adapted to a good and blessed life and fair speech, can bring no trifling advantages not only to private concerns but to cities, nations, and finally to all mankind."[34] The relation of private impulse and public good, the ethically educated regard of the one for the many, is the goal of the whole humanist movement, particularly as

interpreted by those whose native city was, as for Barbaro, the
Venetian or, as for Poggio, the Florentine Republic.

We have seen what in Petrarch was a sense of exile and a
perception of fragmentation become in Poggio and his friends a
triumphant image of return and conviction of integrity. There remains one last text for us to examine in the light of our Aesculapian
concerns, one last document where we can see early Renaissance
humanism asserting its self-consciousness. It falls, in time, between
Petrarch and Poggio. I refer to Giovanni Boccaccio's preface to his
massive *Genealogia Deorum Gentilium,* the *Genealogy of the Gods,*
which occupied the last thirty years of his life, from the 1340s
almost until his death, a year after his beloved Petrarch, in 1375.
The *Genealogia* is an encyclopedic work on myth—on the nature,
relationship and meaning of the Gods of the Gentiles—and it stands
like Janus at the threshold of the new era, looking back at ancient
treatises on the Gods, like Cicero's *De Natura Deorum,* and Hyginus'
Fables, and Fulgentius' sixth century *Mythologiae.* Boccaccio's huge
work gathers in all that flows from ancient treatises and writers,
from Church Father and Christian poet, and then circulates its lore
through later writers, providing in its medieval format an overwhelming image of Renaissance eclecticism. The book is, like its
author, learned, human, genial, devout; though also like its author
it is not a little redundant, too pleased with its own efforts at times,
too deferential before authorities like Petrarch and others. This
splendid monster, like something from the past, could never have
been produced in the past; not only is it written by a man who has
tried to learn Greek, who is aware of the latest discoveries of the
day, but it exudes, in its very syncretism, the spirit of revival and
restoration we have spoken of—although in its own particular way
as a massive prose epic, a work in many ways comparable to the
great epics and romances in verse produced by poets from Pulci to
Milton, save that the subject now is not the death lament of some
chivalric past or the loss of some paradisiacal beginning, but a song
of revival, a huge hymn to ancient culture, now restored.

We catch these notes in his preface, which Boccaccio writes in
the form of a dialogue between himself and one Donino, emissary of

Hugo IV, King of Cyprus and Jerusalem, who had commissioned the work but died in 1359, well before it was completed—though that seemed to bother neither Boccaccio nor his book, both author and subject swelling to fullness, rushing on, one king more or less a mere speck on the landscape. Can it be done? asks Boccaccio.

> Doubtless—if mountains offer easy passage and trackless deserts an open and travelled road; if rivers are fordable and seas tranquil; if Aeolus from his cave sends me in my course strong and favorable winds; or, better still, if a man might have on his feet the golden sandals of Argeiphontes, to fly whithersoever he pleased for the asking. Hardly then could he cover such extent of land and sea, though his life were never so long, and he did nothing else.[35]

Certainly it can be done, says Boccaccio—by an epic hero. But beneath the epic impulse, here presented obliquely, of the author-hero, is the view of Antiquity, its myths and writers, as a landscape, a vast, difficult terrain to be sure, but a landscape that is, with good fortune and great heart, chartable, knowable. For Boccaccio, Antiquity is not a distant shore—as it was for lonely, riven Petrarch; to the more robust, less tentative Boccaccio, it is new world, fabulous but now available. Boccaccio is coy; to handle those languages and people, it will take someone, he says, "strong enough, keen enough, and with good enough memory, first to observe what is relevant, then to understand it, retain it, note it down, and finally reduce it to order."[36] He suggests Petrarch. Donino sidesteps gracefully. When Boccacccio is at last persuaded, he addresses his patron, King Hugo. He will take his frail bark to sea: "I may trace every shore and traverse every mountain grove; I may, if need be, explore dyke and den afoot, descend even to hell, or, like another Daedalus, go winging to the ether."[37] The epic hero, and his labor, are launched: Aeneas, St. Paul, Dante—all are caught up in this epic opening. And what will our hero find? In his words immediately following, we hear the familiar humanist accent:

> Everywhere... I will find and gather, like fragments of a mighty wreck strewn on some vast shore, the relics of the Gentile gods. These relics, scattered through almost infinite volumes, shrunk with age,

half consumed, well-nigh a blank, I will bring into such single genealogical order as I can.[38]

There is the deep preoccupation with assembling the fragments of antiquity and recreating an original shape, the shape of "genealogical order," or "in unum genealogie corpus." Genealogy is humanist philology writ large, the probing for the past, the translation of significance to the present, on an epic scale. That will be Boccaccio's great voyage, a journey of discovery which is a labor of recovery.

Because now not a single lacerated text, nor a series of texts, but rather "almost infinite volumes" confront the humanist, his new book, made up of all these old books, will not "have a body [*corpus*] of perfect proportion. It will, alas, be maimed—not, I hope, in too many members—and for reasons aforesaid distorted, shrunken, and warped."[39] His book, finished, will look like all the fragments it has absorbed and reassembled, and so be a true copy of the originals. Boccaccio's implication is that his book will be an original of its own kind, in which the king will see "not only the art of the ancient poets, and the consanguinity and relations of the false gods, but certain natural truths, hidden with an art that will surprise you, together with deeds and moral civilization of the Ancients that are not a matter of every-day information."[40] As the plan of the book is new, so is the content. This is as close as early humanists ever come or could come to saying they were original.

Boccaccio concludes: do not be surprised at discrepancies, false-hoods, contradictions. They belong to the ancients, not to me. "Satis enim mihi erit comperta rescribere"—"I will be satisfied only to write down [write again] what is found." The humanist epic consists in "rescribere," in rewriting or reassembling in language, what the mind of man has found. Like Apollo's son, who would heal, but not judge, the scattered limbs, the early humanist revives the past; only later generations would criticize. Not now. So, before his final prayer to God for aid, Boccaccio summons in full the image for his effort, for the effort of all of them, that he has twice touched on:

I can quite realize this labor to which I am committed—this vast system of gentile gods and their progeny, torn limb from limb [*membratim discerptum*: Petrarch's word, Virgil's word] and scattered among the rough and desert places of antiquity and the thorns of hate, wasted away, sunk almost to ashes; and here am I setting forth to collect these fragments, hither and yon, and fit them together, like another Aesculapius restoring Hippolytus.[41]

From Petrarch gazing at the mutilated body of one old book, through the whole—entire—bodies of Poggio's books by way of the mighty corpus of Boccaccio's new book, made of the limbs of the old, the humanist has implicitly or overtly seen himself as physician-restorer. But the early humanist is also Hippolytus, for as he reassembles the past, he assembles himself. The humanist's supreme reaction is finally his own sense of himself; his crucial composition is the reconstitution of self out of what the past has given him—a sense of self that is defined by the activity of making up the self. The humanist is Aesculapius to his own Hippolytus, restorer of himself out of the fragments old and new of his own humanity.

We remember that in the seminal account of Hippolytus in book 7 of the *Aeneid,* Virgil tells us that when Hippolytus was made whole, he went to live "in silvis italis," and was called "Virbius," as his son was called after him. Virbius, of course, means "twice man"— man a second time, man as he is reborn.[42] Let that finally be our emblem for the early humanist—the man made again, whole, assembled out of the fragments of his own past; the humanist, one who, by a sense of loss that is also an effort of historical imagination, has made himself up, his essential self both derivative and integrated; his consciousness old but very new; a scholar confident that, in his Italian woods, his exile is finally over and the Rome he so longed for is again alive.

Notes

1. Honestibus parentibus, Florentinis origine, fortuna mediocri et (ut verum fatear) ad inopiam vergente, sed patria pulsis, Aretti in exilio natus

sum, anno huius aetatis ultimae, quae a Christo incipit, M. CCC. IIII. die
Lunae, ad auroram XIII. Cal. Augusti (*Francisci Petrarcae Epistolae De
Rebus Familiaribus Et Variae*, ed. Giuseppe Fracassetti [Florence: Typis
Felicis Le Monnier, 1859], 1:2; Morris Bishop, trans., *Letters From Pe-
trarch* [Bloomington: Indiana University Press, 1966], p. 7).

2. Ulysseos errores erroribus meis confer: profecto si nominis et rerum
claritas una foret, nec diutius erravit ille, nec latius. Ille patrios fines iam
senior excessit: cum nihil in ulla aetate longum sit, omnia sunt in senec-
tute brevissima. Ego in exilio genitus, in exilio natus sum (Fracassetti,
Epistolae, 1:18; Bishop, *Letters,* pp. 18–19).

3. Et licet filius sibi successerit prudentissimus et clarissimus vir, et
qui per paterna vestigia me carum semper atque honoratum habuit, ego
tamen illo amisso cum quo magis mihi praesertim de aetate convenerat,
redii rursus in Gallias, stare nescius, non tam desiderio visa millies re-
visendi, quam studio, more aegrorum, loci mutatione taediis consulendi.
(Fracassetti, *Epistolae,* 1:11; Bishop, *Letters,* p. 12).

4. See on this theme in later Renaissance epics, A. Bartlett Giamatti,
"Headlong Horses, Headless Horsemen: An Essay on the Chivalric Epics
of Pulci, Boiardo, and Ariosto," in *Italian Literature: Roots and Branches:
Essays in Honor of Thomas Goddard Bergin,* ed. Giose Rimanelli and Ken-
neth John Atchity (New Haven: Yale University Press, 1976), pp. 265–
307.

5. For a later version of this idea as located in lost children and found-
lings, see A. Bartlett Giamatti, "Primitivism and the Process of Civility
in Spenser's *Faerie Queene,*" in *First Images of America: The Impact of the New
World on the Old,* ed. Fredi Chiappelli, Michael J. B. Allen, and Robert L.
Benson (Berkeley: University of California Press, 1976), pp. 71–82.

6. Quod si tu mihi, quicumque a patria absunt exulare sine ulla dis-
tinctione firmaveris, rari ergo non exules. Quis enim hominum, nisi
desidiosus ac mollis, non aliquotiens aut visendi avidus, aut discendi
studio, aut illustrandi animi, aut curandi corporis, aut amplificandae rei
familiaris proposito, aut necessitate bellorum, aut suae reipublicae seu
domini seu parentis imperio, domum linquit et patriam? (Fracassetti,
Epistolae, 1:90; Francesco Petrarca, *Rerum familiarium libri I–VIII,* trans.
Aldo S. Bernardo [Albany: State University of New York Press, 1975], p.
71.)

7. Vidimus in exilium missos, priusquam ad destinatum pervenissent,
immenso patriae desiderio revocatus: alios vero, post tempus, tanto cum
honore ... reversos. ... Nemo unquam tam iniquo loco iacuit, ut non ei
liceret oculos attollere: nemo tam deploratum rerum suarum vidit exitum,
ut prohibetur sperare meliora (Fracassetti, *Epistolae,* 1:90–91; Bernardo,
Rerum familiarium, pp. 71–72).

8. Patriam viro omnem mundi angulum, exilium nusquam esse, nisi quod impatientia fecerit (Fracassetti, *Epistolae* (1863), 3:80; my translation).

9. *The Renaissance Sense of the Past* (London: Edward Arnold, 1969), p. 21.

10. For these matters the basic text is Wallace Ferguson, *The Renaissance in Historical Thought: Five Centuries of Interpretation* (Cambridge: Harvard University Press, 1948).

11. Magnus fateor vir fuisti, sed instituendis formandisque magnis viris maximus. (Fracassetti, *Epistolae*, 3:279; Mario Cosenza, trans., *Petrarch's Letters to Classical Authors* [Chicago: University of Chicago Press, 1910], p. 88. Where I have used Cosenza's translation, I have somewhat modernized his diction.)

12. Oratoriarum institutionum liber heu! discerptus et lacer venit ad manus meas. Agnovi aetatem vastatricem omnium (Fracassetti, *Epistolae*, 3:278; Cosenza, *Petrarch's Letters,* p. 84).

13. Vidi formosi corporis artus effusos: admiratio animum dolorque concussit (Fracassetti, *Epistolae*, 3:278; Cosenza, *Petrarch's Letters*, pp. 84–85).

14. namque ferunt fama Hyppolytum, postquam arte novercae
    occiderit patriasque explerit sanguine poenas
    turbatis distractus equis, ad sidera rursus
    aetheria et superas caeli venisse sub auras,
    Paeoniis revocatum herbis et amore Dianae.
    tum pater omnipotens, aliquem indignatus ab umbris
    mortalem infernis ad lumina surgere vitae,
    ipse repertorem medicinae talis et artis
    fulmine Phoebigenam Stygias detrusit ad undas.

(Text and translation from *Virgil*, Loeb Classical Library, ed. H. R. Fairclough, 2 vols., rev. ed. [Cambridge: Harvard University Press, 1969, 1974]. Although I have used Fairclough's translation, I have modernized his diction and arranged the prose in verse form.)

15. On Virbius, particularly in Dante, see Marguerite Mills Chiarenza, "Hippolytus' Exile: *Paradiso* XVII, vv. 46–48," *Dante Studies* 84 (1966), 65–68.

16. On the tradition of the healer in the Christian middle ages, see Rudolph Arbesmann, "The Concept of 'Christus Medicus' in St. Augustine," *Traditio* 10 (1954), 1–28.

17. Opto te incolumem videre, et sicubi totus es, oro ne diutius me lateas. Vale (Fracassetti, *Epistolae,* 3:280; Cosenza, *Petrarch's Letters,* p. 89).

18. Et fortasse nunc apud aliquem totus es (Fracassetti, *Epistolae,* 3:278; Cosenza, *Petrarch's Letters,* p. 85).

19. Remigio Sabbadini, *Le Scoperte dei codici latini e greci ne' secoli, XIV e XV,* rev. and ed. Eugenio Garin (Florence: Sansoni, 1967), 1:78. For an older account, see J. E. Sandys, *A History of Classical Scholarship* (Cambridge: Cambridge University Press, 1908), 2:27. For further bibliography on Poggio's four expeditions, see the excellent account of Rudolf Pfeiffer, *History of Classical Scholarship from 1300 to 1850* (Oxford: Oxford University Press, Clarendon Press, 1976), pp. 31–34.

20. Vtque Camillus secundus a romulo conditor dictus est: qui ille statuit urbem. hic amissam restituit. Sic tu omnium quae iam amissa: tua virtute ac diligentia nobis restituta fuerint secundus auctor: merito nuncupabere. (*Epistolarum familiarium libri VIII,* ed. Antonio Moreto and Girolamo Squarciafico [Venice: Damianus de Gorgonzola and Petrus de Quarengis, 1495], bk. 4, ltr. 5, n.p.; Phyllis Gordan, trans., *Two Renaissance Book Hunters* [New York: Columbia University Press, 1974], p. 191. I cite the Latin text of 1495 with all abbreviations expanded).

21. Quintilianus enim prius lacer: atque discerptus concta membra sua per te recuperabit. Vidi enim capita librorum Totus est: cum uix nobis media pars & ea ipsa lacera superesset (Moreto and Squarciafico, *Epistolarum,* n. p.; Gordan, *Book Hunters,* p. 192).

22. O lucrum ingens. O insperatum gaudium. Ego te o Marce Fabi totum integrumque aspiciam. Et quanti tu mihi nunc eris: quem ego quamuis lacerum crudeliter ora: Ora manusque ambas: populataque tempora raptis Auribus: & truncas inhonesto uulnere nares. Tamen propter decorem tuum in deliciis habebam (Moreto and Squarciafico, *Epistolarum,* n. p.; Gordan, *Book Hunters,* p. 192).

23. Nos utentes ad exprimendam animi virtutem, ab reliquis animantibus segregamur. Permagna igitur habenda est gratia tum reliquarum liberalium artium inventoribus, tum vel praecipue iis, qui dicendi praecepta, et normam quandam perfecte loquendi suo studio, et diligentia nobis tradiderunt. Effecerunt enim, ut qua in re homines caeteris animantibus maxime praestant, nos ipsos etiam homines antecelleremus (*Poggii Epistolae,* ed. Thomas de Tonellis [Florence: Typis L. Marchini, 1832], bk. 1, ltr. 5, vol. 1, p. 26; reprinted in *Poggii Opera Omnia,* ed. Riccardo Fubini [Turin: Bottega d'Erasmo, 1964], vol. 3; Gordan, *Book Hunters,* p. 193).

24. Is vero apud nos antea, Italos dico, ita laceratus erat, ita circumcisus, culpa, ut opinor, temporum, ut nulla forma, nullus habitus hominis in eo recognosceretur (de Tonellis, *Epistolae,* 1:27; Consenza, *Petrarch's Letters,* p. 92).

25. Tute hominem vidisti hactenus (de Tonellis, *Epistolae*, 1:27; Gordan, *Book Hunters*, p. 194).

26. Atque hic Priamiden laniatum corpore toto
Deiphobum vidit, lacerum crudeliter ora,
ora manusque ambas, populataque tempora raptis
auribus et truncas inhonesto volnere naris.
Fairclough, *Virgil*.

27. squalentem barbam et concretos sanguine crinis
Fairclough, *Virgil*.

28. Cum sit in pristinum habitum et dignitatem, in antiquam formam, atque integram valetudinem ... restitutus (de Tonellis, *Epistolae*, 1:27; Gordan, *Book Hunters*, p. 194).

29. Nam si Marcus Tullius magnum praesefert gaudium pro Marco Marcello restituto ab exilio, et eo quidem tempore, quo Romae plures erant Marcelli similes, domi, forisque egregii, ac praestantes viri, quid nunc agere docti homines debent, et praesertim studiosi eloquentiae, cum singulare, et unicum lumen Romani nominis, quo extincto nihil praeter Ciceronem supererat, et eum modo simili lacerum, ac dispersum, non tantum ab exilio, sed ab ipso paene interitu revocaverimus? (de Tonellis, *Epistolae*, 1:27–28; Gordan, *Book Hunters*, p. 194.)

30. Ut monumenta litterarum e tenebris in lucem erueres (*Francisci Barbari et aliorum ad ipsum Epistolae*, ed. A. M. Quirini [Brescia: Joannes-Maria Rizzardi, 1743], p. 2; Gordan, *Book Hunters*, p. 196).

31. Tu Tertullianum, tu M. Fabium Quintilianum, tu Q. Asconium Pedianum, tu Lucretium, Silium Italicum, Marcellinum, tu Manilium Astronomum, Lucium Septimium, Valerium Flaccum, tu Caprum, Eutychium, Probum Grammaticos, tu complures alios, Bartholomaeo collega tuo adjutore, vel fato functos vita donastis, vel longo, ut ajunt, postliminio in Latium reduxistis (Quirini, *Epistolae*, p. 2; Gordan, *Book Hunters*, pp. 196–97).

32. Cum primus Homerum variis in locis per frustra dispersum ... ex Asia totum Graeciam reportasset (Quirini, *Epistolae*, p. 2; Gordan, *Book Hunters*, p. 197).

33. Aesculapium inter Deos relatum accepimus, propterea quod cum alios nonnullos, tum Hippolytum supremum vitae diem functum, aliquot tamen post annos moriturum, ab inferis revocavit. Cui si populi, nationes, provinciae sacras aedes dicaverunt, quid vobis, nisi haec consuetudo jampridem obsolevisset, faciendum putarem? qui tot illustres, ac sapientissimos viros mortuos in perpetuum resuscitatis, quorum ingeniis, ac institutis non solum nos, sed etiam posteri bene dicere & honeste vivere poterunt (Quirini, *Epistolae*, pp. 2–3; Gordan, *Book Hunters*, p. 197).

34. Sic humanitatem, & disciplinam, quae ad bene beateque vivendum, & ornate dicendum accommodatae sunt, non modo privatis rationibus, sed urbibus, nationibus, universis denique hominibus non mediocres utilitates afferre posse dubitandum non est (Quirini, *Epistolae,* p. 3; Gordan, *Book Hunters,* p. 198).

35. Equidem si prestent montes faciles transitus: & solitudines inuie apertum notumque iter. Si flumina uada: & maria tranquillas undas: ac transfretanti emittat ab antro Aeolus uentos tam ualidos quam secundos: & quod maius est: sint Argiphontis talaria aurea uolucri cuicumque homini alligata pedibus: & pro uotis quocumque libuerit euolet: uix tam longos terrarum marisque tractus. etiam si illi prestetur permaxima seculorum annositas ne dum aliud agat: solum poterit peragrasse (*Genealogia Deorum Gentilium* [Venice: Wendelin von Speyer, 1472], n. p.; Charles Osgood, trans., *Boccaccio on Poetry,* 2nd ed. [New York: Bobbs-Merrill, 1956], pp. 5–6. I cite the Latin text of 1472 with abbreviations expanded).

36. Tam solide: tam perspicax ingenium: tamque tenax memoria: ut omnia queat uidere apposita: & intelligere uisa: & intellecta seruare: & demum calamo etiam exarare: & in opus collecta deducere. (*Genealogia,* n. p.; Osgood, *Boccaccio,* p. 6).

37. Si omnia legero littora & montuosa etiam nemora: scrobes & antra: si opus sit peragrauero pedibus: ad inferos usque descendere & Dedalus alter factus: ad aethera transuolauero undique (*Genealogia,* n. p.; Osgood, *Boccaccio,* p. 10).

38. Non aliter quam si per uastum litus ingentis naufragii fragmenta colligerem: sparsas per infinita poene uolumina deorum gentilium reliquas colligam: quas comperiam: & collectas euo diminutas atque semessas & fere attritas in unum genealogie corpus: quo potero ordine... redigam (*Genealogia,* n. p; Osgood, *Boccaccio,* pp. 10–11).

39. Corpus huiusmodi habere perfectum. multum quippe: & utinam non membrorum plurium & fortasse distortum seu contractum gibbosumque habendum est. Iam rationibus premonstratis (*Genealogia,* n. p.; Osgood, *Boccaccio,* p. 11).

40. Preter artificium fingentium poetarum & futilium deorum consanguinitates & affinitates explicitas: naturalia quedam uidebis tanto occultata misterio ut mireris: sic & procerum gesta moresque non per omne trivium euagantia (*Genealogia,* n. p.; Osgood, *Boccaccio,* p. 12).

41. Satis aduertere possum quid mihi faciendum sit: qui inter fragosa uetustatis aspreta & aculeos odiorum membratim discerptum attritum & in cineres fere redactum ingens olim corpus deorum procerumque gen-

tilium nunc huc nunc illuc collecturus: & quasi esculapius alter ad instar hippolyti consolidaturus sum (*Genealogia*, n. p.; Osgood, *Boccaccio*, p. 13).

42. See Chiarenza, "Hippolytus' Exile," pp. 65–66.

HARRY BERGER, JR.

The Aging Boy: Paradise and Parricide in Spenser's *Shepheardes Calender*

> *They fed him up with Hopes and Air*
> *Which soon digested to Despair.*
>
> —*Marvell, "The Unfortunate Lover"*

When in *December* Colin Clout nostalgically reviews the activities of his lost innocence, he sees them deceptively mantled by the soft Arcadian tradition which promoted the illusion that the paradise of youth is unending: "What wreaked I of wintrye ages waste. / Tho deemed I, my spring would ever laste" (ll. 29–30). This speaks to the couplet that occupies the corresponding place in *Januarye:* "And yet alas, but now my spring begonne, / And yet alas, yt is already donne" (ll. 29–30). The hyperbole of instant senescence serves as a measure of the folly of that illusory expectation and expresses the bitter state of mind which is its dialectical consequence. Colin is justly notorious for having passed from youth to old age in the space of Spenser's twelve *Calender* months. It is a comic instance of the pastoral conversion of great things to small. As I remarked in an earlier essay on *The Shepheardes Calender,* such rapid aging suggests that he is not very durable: to pass a lifetime in a year is to treat a year as if it were a lifetime; within the little world, the restricted possibilities, and the idyllic conditioning characteristic of the pastoral milieu, molehills are mountains.[1] This gives *Age* (and of course *Youth* as well) a very particular symbolic range in the *Calender,* and my thesis in the present essay is that Age can only be understood as a function of what I shall define as the "paradise principle," an analogue if not a source of the more familiar pleasure principle.

We often encounter in both *The Faerie Queene* and the minor poems figures who display various aspects of Spenser's psychology of the have-not. Some examples are Clarion's foe Aragnoll, Mother Hubberd's Fox and Ape, the tearful Muses, Alcyon (the diminished Halcyon of *Daphnaida*), Malbecco, Busirane, Ate, Slander, Radegund, Envy, Detraction, the Blatant Beast, Mutabilitie, and the speaker in several poems, including Book 5 and *The Mutabilitie Cantos*. The condition of the have-not is depicted as a self-willed submission to Tantalean bitterness and pain in response to loss, deprivation, and the inability to appease the "infinite desyre" of eros. Some prospect or hope of paradisal bliss arouses a longing for quick and complete possession which is marked as self-defeating in its hybristic excess, a premature and unrealistic compulsion to assimilate (and so to destroy) the other. This longing for what is unattainably beyond and for what has been irretrievably lost furrows the have-not's spirit with parallel competing impulses—to recreate, worship, replace, disparage, oppress, repress, violate, devour, and destroy the loved and hated other.

I propose to show that something of this spirit infiltrates the condition symbolically specified as Age in the *Calender* and that Spenser locates the condition not merely—not even primarily—in his pastoral speakers, but in the tradition of received opinion that shapes their culture, values, norms, and expectations. I shall argue that Age and Youth are two versions or phases of the condition and that since the elders bemoan their lost youth and try to project it into the next generation, youthful and aged speakers share the same values in spite of their apparent antipathy. Both love of youthful pleasures and bitterness at their loss are sedimented into the tradition, which is handed down from one generation to the next in a cyclic pattern dominated by the paradise principle. Finally, I shall suggest that the *Calender*, by its critique of the tradition it creates as its predecessor, presents itself as breaking the pattern. Spenser uses the resources of the tradition—its languages, motifs, and iconography—in an ironic and ambivalent manner both to express his affinity for it and its continuing hold on his imagination, and to free himself from its limits by a deconstructive literary act. The poem is thus about its own genesis from its peculiar poetic Elysium. Because space will not permit an extended demonstration of these points, I shall devote the major part of my discussion to the *Februarie* and *November* eclogues.

The basic premises of my argument, then, are (1) that the paradise principle as the source both of the have-not response and of its futile attempts to restore and return to the lost paradise is the organizing motif of the *Calender,* and (2) that the paradise principle so conceived is the organizing motif of the literary tradition Spenser imitates, sums up, and deconstructs. As for the paradise principle itself, what I wrote in my earlier essay still seems valid to me, and I hope I may be forgiven for recapitulating it in the following excerpts:

> The fundamental object of . . . criticism is the longing for paradise as the psychological basis of the pastoral retreat from life. This longing may be inflected toward wish-fulfilling fantasy or toward bitter rejection of the world that falls short of such fantasy. These are, in fact, mutually intensifying impulses which often wear moral disguises: the first envisages a perfect world of green or gold; the second paints the actual world pure black. [p. 14]

> The eclogues reveal two essential relations to that ideal [of life as paradise], the recreative and the plaintive. The first is exemplified by those speakers who have found paradise or are in it and who see no reason for leaving it. . . . The second or plaintive relation to paradise is exemplified by those speakers who have lost it, either through thwarted love or through experience of the actual world and its evils. [pp. 142–143]

> The virtues on both sides are usually outweighed by the weaknesses, for the speakers in the second group also have their hearts in Paradise. They are differentiated from the first group primarily because they look back in desire toward a condition the other speakers do not feel they have lost. The longing for paradise is expressed in disappointed as well as unrealistic expectations. The assertion of ignorance, frustration, irreversible decline, general corruption, and any other pains or evils, as the normal way of life, is traced by Spenser to too fixed an attachment to an unattainable state—an attachment in which the

idyllic (what could be) is set up as a model of the ideal (what should
be) or the actual (what is). [p. 143]

By calling this attachment a "paradise *principle*" I mean to suggest
its motivating character as the shaping cause of what appears as a
structure in synchronic perspective and as a process or sequence in
diachronic perspective. The structure is a polarity of recreative and
plaintive attitudes that may in any instance take the disjunctive
form of a conflict or the conjunctive form of ambivalence. The
sequence may be variously viewed as an obsessively repeated alterna-
tion between paradisal expectations and bitterness, or as a "fall"
from the first to the second followed by an effort to return. Both
views, but especially the first, are dramatized in the *Februarie* eclogue.

Patrick Cullen argues that the other shepherds are "comic foils"
to Colin, representing the one-sided and limited but still healthy
values of each of the two perspectives.[2] For example, the February
debate between young Cuddie and old Thenot "is not unnatural; it
is not only expected, it is also necessary and desirable." The two
positions, "neither sufficient unto itself," complement each other to
provide "the balance-in-opposition of the natural year" (p. 41). In
this conflict of limited contraries Cuddie "identifies winter with
parental discipline, with age's dampening of youth's desire," and
his aged opponent, Thenot, "identifies spring with carelessness, the
lack of discipline of youth. The debate over winter and spring is
thus symbolic of the psychological power struggle between youth
and age" (p. 34). Both are partly right, partly wrong, and each,
being incomplete, needs the other. Thenot's emphasis on restraint
and self-control is good practical wisdom, but there is "bias" in his

> contention that old age is "the lusty prime" man should live his life
> for, bias in his unwillingness or inability to see that spring and
> procreative love are as much the function of youth and life as restraint
> is the function of age. . . . There is an obvious aphoristic truth in the
> aged Thenot's contention that "All that is lent to love, wyll be lost,"
> but there is no less wisdom in Cuddie's instinctive knowledge of
> the function and value of spring and youth, fertility and procre-
> ation. . . . The ideal here is a balance, lest age become sterility and
> youth be vainly spent. [p. 38]

Perhaps because he unaccountably finds "obvious aphoristic truth" in Thenot's "contention" Cullen misses its value as an index to the source of the old man's bias, namely, his membership in the devil's party of youth. Cuddie taunts Thenot with his remark that "such an one" as Phyllis "would make thee younge againe," and it is to this that Thenot replies, "Thou are a fon, of thy love to boste / All that is lent to love, wyll be lost." Behind the aphorism is a direct response: "I'll never be young again, and you won't be young for very long." Since Cuddie's boast had been reasonably modest— "Phyllis is myne for many *dayes*," not months or years—Thenot's emphatic answer smacks more of "bias" than of truth. The bias had already been flagged in his earlier statement affirming the philosophy of waste: the common course of the world—and so, presumably, of the life cycle—is "From good to badd, and from badde to worse, / From worse unto that is worst of all," after which it returns not to its "former spring" but ironically to "his former fall"; death precedes another fall and long decline from paradise. The way Thenot sees it, he has "*worne out* thrise threttie yeares," only "*some* in much joy," but "*many* in many teares." Do joys precede tears in life as they do in this line? Do the many sad years follow *because* the joys lasted too short a time?

Thenot's attachment to the philosophy of waste, and his stoic counsel, seem intimately associated with his attachment to the joys of youth, his bitterness at their early, perhaps unexpected loss. We do not seriously question Cuddie's insight that envy and the loss of virility make Thenot a killjoy:

> Ah foolish old man, I scorne thy skill,
> That wouldest me, my springing youngth to spil.
> . . . .
> Now thy selfe hast lost both lopp and topp,
> Als my budding braunch thou wouldest cropp:
> But were thy yeares greene, as now bene myne,
> To other delights they would encline.
>
> {ll. 51–60}

"*Other* delights" is interesting because it implies that railing at Cuddie's youth affords "rusty elde" the only pleasure of which it is now capable, the only way in which Thenot can keep in touch with

what he has lost. To Cuddie's disparaging puns he responds in
kind—"thou kenst little good, / So vainely tadvaunce thy *headlesse
hood*"— and with equal rhetorical verve:

> For Youngth is a bubble blown up with breath,
> Whose witt is weakenesse, whose wage is death,
> Whose way is wildernesse, whose ynne Penaunce,
> And stoopegallaunt Age the hoste of Greevaunce.
>   [ll. 85–90]

After these lines the tone of the debate temporarily mellows as
Cuddie agrees to hear a tale from Thenot's youth, and agrees also on
the "well thewed" and "wise" quality of the tales devised by "that
good old man," Tityrus. It becomes clear that keeping in touch with
youth (or age) is as important as putting it down, that putting it
down is a way to stay in touch.

Thenot's position, as revealed in the above lines and in his other
comments, betrays the crosscutting pressures of two different sentiments: youth is heedless and throws its life away on trifles; youth
is foolish to cling to joys it must lose. The second sentiment implies
that the joys are more than mere trifles. His response is exacerbated
by Cuddie's challenge to his failing powers:

> And as the lowring Wether lookes downe,
> So semest thou like good fryday to frowne.
> But my flowring youth is foe to frost,
> My shippe unwont in stormes to be tost.
>   [ll. 29–32]

For youth the cycle swings upward from fall to prime, from "lowring" to "flowring," and the old man's pessimism can be dismissed
as the natural expression of those in the older generation looking
with envy at what they have lost. To the annual and life cycles
Cuddie's arguments add a third context: the passage from winter to
spring figures the passing of the old generation and the advent of
the new; Thenot's "lowring" is symptomatic of his loss of power, it
presages the rising of the new "Lords of the yeare," and Cuddie can
therefore endure—indeed, enjoy—Thenot's storms more easily than
those of winter. But it is the coupling of the annual with the
generational contexts that gives the seasonal model its power to

deceive the young as Colin was deceived: "What wreaked I of wintrye ages waste, / Tho deemed I, my spring would ever laste."

Thenot speaks to this deception with more animus than it
would seem to call for in a passage which betrays the divergent
pressures of his two arguments:

> The soveraigne of seas he blames in vaine,
> That once seabeate, will to sea againe.
> So loytring live you little heardgroomes,
> Keeping your beastes in the budded broomes:
> And when the shining sunne laugheth once,
> You deemen, the Spring is come attonce.
> Tho gynne you, fond flyes, the cold to scorne,
> And crowing in pypes made of greene corne,
> You thinken to be Lords of the yeare.
> But eft, when ye count you freed from feare,
> Comes the breme winter with chamfred browes,
> Full of wrinckles and frostie furrowes:
> Drerily shooting his stormy darte,
> Which cruddles the blood, and pricks the harte.
> Then is your carelesse corage accoied,
> Your carefull heards with cold bene annoied.
> Then paye you the price of your surquedrie,
> With weeping, and wayling, and misery.
>   [ll. 33–50]

The illogicality of the opening couplet is something Thenot seems
willing to risk for the pleasure of countering Cuddie's "My shippe
unwont in stormes to be tost" with a tart proverb of his own: "Don't
blame the sea god for knowingly and unnecessarily exposing your-
self to storms you've experienced before." It is not at all clear how
"so [in this manner] loytering" and its consequent follows from
this, but Thenot goes on to criticize the young for pasturing their
herds among the budding bushes, for prematurely celebrating their
triumph over winter, and finally for being unable to withstand it
when it comes. He uses the model of seasonal change in a fluid if not
sophistical manner, and the shiftiness of this passage is worth noting: what seems at first to be a deceptive and fleeting harbinger of
spring—one laugh of the sun—turns out to be spring itself, succeeded by the following winter.

Thenot thus rhetorically enhances both the insubstantial brevity of "lusty prime" and the folly of youth's "crowing." Spring quickly gives way to the recurrence of the "former fall," and as he proceeds, the rising intensity of his rhetoric transforms winter to "winter," that is, it works to detach the seasonal model from the annual cycle and associate it with the declining course of life. He personifies "breme winter" as an archer who, despite his age, vigorously and aggressively attacks his foe. The archer is a figure of Panic used to frighten Cuddie with a prospect of his grim future. But it is also a figure of Thenot, who stands before Cuddie as the agent of Elde giving an earnest of that retribution while the wintry dart of his rhetoric allows him to assert his own Nestorian vigor and savor his own revenge. Thenot wants it both ways: "some day you'll be as wrinkled and furrowed as I am; but when you are, you won't have my virile and hardy 'corage'; you'll be an easy target for the old bowman." Spenser ironically points this theme by having Cuddie begin his response with a contemptuous assessment of Thenot's virility, and go on to speak of the pleasures of young love.

It is in terms of this theme that the figure of the old archer takes on depth, suggesting the cause of Thenot's animus and the basic ambivalence of his attitude toward youth. Although at first glance it is a self-portrait, the dart is telltale. The preeminent dart-shooter in the *Calender* is Cupid, who materializes in *March* and whose arrows make wounds that are felt in *Aprill* (l. 22), *August* (ll. 93ff.), and *December* (ll. 93–96). I find compelling the notion that Thenot's archer is a wintry Cupid: a figure of the persistence of desire in old age, the thorn in the flesh, the ghost or afterimage of young Cupid. It is as if this is what the "other delights" of youth inevitably become in the bitter afterwash of so brief a "flowring," as if desire ages with the body and the darts it keeps shooting replace the wounds of love with the "breme" memory of its loss after it has burst the bubble of "Youngth."

However speculative this reading may sound, and however forced its application to these lines, the sentiment is itself a commonplace which Spenser could have found in many sources and which informs his general treatment of the effect of the paradise principle on the mind "drawing to his last age." The rationale is perfectly expressed, for example, by Castiglione in the dedicatory preface to the second book of *Il Libro del Cortegiano*. Chaucer's Reeve provides another precedent:

> But ik am oold, me list not pley for age;
> Gras tyme is doon, my fodder is now forage;
> This white top writeth myne olde yeris;
> Myn herte is also mowled as myne heris,
> But if I fare as dooth an open-ers,—
> That ilke fruyt is ever lenger the wers,
> Til it be roten in mullok or in stree.
> We olde men, I drede, so fare we:
> Til we be roten, kan we nat be rype;
> We hoppen alwey whil the world wol pype.
> For in oure wyl ther stiketh evere a nayl,
> To have an hoor heed and a grene tayl,
> As hath a leek; for thogh oure myght be goon,
> Oure wyl desireth folie evere in oon.
> For whan we may nat doon, than wol we speke;
> Yet in oure asshen olde is fyr yreke.
>   [*Reeve's Prologue,* ll. 3867–82]

The *Calender*'s most direct descendant of the Reeve is Palinode in *May:*

> To see those folkes make such jovisaunce,
> Made my heart after the pype to daunce.
>   [ll. 25–26]

>   (O that I were there,
> To helpen the Ladyes their Maybush beare)
> Ah Piers, bene not thy teeth on edge, to thinke,
> How great sport they gaynen with little swinck?
>   [ll. 33–36]

> Sicker now I see thou speakest of spight,
> All for thou lackest somedele of their delight.
>   [ll. 55–56]

Thenot is superficially more like Piers than Palinode: "For Younkers Palinode such follies fitte, / But we tway bene men of elder witt" (ll. 17–18). But Cuddie's insight is justified by the response that betrays the lurking presence of both Cupids, young and old, in Thenot's "elder witt":

> But were thy yeares greene, as now bene myne,
> To other delights they would encline.
> Thou art a fon, of thy love to boste,
> All that is lent to love, wyll be lost.

Thenot's apparently stoic response *to* life is actually a cynic's view *of* life. His argument is superficially ethical: youth is imprudent, arrogant, self-indulgent, and (taking the moral of his tale into account) ambitious as well as dishonest and malicious in its pursuit of pleasure or power. But at bottom his argument is practical: the pleasures of youth are folly not because they are evil but because they are short-lived and it is painful to lose them. His blanket rejection of youth smacks of the disappointment Cuddie attributes to him, measuring the force of his youthful attachments and the bitterness of his loss. This is further borne out by his tale of the oak and the briar. His anxiety over the declining power and authority of age translates into a diatribe against the "surquedry" of upstart youth. In the tale, the oak is a bathetic distortion of Thenot, the briar an abusive distortion of Cuddie. Thenot's focus is on the oak's loss of his former power, size, status, and nurturant fertility. Passages that express loathing for physical decrepitude are thus assigned not only to the briar (ll. 169–82) but also to the aged speaker himself. On the other hand, the speaker's description of the briar is—in spite of his denunciatory portrait—no less admiring than that which he assigns the briar (ll. 118–23, 129–32). Thenot delights not only in the flowers of spring but also in those of speech; hence he shows his attachment to what he professes to scorn. While disparaging the devious but persuasive language of youth he lards his narrative with it.

Cuddie's brusque interruption shows that he remains unmoved by Thenot's effort to "cruddle" his blood and "pricke" his heart. But this only means that paradoxically he and Thenot represent different phases of the same dialectical attitude. His ad hominem contempt of the Mantuanesque arguments, evident throughout the

eclogue, reveals the lurking influence of the paradise principle
openly expressed in Colin's "tho deemed I, my spring would ever
laste." To have taken Thenot more seriously might have protected
him from precisely the cynicism that Thenot's arguments betray.
And even though his description of youth's delights is relatively
temperate, giving us cause to suspect Thenot's bitter response, his
conception of love is also motivated by the paradise principle. The
modest scale and playful sense of his approach to love provides a foil
to Colin's plaintive excesses, but he shares with Colin the assumption that love involves pursuit, possession, and poetry, that woman
is a trophy to be won, that she can be won by gifts or song, and that
the conquest is matter for further song:

> Tho would thou learne to caroll of Love,
> And hery with hymnes thy lasses glove.
> Tho wouldest thou pype of Phyllis prayse:
> But Phyllis is myne for many dayes:
> I wonne her with a gyrdle of gelt,
> Embost with buegle about the belt.
> [ll. 61–66]

This economic view of *la chasse* is hardly heroic but it reflects
one kind of pastoral convention, reducing love to a game which has
little or nothing to do with the difficulties of sustained personal
commitment. Its recreative expectations are the same as those
shortly to be expressed by Willye in *March:*

> Tho shall we sporten in delight,
> And learne with Lettice to wexe light,
> That scornefully lookes askaunce.
> Tho will we little Love awake,
> That nowe sleepeth in Lethe lake,
> And pray him leaden our daunce.
> [ll. 19–24]

"Scornefully lookes askaunce" describes the expected challenge that
sweetens an expected victory which may last as long as "many dayes."
A love governed in this way by the dictates of the paradise principle
is bound to be lost when the "breme winter," like an aged embit-

tered Cupid, shoots its dart. It is no doubt because it *has* been lost that "breme" Thenot shoots his dreary dart at Cuddie. Thus Cuddie and Thenot are more in agreement than they know.

In this selective reading of *Februarie* I have tried to show that the positions represented by the two speakers are dialectically involved in a single complex attitude, and that the limitations of both derive from their common source in the paradise principle. It can be demonstrated through interpretation that the same unity-in-polarity marks all the other *Calender* debates and is of course preeminently figured in the persona of Colin Clout. The polarized attitude of the paradisal poetic tradition is the *Calender*'s chief object of critical mimesis, and this object is fundamentally abstract, impersonal, collective. Its various aspects, for instance, Youth and Age, are also best viewed as abstractions dissociable from any speaker who argues in their name. What Age and Youth "belong to," what they are part of, is the paradise principle, not this or that speaker. To look at it this way makes it easier to approach the paradisal tradition as a pressure exerted on the speakers who exhibit its influence. And this, finally, allows us to see that the *Calender*'s apparent variety of modes of plurality of values render it not merely a pastoral microcosm of literary modes and values, but a continuous allusion to them, a reconstruction that integrates and targets them as manifestations of the paradise principle.

II

The figure of Thenot provides a convenient medium through which to transfer the Age/Youth theme from the context of *Februarie* to that of the new poet's relation to literary tradition. "Thenot" names a speaker who also participates in *Aprill* and *November* as an auxiliary interlocutor, and some critics have assumed without question that in spite of their differences the latter two and the Mantuanesque *senex* of *Februarie* are the same. Since this hypothesis has been stated without being defended, and since, if it is tenable, it links Thenot more closely to Colin Clout as well as to one of the *Calender*'s more conspicuous precursors, Clément Marot, I should like briefly to make the case for it now.

The evidence is as follows: The old man in *Februarie* fondly remembers the tales of youth, love, and chivalry he heard when he was young (ll. 98–99), though now he is a bitter critic of youth's erotic folly. In *Aprill* Thenot berates Colin for letting love blind man and impair his art (ll. 17–20, 154–57). In *November* his "light virelayes" and "looser songs of love" deserve "Poetes prayse," according to Colin, but his "Oaten pypes" have long been asleep (ll. 21–24), and he once again mentions Colin's disorder ("loves misgovernaunce," l. 4). Although there is some inconsistency here, especially in view of Colin's description of Thenot's poetry, we are encouraged by two relatively superficial indicators to wrest a pattern from the evidence. The first is the famous case of the misplaced zodiacal sign. In *November* Colin says that Phoebus has "taken up his ynne in Fishes haske" (l. 17) which, if this means the sun is in Pisces, he could do more easily in February; whether or not this was accidental on Spenser's part, it does serve to link *November* with *Februarie*. Second, *November* and *Aprill* are linked by close thematic and rhetorical echoes, a linkage which I shall discuss shortly. Thus connections are drawn among the three eclogues in which Thenot appears.

The pattern I mentioned may be extrapolated from Patrick Cullen's remark that in *November* "Colin, ironically, is older than Thenot."[3] Thenot seems to grow younger as Colin grows older insofar as his youthful attachment to poetry receives more emphasis in each succeeding eclogue: *Aprill* displays his command of literary clichés (ll. 5–8), his appreciation of skill in making (l. 19), and his eagerness to hear one of Colin's "ditties . . . so trimly dight" (l. 29); in *November* we learn that he has himself been a practitioner of love poetry and goes so far as to justify love if, as in Colin's case, it improves one's verse. Thenot's image of "breme winter with chamfred browes," applicable to himself in *Februarie,* is echoed in Colin's *December* self-portrait (ll. 133–38). Thus by the end of the *Calender* he and Colin will have changed places: in the first the triumph of Youth in Age, in the second the triumph of Age in Youth. And since *November* and *December* return us most explicitly to Marot's poetry, the literary source of the two names, we may view this as the triumph of the older literary generation over the younger, the triumph of *breme* tradition over the new individual talent. Thus the Panic cycle is transmitted: Colin's fall from the paradise of youth is a mirror inversion (and perhaps a consequence) of the elder's return to it.

The significant references to Marot occur in the *Januarie* and *Februarie* glosses when E. K. reminds us that "Colin" is used by "the French Poete Marot (if he be worthy of the name of a Poete)" (ll. 84–85) and that "Thenot" is "the name of a shepheard in Marot his AEglogues" (*Februarie,* l. 260); in the argument to *November,* which notes that the elegy was "made in imitation of Marot his song"; and at the end of *November,* when Spenser assigns Marot's emblem, *La mord ny mord,* to Colin. The frame of the elegy lends the emblem one meaning, the elegy another, and, as we shall see, the two meanings converge. The frame makes it clear that Thenot's primary interest is in hearing Colin's "rymes": for the pastoral auditor, grief is noted only as an arabesque adorning the pleasures of well-made song, and he looks forward to Colin's "carefull verse" more for its careful turnings than for its sorrowful care. Colin's motive for singing the elegy is no more personal than Thenot's: decorum is the criterion in terms of which he chooses his selection; he sings a sad song not for Dido but for the onset of winter (ll. 13ff.). Thus the plaintive matter of the elegy is subordinated to the recreative occasion. The elegy seems bent on imitating Marot more than *La mord.* And as we listen to Colin canter through a series of elegiac and pastoral commonplaces, we may well agree with our model, Thenot, that the song's the thing.

This emphasis is supported by the varied undersong: "O heavie herse, / Let streaming teares be poured out in store: / O carefull verse" (ll. 60–62). "Herse" is not only a bier or catafalque (*catafalco,* a canopied framework to which epitaphs or short poems were affixed) but also—as E. K. points out—a funeral service. Additionally, "herse" is the noun form of the verb "to hery," to praise, which Colin had used in line 10. "Herse" is therefore virtually identical with "verse," which simply rehearses its meaning. The elegiac movement from "Heavie herse" to "happy herse" and "carefull verse" to "joyfull verse" is already compressed into the meanings of "herse" itself, which enacts the logic of recreative metamorphosis: the birth of verse is the burial of death and the death of grief.

La mord ny mord thus bears a double significance: it emphasizes the fact that this is not so much personal expression as poetic exercise and imitation, and it reminds us that in recreative metamorphosis death has no bite because life gives way to art. But these two senses are further qualified and deepened by another aspect of the poem, one in which the "message" of the imitated conventions comes up for criticism. The essence of the critique may be focused by a glance at the pointed counterpoint between *Aprill* and *November*. Nancy Jo Hoffman has persuasively demonstrated how "the third mourning stanza in 'November' speaks directly to the April eclogue, undoing its festivities before our eyes."[4] Where the April muses bear "Bay braunches," the November muses "that were wont greene bayes to weare,/Now bringen bitter Eldre braunches seare." The lightly voiced rusticity of *Aprill*'s "forswonck and forswatt" swain with his easy access to the beautiful and the good ("Bellibone") embodied as Elisa, the spirit of Elisium, leads to its own subversion in *November*'s grave pronouncement on mortal men "that swincke and sweate for nought."

The *Aprill* song is given as an example of Colin's idyllic preexperiential art, of his ante-Rosalind period when verse flowed and flowered, because nature and poetry were one—which is to say because nature was completely poetized: the song was "made, as by a spring he lay,/And tuned it unto the Waters fall" (*Aprill*, ll. 35–36). Colin's birdlike youth is thus itself a fantasy piped into being by the "systers nyne," and the mythologizing, idealizing, temper of the visionary conventions they inscribe in the *Aprill* poet's "vacant head" (*October*, l. 100) help explain why he deemed his "spring would ever last." The mystifications of the immortal muses spring from their parnassian insulation in a garden whose

"poesyes" are conventions not only of verse but also of thought—
are, that is, expectations about life. In the muses' anthology, to
grow old is to be ruined. This why Spenser's poem for the muses
appears in the volume entitled *Complaints* among the other laments
for the ruins of time. There is, after all, a certain note of self-aware
amusement in the *Epithalamion* poet's insistence on the long face of
the learned sisters:

> And when ye list your owne mishaps to mourne,
> Which death, or love, or fortunes wreck did rayse,
> Your string could soone to sadder tenor turne,
> And teach the woods and waters to lament
> Your dolefull dreriment.
>
> [ll. 7–11]

The repeated "or" in line 8 specifies indifference rather than dis-
junction, for any setback is liable to elicit not only the tears but also
the shrieks of the muses, whose ancient learning leaves them unpre-
pared for anything except eternal youth, which is to say that time
has passed them by.

Aprill shimmers with Elysian lore whose "pierlesse pleasures"
(*June*, l. 32) cast their green shadows over the future. They bemuse
the vacant head with what the bitter elder later castigates as a
"slipper hope" and "marked scope" (a sight or vision, a target or
prey, an object of desire or pursuit) which by its very paradisal
nature could not but be missed, leaving in its wake only the
"trustlesse state of earthly things" (*November*, ll. 153–55). Hence
the elegist counsels neither genuine transcendence nor endurance
and acceptance but the evasive pseudotranscendence of a return to
the lost green world—to "fayre fieldes and pleasaunt layes," to
"fieldes ay fresh" and "grass ay greene" (ll. 158–59); the emphasis is
on *ay,* the difference being not that these fields are spiritual but that
they last longer. "Make haste ye shepheards, thether to revert"
(l. 161): in the vicinity of the phrase "grass ay greene," "revert" becomes "re-green," and the return is to the *Aprill* world of Elisa and
Chloris (which, writes E. K., "signifieth greenesse"), to the green
fields of Elisium "devised of Poetes to be a place of pleasure like
Paradise" (*Aprill,* l. 281).

The meaning of *La mord ny mord* is thus complicated by its different relations to the elegy and to its frame. The double significance I mentioned above is deepened by the fact that if the elegy is conspicuous for its literary and imitative quality, what it imitates is a plaintive response to *mors mordax* which fails to discriminate among life's "mishaps" and, in its radical pessimism, implies that death per se (and not merely Dido's untimely death) is *unkindly,* a paradigm of the hopelessness of the human condition (cf. *November,* ll. 123–62). In this manner the November eclogue reveals itself to be not only an experiment *in* the traditional mode but also a critique *of* that mode. It is mimicry as well as mimesis.

The same is true of the *Calender* as a whole. Beyond its countless literary echoes, references, and allusions stands the profile of what I have been calling *the* tradition. And this is clearly a reductive profile. It is as if, to borrow Harold Bloom's terms, Spenser cleared a space for himself by a combination of "revisionary ratios" that perform a brilliant misreading of the precursor tradition, re-creating it in the antithetical image of the paradise principle. While Spenser shares with Colin the delight in testing his "tender wyngs," he swerves away from him in making him exhibit the motivational effects of the principle. In this swerve (Bloom's *clinamen*) he returns his literary stepchild to its real father, Marot, toward the end of the *Calender.* And though Spenser assigns Marot a special place among his precursors, his genial revisionary slander is exemplary and diffuse rather than narrowly focused. As Richard Mallette observes, the *November* elegy, in which the presence of Marot is most conspicuously and specifically evoked,

> is the most patently "literary" eclogue in the collection. As a pastoral elegy, whose forebears stretch with great distinction from Theocritus and Virgil to Marot and Petrarch, "November" asks to be measured against a redoubtable tradition. It abides virtually every convention of its mode, from the invocation of the Muses, to the questioning of the rural deities and the final consolation.[5]

But of course *November* and the *Calender* as a whole are more aggressive than that: they *measure* the tradition and question its redoubtability by illustrating the tendencies of escape into artifice that make it redoubtable in the wrong way and for the wrong reasons.

So unified, characterized, and criticized, the poetic traditions that fathered *The Shepheardes Calender* become its child, and stand within its readers' purview as the paradisal poetic tradition, or the paradise of poetic tradition. In the introductory section of this essay I suggested that the paradise and its consequences were legacies bequeathed by the poetic tradition to the new poet, and in concluding I would like to amplify this suggestion. Why do the *Calender*'s elders present its youth with a paradisal version of experience which they at the same time condemn, with honey they know will turn to gall? For as Cullen has so cogently shown, the tradition which the *Calender* dramatically constitutes is divided against itself into sweet and bitter, Arcadian and Mantuanesque, recreative and plaintive factions. But this is to be expected. For even the venerable elders were once young, and the monuments of unaging intellect they handed on included the poetry of youth and "matter of love" as well as the wisdom of age "mixed with some Satyrical bitternesse," along with eclogues urging "reverence dewe to old age" and "contempt of Poetrie and pleasaunt wits" (E. K., *Generall Argument*, ll. 33–39).

This polarized tradition brings together two sets of predecessors, one sociopolitical and the other literary:

> Spenser articulates a tense relationship to literary and social patriarchy shared by many in his literary generation: poetic progenitors have shaped a literary tradition within which the new poet must find a place by creative imitation; the elder Tudor generation has shaped and still controls the social institutions and cultural values within which the young, educated gentleman or would-be gentleman must live and write and try to advance himself.

> Colin's pattern of prodigality and misfortune has its origin precisely in his successful embrace of the Renaissance poet's pastoral role; the literary shepherd's otiose environment of eroticism and poetry is being viewed through the stern spectacles of Tudor patriarchal morality. . . . The Vergilian progression puts pastoral at the beginning of the poet's career. . . . Pastoral is persistently associated with new poets and with poets who are young.[6]

> Petrarch's description of himself in his *Epistle to Posterity,* as led astray by youth but corrected by maturity, established a paradigm that

would be repeated again and again, for it continued to serve the purpose for which it was designed. It marked out a space within which the poet and his poetry might enjoy a certain autonomy— though an autonomy based on rebellion and even . . . idolatry.[7]

The presence of these two factions in the *Calender* complicates the notion of *puer senex:* the young poet is *senex* in being imprinted with the culture of the literary elders he imitates, but at the same time the elderly culture preserves and transmits its experience of its own youth. It offers the new poet the opposing values and different phases of the life cycle. Yet the signals these factions give are only superficially contradictory and are, as I have argued, united by their common subordination to the paradise principle. We may call these two factions the Poets and the Stoic Censors. The Poets are the tradition's party of Youth, sweet pastoral and Arcadia; the Censors are its Mantuanesque party of Age and bitter pastoral. The Censor is censorious *because* his youth was dominated by the idyllicism of the Poets and was spent in paradisal pursuit of pleasure. The Poets dominate youth *because* the aging mind of the Censor still affects the paradise it has lost and reinstates its own youthful fantasy in the minds of its successors. Because the Censor is a closet Poet, the Poet is a budding Censor. The Poet is the larva, the Censor the imago, and they continually reproduce each other under the influence of their common parent, the paradise principle.

The limits of the *Calender* world are defined in terms of this conflict between youth and age, and the conflict is dramatized at both the intra- and inter-generational levels. I conclude my study with a brief glance at a passage from *The Faerie Queene* that encapsulates this dialectic, articulating its basic structure and revealing its abiding interest for Spenser. In book 3 there is a nursery that testifies to the same escapist pressure as the poets' nursery of pastoral—testifies to the same fear of mortality, the same bitterness over the human condition, the same desire for eternal return:

> It sited was in fruitfull soyle of old,
>> And girt in with two walles on either side;
>> The one of yron, the other of bright gold,
>> That none might thorough breake, nor over-stride:
>> And double gates it had, which opened wide,

By which both in and out men moten pas;
The one faire and fresh, the other old and dride:
Old Genius the porter of them was,
Old Genius, the which a double nature has.

He letteth in, he letteth out to wend,
    All that to come into the world desire;
    A thousand thousand naked babes attend
    About him day and night, which doe require,
    That he with fleshly weedes would them attire:
    Such as him list, such as eternall fate
    Ordained hath, he clothes with sinfull mire,
    And sendeth forth to live in mortall state,
Till they againe returne backe by the hinder gate.

After that they againe returned beene,
    They in that Gardin planted be againe;
    And grow afresh, as they had never seene
    Fleshly corruption, nor mortall paine.
    Some thousand yeares so doen they there remaine;
    And then of him are clad with other hew,
    Or sent into the chaungefull world againe,
    Till thither they returne, where first they grew:
So like a wheele around they runne from old to new.

[6.31–33]

Old Genius, the Janus guarding the gates of Venus' Garden of
Adonis, is endowed with his etymologically denoted function,
birth-giver. An elder presiding over the birth and rebirth of the
young, his double nature is thus complementary to that of *puer
senex*. But he is double-natured because a birth-giver is also a
death-giver, and the sad antithesis of stanza 31--"faire and fresh" vs.
"old and dride"—prejudices the viewpoint of the describer, and
presumably also that of Old Genius, bound by his epithet more
closely to the "old and dride" than to the "faire and fresh." The
phrase "All that to come into the world desire" seems at first
positive and expansive, but is framed in rhetoric which stabs with
increasing force at the folly of this desire: from "fleshly weedes" to
"sinfull mire" to "fleshly corruption," and from "mortall state" to
"mortall paine." The naked babes who long for mortality do so only

because their heads are vacant—because the promise of new life is coupled with the eradication of old knowledge. Replanted, "they had never seene / Fleshly corruption." As in Plato's myth of Er and Virgil's revision of it in the sixth book of the *Aeneid,* old souls become new, parents become children, only by passing through the Lethe which alone (the elders feel) will protect the young from the truth and delude them into carrying on the burden of mortal life.

The culture inscribed in the young is the product of their elders' attempt to flee from the lessons of experience by forgetting them; the forgetfulness is built into the legacy bequeathed by elders to children. The green world is the lost "place"—the past—which the older generation can recover only by planting themselves anew in their children's minds. So Lévi-Strauss observes, in *Tristes Tropiques,* that "it is not only to deceive our children that we keep up their belief in Father Christmas: their enthusiasm warms us, helps us to delude ourselves and to believe, since they believe it, that a world of one-way generosity is not absolutely incompatible with reality,"[8] that is, a world in which parents give without demanding returns, and in which nature gives life without taking it away. But the contradictions that perpetuate this dialectic convert the delusion to its antithesis; the proffered exemption from reciprocity and death generates the false consciusness of childhood, and the subsequent disenchantment of the naked babes only reproduces in their generation the bitterness from which the elders tried vainly to escape: "So like a wheele around they runne from new to old." And the elders, growing old and dried, eternally demand returns. Having constituted the "pierlesse pleasures" of soft pastoral as the norms of childhood, having trained their children to live out the parental fantasies of youth, they exact the expected price for this gift. The young are made their scapegoats for obediently enacting those fantasies. Thus the elders can validate and vicariously enjoy lost illusions, but at the same time they can validate their own judicious transcendence of the illusions. Yet their wintry spite increases as they watch "the young / In one another's arms," and their one consolation is that they can blame youth's folly on their children rather than on themselves.

NOTES

1. "Mode and Diction in *The Shepheardes Calender*," *MP* 67 (1969), 145.

2. *Spenser, Marvell, and Renaissance Pastoral* (Cambridge: Harvard University Press, 1970), p. 127.

3. Ibid., p. 91.

4. *Spenser's Pastorals: "The Shepheardes Calender" and "Colin Clout"* (Baltimore: Johns Hopkins University Press, 1972), p. 90.

5. "Spenser's Portrait of the Artist in *The Shepheardes Calender* and *Colin Clouts Come Home Again*," *SEL* 19 (1979), 31.

6. Louis Adrian Montrose, "'The perfecte paterne of a Poete': The Poetics of Courtship in *The Shepheardes Calender*," *TSLL* 21 (1979), 36–37.

7. Richard Helgerson, "The New Poet Presents Himself: Spenser and the Idea of a Literary Career," *PMLA* 93 (1978), 895.

8. Trans. John and Doreen Weightman (New York: Athenaeum, 1974), p. 245.

JUDITH H. ANDERSON

"In liuing colours and right hew": The Queen of Spenser's Central Books

Even in the 1590 *Faerie Queene,* Spenser's reverence for Queen Elizabeth is accompanied by a cautionary awareness of the temptations
and dangers of queenly power and by a complementary awareness of the cost—the denial or exclusion of human possibilities—an
ennobling Idea exacts of its bearer. The one is evident in the House
of Pride and Cave of Mammon, and the other in the treatment of
Belphoebe. The attainments of Una, the "goodly maiden Queene,"
are threatened demonically by their perversion in Lucifera, the
"mayden Queene" of Pride, and parodied again in Book II by the
verbally reiterative image of Philotime.[1] Belphoebe, beautiful, inspiring, and goddesslike, is momentarily locked in comic encounter
with Braggadocchio in Book II, an encounter which, though it
leaves the worth of her ideal essentially untarnished, resembles
another famous encounter between honor and instinct: between
Hotspur's extravagant idealism, his "easy leap, / To pluck bright
honor from the pale-fac'd moon," and Falstaff's unenlightened but
earthy sense: "Can honor set to a leg?"[2] Specifically aligned with
Queen Elizabeth in the Letter to Ralegh and in the proem to Book
III, the chaste Belphoebe is in human terms both an aspiration and
an extreme, paradoxically both more and less nearly complete than
ordinary mortals.

In the 1596 *Faerie Queene,* while still persuaded of the value of
the queenly ideal, Spenser is more disillusioned—or at least less
illusioned—with the real Queen and her court. In the notorious
proem to Book IV, he complains openly of misconceived criticisms
of *The Faerie Queene* emanating from Elizabeth's court and goes so far

as to summon help from Eros for "that sacred Saint my soueraigne Queene." He urges "*Venus* dearling doue," a benign Cupid, to "Sprinckle" the Queen's "heart, and haughtie courage soften, / That she may hearke to loue, and read this lesson often." Thus introduced by hope for improvement in queenly attitudes and by implied criticism of her present ones, Books IV to VI are bedeviled by recurrent images of revilement and public infamy: Ate, Slander, Malfont, Envy, Detraction, the Blatant Beast. Most of these glance at the Queen, the Queen's court, or events impossible to dissociate from the Queen without transforming her into a mythic ideal isolated from history—at best a hope or an unrealized promise but no longer, by any stretch of the epic imagination, a present reality. In the proem to Book VI—the beginning of *The Faerie Queene*'s end— this is the route Spenser attempts, but with a trail of hesitation, bitterness, and painful reassessment still fresh behind him.

Despite recognition of the poet's cautionary awareness in Books I to III and despite his more open disappointment in Books IV to VI, we have been reluctant to admit their persistence and strength, especially as they touch the Queen. We rightly note the danger to a mere poet of criticizing his sovereign and the real power the cult of the Virgin Queen exerted over men's imaginations. Nothing in this paper denies these realities, but my argument considers them large designs in the poem's fabric rather than its whole cloth.

Reluctance to see the extent to which Spenser criticizes the Queen does him a particular disservice in Books III and IV. Here it obscures the relation of ideal or antique image to the present age, a relation of which the Queen is the measure throughout the poem, and thus it obscures the developing relation of Faerie to history and of fiction to life. Still more serious, to my mind, this reluctance leads us to pretend that the poet did not really mean certain lines or hear certain verbal ambiguities and, in short, was not fully sensitive to his own words or alert to their surrounding contexts.[3] My present undertaking is to examine several passages in Books III and IV that involve verbal cruxes, the Queen, and the relation of present age to antique image. These passages indicate that Spenser's depiction of the Queen's bright image is more complexly shaded in Book III

than is generally ackowledged and is in Book IV more critical,
perhaps shockingly so. In Book IV, something of the nightmare
image of the slanderous Beast who bites "without regard of person
or of time" at the end of Book VI is already present and implicates
the Queen.

I

In the proem to Book III, the poet observes a distinction between present and past and between truth and Faerie image that is
absent from the proems to Books I and II, and without them, its
significance could easily pass unnoticed. In the first of these proems,
the living Queen, "Great Lady of the greatest Isle," is a "Mirrour of
grace and Maiestie diuine," and the poem is a reflection, in effect
itself a mirror, of "that true glorious type" of the Queen. In the
proem to Book II, despite poetic play about the location of Faerie,
the Queen is the living reflection of the "antique Image," and so the
poem, or Faerie image, is a "faire mirrhour" of her "face" and
"realmes." The first two proems present one continuous, unbroken
reflection: the Queen reflects Divinity; like the Queen herself, the
poem reflects the glorious origins, person, and reign of the living
Queen.

Referring to the Queen's face, realms, and ancestry, the final
stanza of Proem II offers an apology for the antique Faerie image
that is in fact a confident justification of it:

> The which O pardon me thus to enfold
> In couert vele, and wrap in shadowes light,
> That feeble eyes your glory may behold,
> Which else could not endure those beames bright,
> But would be dazled with exceeding light.

The dazzling brightness of the living Queen is enfolded in shadow
to enlighten feeble eyes, enabling them to behold true glory. This
veil reveals a single truth instead of obscuring it, and these shadows,
unlike those in the second three books, do not splinter truth or
transform its character. They do not make true glory truly fictive.

In the proem to Book III, the poem continues to be the Queen's mirror, and although she is now invited to view herself "In mirrours more then one"—that is, in Gloriana or in Belphoebe—both glasses are essentially virtuous and can be seen primarily as an outfolding of the good Queen rather than as a dispersion of her unity. But as I have noted elsewhere, in this proem the present embodiment also begins to vie with the antique image, living Queen with Antiquity, and, indeed, to challenge it.[4] Uneasy nuances (not quite tensions) cluster around the word "living." In order to perceive the fairest virtue, chastity in this case, one "Need but behold the pourtraict of her [the Queen's] hart, / If pourtrayed it might be by any liuing art." The poet continues, "But liuing art may not least part expresse, / Nor life-resembling pencill it can paint . . . Ne Poets wit, that passeth Painter farre." Then comes a plea for pardon that recalls the one in the second proem:

> But O dred Soueraine
> Thus farre forth pardon, sith that choicest wit
> Cannot your glorious pourtraict figure plaine
> That I in coloured showes may shadow it,
> And antique praises vnto present persons fit.

More opaque than the "shadowes light" of Proem II, these shadows testify to the poet's "want of words" and wit more than they serve the purpose of revelation. The poem here becomes a slightly compromised "coloured show" that can only shadow the Queen's "glorious pourtraict" and tailor antique praises to present persons, a "fit" that sounds neither so natural nor so close as the continuity of bright reflections in Proems I and II. The poem becomes the glass through which the living sovereign's true portrait is somewhat obscurely seen.

The difference in tone and emphasis between Proems II and III might, I suppose, be attributed to an unusually severe onset of the modesty topos or, that failing, to one of Spenser's regrettable catnaps, this time right on the threshold of Book III. But if these dismissals of particular significance were adequate, the lines that directly follow Spenser's apology for "coloured showes" and "antique praises" would positively resonate with his shameful snoring.

They refer to the depiction of Queen Elizabeth in Sir Walter Ralegh's *Cynthia:*

> But if in liuing colours, and right hew,
> Your selfe you couet to see pictured,
> Who can it doe more liuely, or more trew. . . ?

When Spenser thus sets the "liuing colours" and "right hew" of his sovereign, Queen Elizabeth, against his own "coulord showes" and "antique praises," he introduces into the poem a far-reaching distinction between life and antiquity, historical present and mythic past, current truth and Faerie image. Spenser himself glosses and simultaneously reinforces the startling phrases "liuing colours" and "right hew" two lines later: *living* colors are "liuely" or lifelike, and the *right* hue is true-to-life or, more simply, "trew."

Referring a true and lively picture of the Queen to Ralegh's *Cynthia,* Spenser is unlikely to have meant a picture that is merely realistic or unembellished by art. Ralegh's fragmentary *Ocean to Cynthia,* much of which relates to Ralegh's imprisonment in 1592, a disgrace subsequent to publication of Book III, is the best indication of *Cynthia*'s nature we have, and while Ralegh's voice in it is distinct, individual, and passionate, such highly artificial modes as the Petrarchan ("Such heat in Ize, such fier in frost") and the pastoral ("Vnfolde thy flockes and leue them to the feilds") are also much in evidence.[5] The nostalgic—indeed, the bereaved— employment of pastoral in *Ocean to Cynthia* suggests that the Shepherd of the Ocean's earlier versions of *Cynthia,* written in less desperate straits, might have been more conventional than less so.[6] When Spenser writes of the living colors and right hue of *Cynthia,* he implies a portrayal that is less hieratic and allegorical but more contemporary and personal than his own. Such a portrayal as Ralegh's might be less universal and more ephemeral, but it belongs more truly to time.

Spenser's reference to Ralegh certainly does not discredit the Faerie image but does limit its authority unless that image itself can be expanded to embrace life more closely. The third proem provides a particularly apt introduction to a book in which time and eternity or present age and ideal image are not so smoothly continuous.

Nothing quite like the "heauenly noise / Heard sound through all
the Pallace pleasantly" at the betrothal of Una—a noise like the
voices of angels "Singing before th'eternall maiesty, / In their trinall
triplicities on hye"—reverberates through Book III, and no one
quite like the brilliantly winged angel who succors Guyon materializes to rescue its heroes. In fact, the closest we get to an angel in
this book is Timias' illusion that Belphoebe is one when he wakens
from his swoon to fine her ministering to his wounds: "Mercy deare
Lord . . . what grace is this," he asks, "To send thine Angell from
her bowre of blis, / To comfort me in my distressed plight?" (v. 35).
And even he adds on second thought, "Angell, or Goddesse do I call
thee right?" thereby echoing Virgil's famous lines from Aeneas'
meeting with Venus in the guise of Diana's maiden and avouching
his perception that this angelic illusion originates in a more worldly
pantheon than Una's "trinall triplicities."[7]

A blushing Belphoebe disclaims the angelic or godly status
Timias imputes to her and declares herself simply a maid and
"mortall wight" (36). Unfortunately her declaration is exactly what
Timias might have longed, but should never have been allowed, to
hear, for he falls irrevocably and irremediably in love with her.
Belphoebe not only denies him a reciprocal love but also fails to
comprehend or even to recognize the nature of his response to her.
More than once the poet criticizes her failure as a "Madnesse" that
saves "a part, and lose(s) the whole" (43, cf. 42).

While Timias languishes in love's torments, Belphoebe spares
no pains to ease him, but still not comprehending his malady, "that
sweet Cordiall, which can restore / A loue-sick hart, she did to him
enuy," or refuse to give. Few readers or rereaders of these lines are
prepared for those that follow, in which "that sweet Cordiall
. . . that soueraigne salue" is suddenly transformed to "That dainty
Rose, the daughter of her Morne," whose flower, lapped in "her
silken leaues" she shelters from midday sun and northern wind:
"But soone as calmed was the Christall aire, / She did it faire dis-
pred, and let to florish faire" (51). As Donald Cheney has
suggested, precise equivalents for these lines do not exist. "For
her," he adds, "the rose is a rose, not a euphemism."[8]

But surely not just a rose, either. Belphoebe's dainty blossom soon opens into a flower strongly redolent of myth: "Eternall God," we learn, "In Paradize whilome did plant this flowre" and thence fetched it to implant in "earthly flesh." Soon we recognize the flower as the ur-rose that flourishes "In gentle Ladies brest, and bounteous race / Of woman kind" and "beareth fruit of honour and all chast desire" (52). A truly marvelous hybrid, this is none other than the *rosa moralis universalis.* It is hardly surprising that one of Spenser's eighteenth-century editors compared the rose to Milton's "Immortal Amarant" in the third book of *Paradise Lost,*

a flow'r which once
In Paradise, fast by the Tree of Life,
Began to bloom.[9]

In Belphoebe's transformation from uncomprehending nurse to vestal votaress of the rose, to antique origin and a fructifying virtue undifferentiated by time, person, or place, Timias is forgotten. Her specific relation to him will not align with the general moral statement into which it is transformed. Honor and chaste desire, the fruit of the flower, are indeed virtuous, but Timias' love is honorable in Book III, and his desire, if not virginal, is decent and pure and, in these senses, chaste. The general moral statement not only transcends the particular case but wholly misses it. Timias is one person these antique praises of the flower do not fit, and when we consider that Belphoebe's use of tobacco (v. 32) to heal Timias' wounds signals an obvious allusion to Ralegh, we might also think one "present person."

Having glorified the rose, the poet appears in no hurry to return from antique ideal to the person of Belphoebe. He directly addresses the "Faire ympes of beautie" and urges them to emulate their origin by adorning their garlands with "this faire flowre . . . Of chastity and vertue virginall." These "ympes" (shoots, scions) of beauty are preeminently the "Ladies in the Court," to judge both from the poet's present address and its resemblance to the final dedicatory sonnet of *The Faerie Queen.*[10] Timias aside, the poet opts for the general application of the antique ideal to his present world of

readers. But with the poet's final promise that the flower will not
only embellish the ladies' beauty but also crown them "with
heauenly coronall, / Such as the Angels weare before Gods tribunall," we might feel for a moment that we have somehow traveled
beyond even Timias' first flush of illusion to a still simpler, purer,
less earthly vision (53).

The poet's address to the ladies continues in the next stanza,
where he now commends to their attention not the beatifying rose,
upon which he has spent the mythmaking of the previous stanzas,
but Belphoebe herself as true exemplar of its virtue. In effect he
returns the rose, but now in its glorified form, to her person. Of
particular note in the present stanza are the initial occurrences of the
word "faire" and the phrases "none liuing" and "ensample dead,"
curious phrases whether taken alone, together, or with the "liuing
colours and right hew" of the third proem:

> To youre faire selues a faire ensample frame,
> Of this faire virgin, this *Belphoebe* faire,
> To whom in perfect loue, and spotlesse fame
> Of chastitie, none liuing may compaire:
> Ne poysnous Enuy iustly can empaire
> The prayse of her fresh flowring Maidenhead;
> For thy she standeth on the highest staire
> Of th'honorable stage of womanhead,
> That Ladies all may follow her ensample dead.

The repetition of "faire" is insistent, even anxiously so, but it
enforces a link between present persons and Belphoebe. This link, if
only a matter of rhetoric and fair appearance, suggests a series of
steps from the ladies' "faire selues," surely many of whom were
bound to marry; to a generalized "ensample" of purity, to its more
exclusive, or higher, form, virginity; and finally to the individual
fulfillment of virginity in fair Belphoebe herself, who is found on
the "highest staire . . . of womanhead."[11] The poet's conception of a
series of steps—that is, a "staire"—becomes additionally significant
once we have looked closely at the other verbal oddities in the
stanza.[12]

The first of these, the phrase "none liuing," presumably means "none of you ladies" or "no one living," since the poet here addresses his present audience, "youre faire selues," and compares them to Belphoebe, the exemplar of ideal chastity, to which "none liuing" has yet attained. Alternatively, if we take the word "liuing" to be applicable to Belphoebe, the phrase could mean "no other living lady" except Belphoebe herself. This is the meaning of a remarkably similar claim about chaste Florimell earlier in the same canto where her dwarf declares of her, "Liues none this day, that may with her compare / In stedfast chastitie" (v. 8).[13] But there are also significant differences between a claim made by a distraught dwarf within the narrative context of Faerie and one made by the poet himself and addressed to an audience outside the poem. We readily see that the loyal dwarf speaks loosely or hyperbolically. He really means no *other* living lady in all the realm of Faerie is chaster than Florimell or simply that she is the chastest lady imaginable. The word "liuing," however, is not so readily defused in relation to Belphoebe, who mirrors the chastity of the living Queen, especially when it occurs in a direct address to the poet's living audience. If in this context we were to consider Belphoebe "liuing," then she seems actually to become the Queen, a development at variance with statements in the proem to Book III and downright embarrassing when we reach "her ensample dead" in the alexandrine of this stanza. Such a radical dissolution of the fictional character of Belphoebe is entirely unexpected and would probably be largely wasted or, worse, misunderstood.

The natural reading of the phrase "none liuing" is, as suggested, the obvious one, "no one living" or simply "no living lady." While this reading does not refer specifically or directly to the Queen, it increases the distance between Belphoebe as a mythic ideal and any living referent, including the Queen, and thus the distance between antiquity and present age. The increased distance reflects the strains between ideal exemplar and human response in the story of Belphoebe and Timias and helps to bring their story to an appropriate conclusion in 1590.

But if the obvious reading of "none liuing" is also the right one, it is designed to give us another, longer pause for thought when we

reread the alexandrine that succeeds it: Belphoebe "standeth on the
highest staire . . . of womanhead, / That Ladies all may follow her
ensample dead." If Belphoebe is a mythic ideal who has moved
farther away from a living referent, what has she to do with death?
First she seems to be mythic in this stanza and now to belong to
history. The obvious reading of "none liuing" and the alexandrine
clearly do not as yet accord.

The phrase "ensample dead," when glossed at all, is taken to be
an ellipsis of the clause "when she is dead,"[14] and it can be referred
to the occurrence of a parallel construction in Merlin's prophecy to
Britomart of the child or "Image" Artegall will leave with her when
he is dead (III.iii.29):

> With thee yet shall he leaue for memory
> Of his late puissaunce, his Image dead,
> That liuing him in all actiuity
> To thee shall represent.

But the phrase "ensample dead" could just as well mean "her dead,
or lifeless, example." At first glance, before we are startled into
reassessment, this is exactly what it seems to mean, and if this were
in fact all it meant, it would serve as a chilling comment on the
ideal Belphoebe embodies and, although at a distinctly greater remove than before, on that of the Queen as well. This alternative
meaning of "ensample dead" also finds a relevant parallel in an
alexandrine of Book III. It occurs when the witch creates false
Florimell, that parody of coldly sterile, lifeless Petrarchism: "and in
the stead / Of life, she put a Spright to rule the carkasse dead"
(viii.7). Death is this carcass' present condition (dead carcass), not
its future one (when dead).

The occurrence in a single stanza of two verbal cruxes as immediately and obviously related as life ("none liuing") and death
("ensample dead") is unlikely to be adventitious. The reading "dead
example"—the more obvious reading of "ensample dead"—accords
better with the more obvious reading of "none liuing," since it does
not require, as does the alternative "when she is dead," an abrupt
and irrational shift from mythic to historical reference and, to put it
bluntly, from an ageless Belphoebe to an aging Elizabeth. There is

no way for us to cancel the obvious reading of "ensample dead," but perhaps we need not stop with its dispiriting message. In the context of Timias' highly Petrarchan adoration and idealization of Belphoebe, the alternative reading, "ensample [when she is] dead," need not refer to death as an exclusively physical event. It can also be taken in a way that makes sense of the mythic Belphoebe's connection with death and offers the positive reflection on her ideal that balances, though it cannot wholly offset, the negative one.

In its Petrarchan context, the reading "when she is dead" points to the resolution of the conflict between body and spirit that comes with the lady's physical death and spiritual transcendence. The phrase "ensample dead" therefore implies the ideal, the life-in-death, that the deadly carcass, the death-in-life, of false Florimell parodies. This reading of the phrase balances the cold reality of human loss—death, denial, lifeless example—with high praise of Belphoebe and of the Queen whose chastity, if only dimly, she still mirrors. At the same time, it continues Belphoebe's movement away from an earthly reality and suggests the only possible solution of Timias' dilemma—and seemingly the destined conclusion of Ralegh's—to be the symbolic or actual transfiguration of Belphoebe into pure spirit.[15]

Looking back at the same stanza with our Petrarchan reading in mind, we might be struck anew by the phrases "perfect loue" and "spotlesse fame." It suddenly makes more sense that "none liuing" should be perfect or spotless in Book III, where the possibility of a living Una has receded like a setting sun, and that the "highest staire . . . of womanhead" should be reached with the lady's transformation through death into spirit. Presumably this is also the "staire" on which worthy emulators of the true rose are crowned "with heauenly coronall . . . before Gods tribunall."

It is even tempting to see a relation between the Petrarchan praise of fair Belphoebe in Book III and the first of Ralegh's commendatory sonnets to accompany *The Faerie Queene:*

Me thought I saw the graue, where *Laura* lay
Within that Temple, where the vestall flame
Was wont to burne, and passing by that way,
To see that buried dust of liuing fame,

Whose tombe faire loue, and fairer vertue kept,
All suddenly I saw the Faery Queene:
At whose approch the soule of *Petrarke* wept,
And from thenceforth those graces were not seene.
For they this Queene attended, in whose steed
Obliuion laid him downe on *Lauras* herse.

But there is also a significant distance between this vision of Laura's
living successor and Spenser's fully idealized Belphoebe, whose rose
opens fully only in death. Perhaps because farther removed from it
personally, Spenser saw more clearly the temporal, human cost—to
Belphoebe and Timias both—of the fully realized Petrarchan vision.
By the writing of Book III, he certainly knew that in time Laura's
tomb could only be replaced by another's "ensample dead."[16]

II

When Belphoebe is last seen in Book III, response to her is
poised between timeless and temporal truth, rather than being torn
apart by their conflict. In Book IV, Belphoebe's next and also her
last appearance, this duality of response to her remains, but with a
difference. Her estrangement from Timias intersects with his relation to Amoret, Belphoebe's twin sister; and Belphoebe's reconciliation with Timias clashes conspicuously with the abandonment and
slander of Amoret. With Timias' reconciliation and Amoret's revilement, duality of judgment and of truth can no longer be contained in a single phrase or image or even in a single character or
event. Belphoebe herself—or what she was in Book III, an ideal
maintaining some relation to worldly reality—is fractured. The
alternatives of love and loss, of timeless and temporal truth, are no
longer grasped together, no longer simultaneous and complementary dimensions of awareness, as they were in the phrase "ensample
dead." They have become sharply distinct and are in danger of
becoming mutually exclusive. The distance between ideal image
and present age, antique praises and living colors, is widening
rapidly.

The story of Belphoebe and Timias is inseparable from the last

stages of Amoret's story in Book IV. Wounded and then tended by
Timias, Amoret becomes the unwitting cause of Belphoebe's estrangement from him. She is part of their story, and when she is
simply abandoned by them in the middle of it, she becomes, both
narratively and morally, a loose end waiting to be woven into the
larger design. Amoret's ties with the story of Belphoebe and Timias
are also symbolic and thematic. The ruby that helps to bring Belphoebe back to Timias is "Shap'd like a heart, yet bleeding of the
wound, / And with a little golden chaine about it bound" (viii.6). A
jeweler's replica of Amoret's heart in the Masque of Cupid, this
lapidarian heart that Belphoebe once gave Timias alludes to
Amoret's real one, suggesting contrast with, as well as resemblance
to, it. The twin birth of Belphoebe and Amoret, the complementary
maids of Diana and Venus, provides a richly allegorical backdrop to
their aborted reunion, and although Amoret is much more complexly human than an abstract conception of Love or Amor, the
latter is one kind of meaning she carries when she is wounded, then
abandoned, and later reviled. The most provocative imitation of
Amoret's thematic congruence with Belphoebe comes when the poet
interrupts his narrative during Slander's revilement of Amoret to
recall an Edenic age when the "glorious flowre" of beauty flourished,
a time when

> . . . antique age yet in the infancie
> Of time, did liue then like an innocent,
> In simple truth and blamelesse chastitie.
> [IV.viii.30]

Antiquity, ideal image, mythic flower, even chastity—the poet
associates them all now with Amoret or, more accurately, with her
revilement.

In addition to the connections between the stories of Amoret
and of Belphoebe and Timias sketched above, there are pointed
contrasts. The reconciliation of Belphoebe and Timias is extremely
artificial, effected through the agency of a sympathetic turtle dove
and a lapidary's heart and totally removed from temporal reality.
When he is reconciled, Timias' condition anticipates Melibee's

self-enclosed vulnerability: he is "Fearlesse of fortunes chaunge or enuies dread, / And eke all mindlesse of his owne deare Lord" (viii. 18). Still more noticeable, even while the estrangement of Belphoebe from Timias alludes unmistakably to Ralegh's fall from queenly favor, their reconciliation in Book IV conflicts with the real state of Ralegh's affairs in 1596.[17] After Ralegh's secret marriage to Elizabeth Throckmorton, one of the Queen's maids of honor, and the consequent imprisonment of them both in 1592, he was, although released fairly quickly from prison, not in fact reconciled to the Queen until 1597. His wife, left to languish in prison longer than he, never returned to favor with the Queen. In the reconciliation of Timias and Belphoebe, artificial thus means twice unreal—unreal at once in manner and in reference.

The abandonment of Amoret contrasts sharply with the artifice of reconciliation. When Arthur finds her in the forest, she is "almost dead and desperate," ingloriously wounded and unromantically in need. In his effort to shelter Amoret (and her less vulnerable companion, Aemylia), Arthur unwittingly takes her to the House of Slander, a foul old woman "stuft with rancour and despight / Vp to the throat" (24). Once they are within her house, an indignant and somewhat bitter poet intrudes at length in the narrative to connect Slander to the present age ("Sith now of dayes") and to oppose this age to the ideal or antique image. Slander's railings therefore have a general historicity or timeliness pointedly attributed to them for which Amoret's own adventures—apart from the topicality of her relation to Timias' estrangement from Belphoebe—fail to account. In short, what befalls Amoret in the two cantos she shares with Belphoebe and Timias looks very much like the other half of their story, the half muted in Belphoebe's withdrawal from Timias and suppressed in her return to him. What befalls Amoret unfolds the "inburning wrath" of Belphoebe (viii. 17) and gives tongue to the revilement and infamy that Ralegh's secret marriage incurred.

Writing presumably in 1592 from the Tower, Ralegh contrasted the Queen's formerly gracious favor to him with his present state:

Thos streames seeme standinge puddells which, before,
Wee saw our bewties in, so weare they cleere.
Bellphebes course is now obserude no more,
That faire resemblance weareth out of date.
Our Ocean seas are but tempestius waves
And all things base that blessed wear of late.

[ll. 269–74]

If we remember Spenser's final vision of Belphoebe in 1590, with its series of "faire" steps from living audience to the highest ideal, these words from *Ocean to Cynthia* have an added edge. But even without this refinement, they afford a commentary on the distance we have seen opening between living Queen and ideal image, in this case, Belphoebe: as the imprisoned Ralegh again observes of this distance, "A Queen shee was to mee, no more Belphebe, / A Lion then, no more a milke white Dove" (ll. 327–28). The extreme artificiality of the reconciliation of Belphoebe and Timias in Book IV bears a similar testimony. As the distance widens, as an ideal Belphoebe becomes further detached from living reference, other kinds of references to the present age build up and push intrusively into Faerie. Their violence and their ugliness, unparalleled by the more controlled images of evil in Books I, II, and even III, do not just threaten the Faerie vision but actually violate it.

The old hag who reviles Amoret, her companion, and her would-be rescuer is nothing short of hideous, as extreme in her violent ugliness as conciliatory dove and ruby-heart are in their artificiality. The poet seems almost unable to put a stop to his description of her. "A foule and loathly creature" with "filthy lockes," she sits in her house "Gnawing her nayles for felnesse and for yre, / And there out sucking venime to her parts entyre" (23–24). The description continues for another two stanzas with a reiterative emphasis and expansiveness that partial quotation hardly conveys. She abuses all goodness, frames causeless crimes, steals away good names. Nothing can be done so well "aliue"—that is, in life—without her depriving it of "due praise." As the poet continues, castigating the verbal poison Slander spues forth from her

hellish inner parts, she becomes an unmistakable precursor first of
Detraction and then of that poet's nightmare, the Blatant Beast,
"For like the stings of Aspes, that kill with smart, / Her spightfull
words did pricke, and wound the inner part.[18]

"Such was that Hag," the poet concludes, "vnmeet to host such
guests, / Whom greatest Princes court would welcome fayne" (27).
Then, just before the poet in his own voice breaks into the narrative
for five stanzas to decry the distance between antique age and present corruption, he praises the patience of Slander's "guests," who
endure every insult she can offer,

> And vnto rest themselues all onely lent,
> Regardlesse of that queane so base and vilde,
> To be vniustly blamd, and bitterly reuilde.
> [IV.viii.28]

Quean, meaning 'harlot,' 'hussy,' or in Spenser's case, 'hag,' is not
the same word as *queen,* and it should be obvious from the poet's
virulent description of Slander that she is not an image of the Virgin
Queen.[19] But the word "queane" in this context is not disposed of
so easily, nor is the possibility that for one awful moment the image
of the bitter old woman glances at the living Queen.

Philologists have been reluctant to recognize the likelihood of
the homonymic pun on *quean/queen* in Renaissance English that
exists in modern English. Kökeritz notes that contemporary
philological evidence proves the possibility of such a pun in colloquial speech but doubts that polite speakers would have found the
pun readily accessible. Dobson likewise notes the distinction in
pronunciation of the two vowels in educated southern speech but
allows for vulgar or dialectical variations in which the pun would
exist.[20] The pun is therefore possible but unlikely or inappropriate
in a polite context, an argument that might, indeed, recommend it
on grounds of aesthetic decorum—not to say political prudence—
for the impassioned description of an impolite hag. The historical
imagination is hard pressed to picture a courtier who would be
likely to explain such a pun to the Queen or even willing to admit
recognition of its presence.

Admitting the pun in Spenser's use of *quean,* we might regard it as one of the many signs in Book IV that the poem is becoming more private and personal, but we can do so without having to argue that the pun or at the very least the possibility of wordplay would not have been recognized by a number of Spenser's readers. Wordplay on the combination *quean/queen* has a long history, in part because of its alliterative potential, as, for example, in Langland's lines, "At churche in the charnel cheorles aren vuel to knowe, / Other a knyght fro a knaue, other a queyne fro a queene."[21] In passing, I should also note that in an age of printing like the Renaissance the spelling of *quean*—"queen" and "queyn" in Thynne's Chaucer—was a visual invitation to wordplay, which philology would be inclined to discount.[22] Whatever its causes, the pun on *quean/queen* almost certainly exists in Shakespeare's *Antony and Cleopatra* when Enobarbus quips that Apollodorus has carried "A certaine Queene to *Caesar* in a Matris" (II.vi.72).[23] The same pun also occurs in Middleton's *A Trick to Catch the Old One* when Witt-Good disclaims youth's follies, including "sinfull Riotts, / Queanes Evills, Doctors diets" (V.ii.185–86). The evils of queans are venereal, but highly qualified readers agree that the pun on *quean/queen* and the consequent play on *king's evil* (scrofula) is present here.[24] Contemporary dramatic use of a pun argues its accessibility to auditors, and a play on diseases dependent on the pun urges this fact.

To my mind, the most illuminating information about Spenser's calling Slander a "queane" is that this is his sole use of the word. Occasion, Duessa, Impatience, Impotence, the witch who creates false Florimell—not a one of these hags wears this common Renaissance label, and we might almost suppose that Spenser was deliberately avoiding it. That he should suddenly have used the word "queane" accidentally or innocently in a context inseparable from Belphoebe, Timias, and the relation of Faerie ideal to present age defies credibility, and does so much more, in view of Spenser's verbal sensitivity, than does the possibility that he alludes momentarily to the Queen.

As with Belphoebe's rose in Book III, there are now no precise or steady equivalents for the figures gathered in Slander's House:

Amoret does not equal Elizabeth Throckmorton, Arthur does not equal Ralegh, Aemylia does not equal anybody, and Slander certainly does not equal the Queen.[25] In the moments and ways I have suggested, however, what happens to Amoret reflects on one level the scandal, wrath, and disgrace Ralegh's marriage unleashed, and briefly the poet holds up to his sovereign the kind of distorted reflection found in a hideous cartoon. The figures of Lucifera, Philotime, and false Florimell bear witness that such a distorted image—such parody—is not entirely alien to the poet's techniques in earlier books, but it recurs here with a difference. Lucifera is not a missing side of Una or of the Queen but a denial of what they truly are. Where she is a possible threat, Slander is a present reality.[26] Complex yet still balanced and grasped together in Book III, contrasting violently and centrifugally in Book IV, opposite words, opposite meanings, and opposite realities figure crucially in the troubled process of reassessing the relation of the Faerie vision to the living Queen.

Notes

1. *The Faerie Queene* I.xxi.8, 23; iv.8, II.vii.44–45. All Spenserian references are to *Works: A Variorum Edition,* ed. Edwin A. Greenlaw et al., 11 vols. (Baltimore: Johns Hopkins University Press, 1932–57), cited hereafter as *Var.*

2. *Henry IV* I,iii.201–02, V.i.131, ed. Herschel Baker, in *The Riverside Shakespeare* (Boston: Houghton Mifflin, 1974).

3. Long since, in an illuminating and liberating article, Louis Martz showed that Spenser was not unaware of comic nuances in his sonnets: "The *Amoretti:* 'Most Goodly Temperature,'" in *Form and Convention in the Poetry of Edmund Spenser,* ed. William Nelson (New York: Columbia University Press, 1961), pp. 146–68. We continue to make progress regarding the poet's control of his meaning elsewhere, but slowly sometimes.

4. This paragraph borrows from my "What comes after Chaucer's *BUT:* Adversative Constructions in Spenser," in *Acts of Interpretation: The Text in Its Context,* ed. Mary J. Carruthers and Elizabeth D. Kirk (Norman Okla.: Pilgrim Books, 1982), n. 6.

5. "The 11th: and last booke of the Ocean to Scinthia," ll. 69, 497 ff., cf. 29–30, *The Poems of Sir Walter Ralegh,* ed. Agnes M. C. Latham

(London: Routledge & Kegan Paul, 1951). All references to *Ocean to Cynthia* are to this edition. On the dating of *Cynthia*, see Latham's introduction, pp. xxxvi–xl; and Stephen J. Greenblatt, *Sir Walter Ralegh: The Renaissance Man and His Roles* (New Haven: Yale University Press, 1973), pp. 12–13.

6. In "Colin Clovts Come Home Againe," Spenser calls Ralegh "shepheard of the Ocean" (l. 66); see also ll. 164, 174–75 in connection with the dating of *Cynthia*. On possible earlier versions of *Cynthia*, see Agnes M. C. Latham, ed., *Sir Walter Raleigh: Selected Prose and Poetry* (London: Athlone Press, 1965), p. 25, and on the style of *Cynthia*, pp. 210–11. Greenblatt's discussion of *Cynthia* is invaluable (pp. 77–98); his remarks on pastoral are especially pertinent (pp. 80, 84–85).

7. See *Var.*, 3:245–46 (xxvii ff.), but also 3:247 (xxxv). The Virgilian text is available in *Var.*, 2:219 (xxxii.6–xxxiii.4): "O—quam te memorem, virgo? Namque haud tibi vultus / Mortalis, nec vox hominem sonat; O, dea, certe." Given Spenser's earlier association of this passage with Belphoebe (II.iii.33), its bearing on Timias' lines is unmistakable.

8. *Spenser's Image of Nature: Wild Man and Shepherd in "The Faerie Queene"* (New Haven: Yale University Press, 1966), p. 102.

9. *Var.*, 3:248 (lii). The reference is to Ralph Church's edition, 1758.

10. *Var.*, 3:198. The full title of the final sonnet is "To all the gratious and beautifull Ladies in the Court."

11. Cf. *Faerie Queene* III.v.53: "Of chastity and vertue virginall." Chastity and virginity are not identical in this line.

12. *OED*, s.v. *Stair sb*, 1: "An ascending series . . . of steps"; 2: "One of a succession of steps"; 2d. *fig:* "A step of degree in a (metaphorical) ascent or in a scale of dignity"; 2e: "A high position."

13. A. C. Hamilton, ed., *The Faerie Queene* (London: Longman, 1977), p. 354, aligns this claim about Florimell with that about Belphoebe.

14 Hamilton, ed., *The Faerie Queene*, p. 354. Hamilton's sensitivity to the need of a gloss is notable.

15. Cf. Louis Adrian Montrose's highly provocative analysis of Petrarchan sublimation in "'The perfecte paterne of a Poete': The Poetics of Courtship in *The Shepheardes Calender*," *TSLL* 21 (1979), 34–67, esp. p. 54 (November Eclogue: Dido/Elissa).

16. In *Mirror and Veil: The Historical Dimension of Spenser's "Faerie Queene"* (Chapel Hill: University of North Carolina Press, 1977), pp. 113–14, Michael O'Connell rightly locates a "sense of paradox" in the final stanza of III.v, the result especially of the word "Nathlesse." Although I do not agree with all of O'Connell's views on p. 114, this sense of paradox follows naturally from my own reading of the penultimate stanza ("ensample dead") and fittingly concludes the canto.

17. See O'Connell, *Mirror and Veil*, p. 116; and A. L. Rowse, *Ralegh and the Throckmortons* (London: Macmillan, 1962), pp. 164, 204–06.

18. Cf. *Faerie Queene* V.xii.36, VI.vi.1.

19. *OED*, s.v. *Quean*, 1; s.v. *Queen* (etymology): *quean* and *queen* have an ablaut-relationship. Thomas P. Roche, Jr., ed., *The Faerie Queene* (Harmondsworth, Middlesex: Penguin, 1978), p. 1176, glosses *quean* as *hag*. This meaning seems obvious from several examples in the *OED* and is the most appropriate one for Spenser's context.

20. Helge Kökeritz, *Shakespeare's Pronunciation* (New Haven: Yale University Press, 1960), p. 88; E. J. Dobson, *English Pronunciation 1500– 1700* (Oxford: Oxford University Press, Clarendon Press, 1968), 2:640, 612, n. 2.

21. *The Vision of William concerning Piers the Plowman in Three Parallel Texts*, ed. Walter W. Skeat (London: Oxford University Press, 1886), C.IX.45–46 (my punctuation). For a concise discussion of Langland's "punning" on quean/queen and its basis in Old English, see Mary Carruthers, *The Search for St. Truth: A Study of Meaning in "Piers Plowman"* (Evanston: Northwestern University Press, 1973), pp. 60–61, n. 19. Carruthers discusses a second instance of wordplay in Langland's line "*here* nis no quen queynt*ere þat* quyk is o lyue" (A.II.14: George Kane, ed.).

22. Chaucer, *Works 1532*, supplemented by material from the editions of 1542, 1561, 1598, and 1602 (London: Scolar Press, 1969), fol. 104, verso, Manciples Prologue, l. 34; fol. 165, verso, column a, l. 19.

23. From the Norton facsimile of the First Folio.

24. Quotation from Middleton is from Charles Barber's edition (Berkeley: University of California Press, 1968); Barber considers the play on *king's evil* "doubtless." For the same view, see James T. Henke, *Renaissance Dramatic Bawdy (Exclusive of Shakespeare): An Annotated Glossary and Critical Essays, Jacobean Drama Studies*, 39 (Salzburg: Institut für Englische und Literatur Universität Salzburg, 1974), 2:249.

25. On the presence of Aemylia and other levels of meaning in IV.viii, see my "Whatever Happened to Amoret? The Poet's Role in Book IV of *The Faerie Queene*," *Criticism* 13 (1971), 180–200, esp. 181–85.

26. Near the end of the poet's praise of antiquity and denunciation of the present, he first appears to compliment the Queen but does not in fact do so. Instead he speaks with an evasive ambiguity that is to become increasingly characteristic of his compliments to her and, it would appear, of his disillusionment with her. In xxxii.8, "her glorious flowre" is beauty's (l. 1). In xxxiii.5, the word "her," while ambiguous, logically refers to beauty's glorious flower in l. 6 (chastity, to judge from Book III); from this flower proceed the "drops" or dew or nectar of virtue. The near, but failed, reference of the pronouns in these stanzas to the living Queen is further testimony of the distance between her and the ideal image.

E. TALBOT DONALDSON

Cressid False, Criseyde Untrue:
An Ambiguity Revisited

When Shakespeare's Ulysses begins his famous condemnation of
Cressida—

> Fie, fie upon her!
> There's language in her eye, her cheek, her lip,
> Nay, her foot speaks; her wanton spirits look out
> At every joint and motive of her body—[1]

he is responding to one of Chaucer's narrator's not very informative
descriptions of Criseyde in the first book:

> She nas nat with the leste of hire stature,
> But alle hire lymes so wel answerynge
> Weren to wommanhod, that creature
> Was nevere lasse mannyssh in semynge.
> And ek the pure wise of hire mevynge
> Shewed wel that men myght in hire gesse
> Honour, estat, and wommanly noblesse.[2]

Ulysses has apparently been reading Chaucer, but he is not one of
those men who Chaucer says may, on the basis of the very way
Criseyde-Cressida looks, guess that she possesses honor, estate, and
womanly noblesse. On the contrary, the very way she moves be-
speaks slut; and Ulysses thinks that old Nestor, who has just remarked rather admiringly that she is "a woman of quick sense," is
silly not to recognize her at once for what she is.

The two quotations dramatize the problem of the relation of
Shakespeare's heroine to Chaucer's. The two women are artistic
realizations of the same legendary figure, but they have very dissimilar personalities, so dissimilar that some scholars deny that
Chaucer's Criseyde had any significant influence on Shakespeare's

Cressida. But one critic, John Bayley, has wondered out loud
whether the two women "are not in fact based on the same kind of
interest and understanding on the part of the two writers; and even
whether Shakespeare, with that sureness of instinct which makes it
irrelevant to ask whether or not he was 'interested' in such a character, may not have formed his Cressida from Chaucer's."[3] I think
that is precisely what Shakespeare did; here I shall consider Shakespeare's Cressida in the light of Chaucer's Criseyde—rather than in
the darkness cast by her shadow, as is too often done.

From Benoît de Sainte Maure, who invented her, up to Dryden,
who destroyed her by making her faithful, the Cressid figure had
only a single raison d'être, her infidelity. In the end she had always
behaved the same, no matter who was telling the story, having
exercised what is for a heroine of romance a sadly limited potential
—to betray her lover. I emphasize this obvious point because
critics have often made it seem that Chaucer's Criseyde is a better and more moral unfaithful woman than Shakespeare's Cressida. Yet Thersites' comment on Cressida's last words in the play
applies just as exactly to Criseyde's longest speech to Diomede in
book 5 of the poem. Indeed, Criseyde's equivocal monologue, in
which she manages to keep one eye on Troy and one eye on
Diomede, is even better characterized by Thersites' words than is
Cressida's admission that she is following the "error" of her eyes.
Says Thersites,

> A proof of strength she could not publish more,
> Unless she said, "My mind is now turn'd whore."[4]

Though harshly expressed, this is the appropriate last word on both
Cressida and Criseyde, and on all the Cressid-kind.

I suppose that Shakespeare chose to recreate Cressida simply
because she was such a celebrated example of human inconstancy,
the appropriate heroine for a play in which one of the major themes
is human inconstancy and inconsistency—the passion with which
people express ideals combined with the ease with which they disre-
gard them. One of the themes of Chaucer's poem—perhaps its
major theme—is the medieval commonplace, the instability of

worldly happiness. Shakespeare seems to have been more concerned with human instability, that great source of worldly infelicity. Every man in his play—except perhaps Pandarus and Thersites—is inconsistent: Troilus, at first rendered by love too woman-weak to fight, later fighting and urging Hector to fight like a merciless madman; in council arguing that one must at all costs hold on to the things in which one places value and then making no effort to prevent Cressida's transfer to the Greek camp; Hector, splendidly arguing that Helen be returned to the Greeks and then abruptly turning his back on his own argument; later allowing a whimsical desire for a suit of gold armor to obliterate both his chivalry and his prudence: Achilles, the great martial hero, playing silly charades with Patroclus in his tent, refusing to fight even after he has undertaken to, and when he finally fights, fighting like a coward; and Ulysses, whose assumed horror at Patroclus' mockery of Agamemnon and Nestor is wholly belied by his own carefully detailed account of that mockery to Agamemnon and Nestor; who discourses magnificently on human behavior and behaves himself like a second-rate—and incompetent—Machiavel. For a world in which virtues blaze up, sputter, and go out, what better symbol could there be than the Cressida of literary tradition?

Chaucer's great achievement was to invoke so much sympathy for his heroine in the earlier part of the poem that her foreknown act of treason comes as a shock—not unlike the shock of tragedy—to the reader when that which his mind knows all along will happen happens against the expectation of his heart. This sympathy for Criseyde is largely produced by Chaucer's narrator,[5] who, being head over heels in love with her, suffuses his characterization of her with adoration. For the most part of four books all propositions relating to her—her appearance, her behavior, her motives— whether the propositions are self-evidently true or wholly dubious, are relayed to us with loving appreciation. She does indeed have some attractive qualities which we can perceive without the narrator's working overtime—gaiety, grace, elegance, in short, great female charm—but many of our sympathetic responses to her are actually responses to the narrator's manipulation of her and of us.

While she is surely in a precarious position in a Troy to which her father has proved traitor, the narrator's introduction of her is more emotional than candid: we meet her, poor thing, in peril from an outraged populace, "allone / Of any frend to whom she dorste hir mone."[6] Who will not pity so forlorn a creature, who also happens to be, according to the narrator's own eyewitness, the loveliest woman in the whole city? And so we pity her, and gladly forgive both her and her narrator when it turns out that, far from being alone and friendless, she has a couple of nieces and a dozen or so attendant women residing with her in a well-equipped house, and an uncle who drops in often for a chat and in whom she can confide. Somehow we are made to feel that this is the proper comfortable environment for so elegant a damsel in distress to enjoy her distress in.

Out of respect for Chaucer's celebrated insight into the human psyche I should like to credit him with having created a woman we can understand as well as love. But the fact is that while the narrator often seems to be probing Criseyde's behavior and motives, he gives us remarkably little firm information. From the description I quoted earlier we learn, for instance, that while she was not among the smallest of women, all her limbs corresponded so well to womanhood that no one ever seemed less masculine—a collection of data from which it is hard to infer much. What we are given in Criseyde is the portrait of a woman of almost mythological femininity, and readers presented with such a portrait become their own myth makers. And what an abundance of ambiguities and contradictions they have to work on! Criseyde is the timidest creature in the world, afraid of Greeks, and of love, and of steel weapons; she is also of "ful assured lokyng and manere,"[7] and almost never loses her poise or self-assurance; she trembles like an aspen leaf in Troilus' embrace—a lark in the clutches of a sparrowhawk, to whom, a few minutes earlier, she has had to administer first aid for a fainting fit. Despite the strong impression we are given that she is a modest chaste widow with no interest in the opposite sex, she observes, on the first occasion Troilus rides by her window, that his body shows good potential for performing an unspecified "thing," an observation at which she blushes.[8] Initially she wonders whether Troilus can speak well of love, but when on their first night together he goes on and on speaking well of love, she interrupts with a tactful suggestion that it is perhaps time for deeds. And on their last night together, when it appears that they are likely to waste it in lamentation on the floor, she suggests that it is time for them to rise and go to bed.

Such actions provide material to those readers who wish to find in Criseyde prognostications of her future behavior, and that Chaucer was anxious to provide such material is shown by his allowing his narrator occasionally to engender suspicion of Criseyde by trying to quell it: thus when in book 2 she is considering whether to accept Troilus, the narrator suddenly intrudes to scold any readers who think she is falling in love too fast—a possibility that few would have entertained if the narrator had not mentioned it. Of course, once a reader has been made suspicious, even the most innocent statements develop ambiguity. Thus such seemingly laudatory comments by the narrator as "For she was wis," or reports of her own thoughts such as "It nedeth me ful sleighly for to pleie"[9] strike some readers as sinister betrayals of a romance heroine's obligation to be as stupid as she is beautiful, and lead to suggestions that she is like her father Calchas, calculating. Perhaps the best example of the technique of ambiguity that Chaucer uses with Criseyde occurs when, in the small chamber at Deiphobus' house, Pandarus is urging her to take pity on the bedridden Troilus. Her response is described thus:

> With that she gan hire eyen on hym caste
> Ful esily and ful debonairly,
> Avysyng hire, and hied nought to faste
> With nevere a word.[10]

"Hied nought to faste": did not hurry too fast. The suspicious reader will hear the verb "hied" and have his impression confirmed that Criseyde is indeed hurrying, but is disguising the fact ("nought to faste"), and his suspicion may be reinforced by the phrase "Avysyng hire," keeping her mind in control of the situation. The sympathetic reader, on the other hand, will understand the words to mean that she is proceeding at precisely the right modest speed expected of a heroine whom one wishes to see give in, but not too fast; such a reader will congratulate her on her intelligence in looking before she leaps. Chaucer would be happy with either impression, and happier with both, though his narrator would be horrified at the first. For here he is, crediting his heroine with the ability to execute the impossible maxim *festina lente:* make haste slowly. As I have said elsewhere,[11] most members of the human race simply cannot festinate with lentitude—only Chaucer's myth of lovely femininity, his not unimpossible she, could pull it off. How, after all, would an actor on the stage make haste slowly?

It is a principle in physics that transparent bodies refract part of the light incident upon them and reflect another part. I suppose it is unfair to liken some one whom I have just presented as an optical illusion to a transparent body, but Criseyde's qualities appear both refracted and reflected in Shakespeare's Cressida. John Bayley believes that what the two women "chiefly have in common is that neither of them know what they want, and so they become the victims of what other people want."[12] This is a shrewd observation, though it seems to me to apply rather better to Criseyde than to Cressida. But it does not take sufficiently into account the fact that there is something both of them want and want desperately, Cressida even more than Criseyde because she has less of it, and that is security from the perils of life in Troy. I think that Shakespeare was particularly struck by the dramatic possibilities offered by the vulnerability of Chaucer's heroine, her precariousness in a city at war, the daughter of a traitor. I'm sure Shakespeare was not fooled by Chaucer's narrator's misleading introduction of Criseyde as "alone, without a friend to whom she dared complain," but he adopts its suggestion for the predicament into which to place his Cressida: war is a presence far more real in his play, and Cressida is not a well-to-do widow with a large household and much female companionship. Rather, she is a young unmarried woman, presumably with a house, though not one that gives us the impression of stability and ease imparted by Criseyde's paved parlor, gold-embroidered cushions, garden with sanded paths, and, above all, attendant women. Cressida is one of Shakespeare's few unmarried women without a confidante—no Celia, no Nerissa, not even a Nurse. Miranda at least had a wise if somewhat grumpy father. But poor Cressida has no one to confide in but Pandarus, in whom she does not confide, for he is a very seedy uncle compared to Criseyde's, and one intent on serving her up on a platter to his friend Prince Troilus. In this last respect he resembles his forerunner, but the danger to Cressida is far greater since she already loves the man he is trying to serve her up to. Cressida's infatuation with Troilus before the action begins is perhaps Shakespeare's most radical alteration in the story. Most of the leisurely development of Chaucer's Criseyde's character occurs not when she is in love, but while she is deciding whether or not she will accept the service of a man with whom she may, in some remote future, fall in love, if she feels like it. She is not under pressure from her heart, only from her uncle. It is not even clear at what point she moves from courtly pity for Troilus to love for him, and ultimately she seems more to slide into love than to fall into it. But with Cressida love is not merely an alternative lifestyle, something one is free to choose or reject; it is a fact of her young life, and one that hurts while it frightens. We have only to watch Rosalind to see the unnerving effect falling in love has on even Shakespeare's nicest heroines; and they at least have the comfort of hoping they may wind up with a husband, not just a lover, which seems to be the most a Trojan girl can expect.

That, from the very beginning of the play, Cressida is not a nice girl is a proposition that seems to have great appeal for moralistic critics,[13] who find even such a natural action as her having fallen in love proof of her innate light-mindedness. Though she has had some defenders, the majority of those who write about her seem to be critical followers of Ulysses, the first high-minded intellectual to settle her business by calling her a slut. At least he is terse about it, while some of her modern nonadmirers go on at great length demonstrating her bad character, as if they were anxious to stop us from wasting emotions on the wrong kind of women. Such preoccupation with establishing Cressida's sluttishness seems itself to reflect a kind of emotional involvement with her that is less literary than personal.

Like the stern parents of a bad Victorian girl in a bad Victorian novel, critics turn Cressida's picture to the wall on which they leave it hanging, dramatizing at once their disapproval of her and their involvement with her. Indeed, Shakespeare had done, in a refractory way, what he saw Chaucer had done before him, that is, involve the onlooker's personal emotions with his heroine. I can think of no literary characters who have been subjected to criticism less cool-headed than Criseyde and Cressida; and when they are treated together, they tend to become the two sides of a companion picture, in which the good qualities of the one are exactly balanced by the bad qualities of the other. Here I am suggesting that Criseyde has been written up at Cressida's expense, and Cressida written down to Criseyde's advantage.

Bernard Shaw is reported to have considered Cressida Shakespeare's first real woman,[14] and while her morality may be dubious, her vitality is not—the hostility she arouses in moralistic critics is indeed a testimony to her vitality. Yet her speaking role in the play is small: she speaks only 117 times, and a hundred of her speeches are of less than twenty words; eighty of less than ten. She has only a half-dozen longish speeches in the whole play. Moreover, more than a third of her speeches are or contain questions—a percentage that I doubt is exceeded by any other considerable character in Shakespeare. The brevity of her remarks, their quick staccato quality, impart vitality to her; and her questions establish her as some one unsure of herself, but alert and seeking facts. Lacking Chaucer's narrator as a companion, she seems more independent than Criseyde; and lacking his total control of the perspective and his ability to manipulate what we see, she cannot share her predecessor's glamorous mystery, and her motives may not be so veiled in ambiguity. Cressida has to hold her own on the stage in full view of us all. But her character has a marked ambiguity, though it is of a different sort from Criseyde's. What Shakespeare does is exploit the fact that all young people, and especially attractive young women with independent minds, possess all sorts of potentialities, of qualities that may with equal probability develop into something moralists will call good or something they will call bad. Since our judgment of her must depend wholly on her words, he assigns her a number of speeches of a kind that, since we are aware of the happy outcome of the plays in which Beatrice or Rosalind appear, we should forgive in those heroines but, since we know the different outcome of Cressida's play, we are less ready to forgive in her. When it is known that a woman will become a slut, any bawdiness she speaks before she actually does so is naturally understood as an appropriate indication of her true character.

Actually, since no one has invented a scatologometer by which to establish standards of indecency, we cannot measure Cressida's bawdiness against that of heroines of better reputation. She does, however, appear no more prominently in Eric Partridge's study of Shakespearean obscenities than some of her more innocent sisters.[15] Yet even if it could be proved that she was no worse than they, the brevity of her whole role would exaggerate the effect of whatever bawdiness it contains. And I note here that bawdiness has sometimes been thrust upon her: one editor suggests that for one of her remarks, unexplained by him, the "best scholiast" would be Aristophanes, and other editors are occasionally too busy blushing at her words to tell us exactly what they're blushing at.[16] Many of her witticisms either are or appear to be double entendres, and I think that it is by a kind of extended use of double entendre that Shakespeare imparts to her much of her ambiguity. What she says often has enough suggestion of submerged indecent meaning to arouse the suspicion of an unprejudiced reader, but on a number of occasions an honest reader will wonder whether his suspicion was not wrongly aroused.[17] Is, for instance, the exchange between Troilus and Cressida on the monstrosity in love full of phallic references as virtually all my students immediately assume, or are such reactions the result of a reader's expectation of the worst from Cressida on all occasions?

For another instance, how one reads Cressida's first soliloquy will depend on one's initial prejudices, for the speech itself has a large potential for variation in interpretation. It is in this that she informs the audience that she loves Troilus passionately, but will "hold off" because, while "men prize the thing ungained," "love got" is not "so sweet as when desire did sue."[18] That is, after one gives in, men cool off and become bossy. One critic thunders that this soliloquy "proclaims her simple creed, the art of the coquette raised to a Rule of Life, based on the assumption that what is to be looked for in Man is simply 'lust in action.'"[19] To me her rhyming couplets sound like memorized advice from her mother, recited by a girl of no experience—straightforward self-preservative counsel based on the not wholly misguided assumption (in Troy, at least) that what is to be found in man *is* lust in action. Indeed, in Troilus' matching soliloquy, spoken later, just before his assignation with Cressida, he looks forward to "wallow[ing] in the lily-beds / Propos'd for the deserver" of her favors—a not unlustful program of action.[20] The critic who points out the similarity of Cressida's prudential soliloquy to Mrs. Peachum's advice to Polly in *The Beggars' Opera* is rendering Cressida a service he never intended, for he helps establish the universal applicability of her maxims;[21] and in the Quarto of the play three of them are accorded the quotation marks that frequently set off gnomic sayings in Elizabethan play texts. But the resolution that Cressida expresses here—what she later admits is impossible for mortals, to love and to be wise— arouses no sympathy in those who disapprove of her, who see in her attempt at self-preservation only flirtatiousness.

But if she is a flirt, she is an incompetent one, since she fails to hold off from Troilus; and I note that those critics who condemn her for the selfishness of her resolution to hold off not only fail to congratulate her for the generosity of her surrender, but take it as further evidence of her bad character. Further evidence of this is found in her first meeting with Troilus, where we are told that her embarrassed speech, in which she is explaining to Troilus why she was hard to win, is insincere—though the critics fail to explain how they know. They tell us also that when she says to Troilus, "Stop my mouth,"[22] she is really begging for the kiss she denies she is begging for. Yet considering that she and Troilus have just completed a remarkably prolonged kiss, measured by the duration of Pandar's verbal accompaniment, and that the immediate future threatens no dearth of kisses, her speech seems, as an act of flirtation, extremely redundant. Nor does her earlier speech, which even her harshest critics grudgingly admit she thinks is sincere, exhibit any of the speciousness of a flirt:

> Boldness comes to me now, and brings me heart.
> Prince Troilus, I have lov'd you night and day
> For many weary months.[23]

These are the words of any good Shakespearean heroine confessing her love with most engaging candor.

In stressing the potentiality for innocence in Cressida I am not denying the other side: I am merely trying to restore a more equal balance between the two faces of ambiguity. In the curious physics of literature, suspicion of absence of innocence always seems to have greater specific gravity than recognition of the possibility of its presence. But of course I cannot deny that it is sometimes proper if not inevitable to assign the less decent meaning of her words to Cressida's conscious intention, even where the possibility of the more decent meaning persists. When she says to her lover, all too hurriedly departing at dawn,

> Prithee tarry,
> You men will never tarry.
> O foolish Cressid! I might have still held off,
> And then you would have tarried,[24]

she may only be voicing, wryly, the truth of the maxims she recited earlier and has ignored; or expressing the ancient female complaint that men ration their moments of tenderness too severely and end them too abruptly. But that the words could come naturally from a woman of experience in bed-matters is undeniable. And even the reader most anxious to see innocence in Cressida is not much supported by her lover. When, a little later, hearing knocking at the gate, Cressida says to Troilus, "My lord, come you again into my chamber" and then adds, to the surprise of many readers, "You smile and mock me, as if I meant naughtily," his reply is a rude "Ha, ha!"[25] Her denial that she intended the pun on the word "chamber" that he has heard is justifiably indignant: he's treating her as if she were a whore.

The exchange again reveals an ambiguity attached to Cressida, but it tells us even more about Troilus. Chaucer's hero is an inexperienced idealist, capable of getting so lost in his own thoughts as to become paralyzed; but with Criseyde he is a thoughtful and considerate lover. Even so, though the narrator never mentions it, the pair seem to be something of a mismatch. They are in a common situation in which one of the partners in a love affair possesses high ideals which the other admires—even loves—without sharing, and which may at times prove exasperating to one who feels that adjustment to reality is more important than upholding ideals. Criseyde is always gayer and more relaxed with her realistic uncle than with her lover, and one wonders whether her resigning herself so easily to going to the Greek camp is not in part the result of a certain fatigue from living up to Troilus' ideals. I think Shakespeare noted this mismatch, and imitated it while altering its nature. He awarded his Cressida a much less sensitive and suitable lover than Chaucer's Troilus. Shakespeare's Troilus has his forerunner's ability to get lost in his own head, so lost, indeed, that he seems hardly aware that Cressida is a person as well as a mistress: his sensuous soliloquy, mentioned earlier, on what it will be like to lie with her somehow manages to omit her entirely—it's all about Troilus;[26] his *alba* on leaving her in the morning is one of the shortest and most reluctant on record—he's capable of marvelous poetry, but it's generally to or about himself; and finally, when Cressida, hearing of her exchange for Antenor, says she will not leave Troy, Troilus informs her bluntly that she will. Chaucer's Troilus had begged Criseyde to steal away with him, and she had refused; Shakespeare's Cressida asks Troilus four times whether she must leave, and four times he tells her yes, she must. From the beginning he has been preoccupied with his ability to be true in love, and it almost seems as if Cressida's departure—even her possible infidelity—were to be welcomed as providing the most favorable circumstances in which to prove his fidelity. Cressida's potentiality for infidelity, indeed, becomes an inseparable element of the rhetoric by which, at their parting, he expresses his own high resolve to be true to her: he can't mention his truth without suggesting her untruth. He even manages to put

himself into the position of Chaucer's Troilus by lecturing her on
the temptations she will meet in the Greek camp, as if he too were
addressing a woman who was willing to go and whom he was trying
to stop from going—the exact opposite of the facts of the situation.
Before Shakespeare's lovers finally part, one begins to feel that
Chaucer's Troilus, who tries to stop Criseyde from going, would
have been a better mate for Shakespeare's Cressida, who doesn't
want to go, and Chaucer's Criseyde, who is willing to go, a more
appropriate one for Shakespeare's Troilus, who is not trying to stop
anyone. Considered in relation to her lover's character and his behavior to her, Shakespeare's Cressida's decision to take up with
Diomed is more understandable than was Criseyde's, who abandoned her lover before he could abandon her—as he never did.

But of course Cressida remains unforgivable: she fulfills her
literary responsibility and becomes a daughter of the game, thus
making an honest man out of Ulysses. But up until the final scene
in which she appears she maintains her ambiguity, for even her
penultimate scene, in which she presumably performs the actions
for which Ulysses condemns her, is ambiguous. She enters with
Diomede to the Greek generals and is greeted by Agamemnon with
a polite speech and a kiss of welcome, which I take to be his
privilege as commander-in-chief of the Greeks. Nestor then diplo-
matically informs her who it is who has just kissed her—"Our
general doth salute you with a kiss."[27] It is here that Ulysses,
apparently already noting the silent Cressida's wanton spirits looking out at every joint and motive of her body, makes his witty
suggestion:

> Yet is the kindness but particular,
> 'Twere better she were kiss'd in general—

a nice use of the passive voice to establish Cressida's status as an
object to be acted upon by the Greek brass. Nestor then begins the
kissing game, followed by Achilles, followed by Patroclus—who
kisses her twice, once for himself and once for Menelaus. Cressida is
thus kissed five times without speaking a word:[28] presumably by
this point in the play she is used to being treated as if she had no

feelings worth anyone's consulting. It is not until Menelaus insists
upon having his own kiss that she speaks—wittily, offensively in
both senses of the word, but defensively too. Indeed, the text indicates that she does not kiss Menelaus. Ulysses, the next officer in
line, fares as badly, or worse, with his request:

> *Ulysses,* May I, sweet lady, beg a kiss of you?
> *Cressida.* You may.
> *Ulysses.*   I do desire it.
> *Cressida.*   Why, beg then.

She has caught the old fox with a very old trick: he has her permission to beg a kiss, but that is all. Ulysses' attempt to recover from
this setback is less than impressive:

> Why then for Venus' sake, give me a kiss
> When Helen is a maid again and his.

Wit that should be crisp and salty is instead soggy and merely
bitter. Cressida fields this weakly hit ball tidily enough: "I am your
debtor, claim it when 'tis due." This is a not unwitty way of saying
that never is for her a perfectly satisfactory time for Ulysses to claim
his kiss. At this point Ulysses, in apparent exasperation that she has
anticipated his own "Never," gives up trying to be witty and resorts
to the insult direct: "Never's my day, and then a kiss of you." As
Cressida is led away by Diomed, Nestor's exclamation, "A woman
of quick sense," precipitates Ulysses' condemnation of her with
which I began this paper. I give the conclusion of his speech:

> O, these encounterers, so glib of tongue,
> That give ac[co]sting welcome ere it comes,
> And wide unclasp the tables of their thoughts
> To every ticklish reader! set them down
> For sluttish spoils of opportunity,
> And daughters of the game.

If one looks at the written text of the scene this seems mere assertion, unsupported by evidence. Cressida's glib tongue has been
silent until late in the action, and indeed she utters only a few more
than seventy words in the whole scene. It is true that she manages to

strike Ulysses down with thirteen of them, but it is not true that she has wide unclasped the tables of her thoughts to any reader less ticklish than Ulysses. Nor has she given a welcome to accosting before it comes, having received five kisses in total silence. Moreover, Ulysses' pluralization of Cressida, his multiplying her from the individual to a species, enables him to pin all the hypothetical sins of the species on her, the individual; as we might say, "She's one of those girls who does such and such," or, in Elizabethan, set her down as one of those sluttish spoils of opportunity and daughters of the game—you know the kind I mean. It is clear that a pretty young woman should not beat a middle-aged self-proclaimed thinker in a small battle of wits, or deny him a kiss others have received. Sour are the grapes of his wrath.

Naturally the play's director in this scene can so direct the actors who play Cressida and Ulysses as to remove all ambiguity either by fully rebutting Ulysses' speech by following the written text or fully justifying it by reading it wholly in terms of Cressida's subsequent behavior. The potentiality for ambiguity is great. My point is that until the very last scene in which she appears Cressida's ambiguity persists, and that because it does, she is both unforgivable and yet one for whom, like Chaucer's Criseyde, it is necessary to feel sympathy. Because she is both unforgivable and understandable the play she is in presents a vision sadder and deeper than what Ulysses, for all his wiliness, can see. And for us to see from the beginning of the play no potentiality in Cressida for a future better than the one we know she will have is to reduce the play's vision to that of Thersites, which is a vision beyond faith, beyond hope, beyond the charity of imagination, and beneath humanity.

NOTES

1. *Troilus and Cressida*, 4:54–57. Citations from Shakespeare's play are from Anne Barton's edition in *The Riverside Shakespeare,* ed. G. B. Evans et al. (Boston: Houghton Mifflin, 1974).

2. *Troilus and Criseyde*, 1.281–87. Citations from Chaucer's poem are

from *The Works,* ed. F. N. Robinson, 2nd ed. (Boston: Houghton Mifflin, 1957). Shakespeare's copy of Chaucer probably read "moste" for "leste" in the first line, and "meaning" for "mevynge" in the fifth.

3. "Time and the Trojans," *EIC* 25 (1975), 68.

4. *Troilus and Cressida*, 5.2.113–14; *Troilus and Criseyde*, 5.956–1004.

5. Since the conception of Chaucer's heroine on which this essay is based is my own and varies greatly from the conception held by most Shakespeareans, I repeat here material which has been much more fully presented elsewhere: "Troilus and Criseide," in my *Chaucer's Poetry: An Anthology for the Modern Reader*, 2nd ed. (New York: Ronald Press, 1975); "The Masculine Narrator and Four Women of Style" and "Criseide and Her Narrator," in *Speaking of Chaucer* (London: Athlone Press, 1970), pp. 46–64, 65–83; "Chaucer and the Elusion of Clarity," *E&S* (1972), 23–44; "Briseis, Briseida, Criseyde, Cresseid, Cressid: Progress of a Heroine," in *Chaucerian Problems and Perspectives*, ed. Edward Vasta and Z. P. Thundy (Notre Dame: University of Notre Dame Press, 1970), pp. 1–12; "Chaucer in the Twentieth Century," *Studies in the Age of Chaucer* 2 (1980), 7–13. In her recent excellent book, *Shakespeare's Chaucer* (Liverpool: Liverpool University Press, 1978), Ann Thompson shows more sympathy for Cressida and less for Criseyde than is customary, but has not quite shaken off received prejudices.

6. 1.97–98. Shakespeare's Chaucer probably said that she was "alone, and did not know to whom she might complain."

7. 1.182.

8. 2.631–37, 649–52.

9. 3.86; 2.462.

10. 3.155–58.

11. Donaldson, "Chaucer in the Twentieth Century," p. 10.

12. Bayley, "Time and the Trojans," p. 68.

13. For a sampling of often vehemently disapproving characterizations of Cressida one has only to consult the New Variorum *Troilus and Cressida*, ed. H. N. Hillebrand and T. W. Baldwin (Philadelphia: Lippincott, 1953), pp. 552–59. Tucker Brooke's defense of her in *The Yale Review* in 1928 provides an honorable exception among the critics included in the Variorum. The chorus of those declaiming Cressida has lost little of its shrillness since 1953, and both full-length books on the play are hostile to her: R. K. Presson, *Shakespeare's Troilus and Cressida and the Legends of Troy* (Madison: University of Wisconsin Press, 1953) and R. T. Kimbrough, *Shakespeare's Troilus and Cressida and Its Setting* (Cambridge: Harvard University Press, 1964).

14. See R. F. Rattray, *Bernard Shaw: A Chronicle* (Luton: Leagrave Press, 1951), p. 47. Shaw found Cressida "enchanting."

15. *Shakespeare's Bawdy* (New York: Dutton, 1948). A scene involving Hero, Beatrice, and Margaret seems to set the record for feminine bawdiness.

16. K. Deighton, ed., *Troilus and Cressida,* The Arden Edition (Indianapolis: Bobbs-Merrill, 1906), n. to 1.2.277–79 (256–57 in *Riverside*): the "minc'd man" speech, which seems now generally considered inoffensive. In The Pelican Edition of Virgil K. Whitaker (Baltimore: Penguin Books, 1970) the note to 1.2.252 (268), the "watch and ward" speech, tells us that the "passage fully establishes Cressida's moral level" but fails to tell us precisely what sense Cressida's speech makes: until that is determined—and I know of no edition that grapples with the problem—it seems harsh to condemn Cressida for gratuitous obscenity.

17. Arnold Stein remarks that Cressida "has a trick, which might have provided Freud with useful examples, of slyly provoking indecent jokes at which then she can be embarrassed": "*Troilus and Cressida:* The Disjunctive Imagination," *ELH* 36 (1969), 149. Stein offers no evidence that Cressida does this intentionally.

18. 1.2.282–95.

19. M. C. Bradbrook, "What Shakespeare Did to Chaucer's *Troilus and Criseyde,*" *SQ* 9 (1958), 314. Bradbrook's conception of Chaucer's Criseyde is very different from mine, for she sees none of the ambiguities I have emphasized.

20. 3.2.12–13.

21. A. P. Rossiter, *Angel with Horns* (London: Longmans, 1961), p. 132.

22. 3.2.133.

23. 3.2.113–15.

24. 4.2.15–18.

25. 4.2.36–39.

26. The remarkable exclusion of Cressida as a person from this speech has been noted by David Kaula, "Will and Reason in *Troilus and Cressida,*" *SQ* 12 (1961), 272.

27. 4.5.19.

28. Cressida's silence has often been noted, especially by Hamill Kenny, "Shakespeare's Cressida," *Anglia* 61 (1937), 168, but few critics seem disposed to argue with Ulysses' insistence that she is glib of tongue.

GEORGE K. HUNTER

Tyrant and Martyr: Religious Heroisms in Elizabethan Tragedy[1]

It is often said, and with good reason, that Christian tragedy is an oxymoron.[2] The idea of a catharsis, of an inexplicable mixture of pity for the hero's unjust individual fate and of terror that the same fate could fall on any man—this is hardly compatible with a strongly represented system of total justice post mortem when tears will be wiped away and unjust gains melted in the fire. And yet tragedy of undoubted power and generic centrality has flourished in periods of widely diffused faith, in the France of Racine no less than the England of Shakespeare, written by authors whom we have no reason to suspect of infidelity and for whom there is considerable evidence of religious assent. It looks as if Tragedy, like Heaven, has many mansions. The sense of tragic mystery in human experience seems to be basic enough to show up true in the theater even in periods of dogmatic faith and to be available to those who, elsewhere in their lives, will invoke specifically religious explanations of the same experience.

The tightrope upon which the tragic artist of an age of faith must dance obviously stands in tension between polarities. At one end stands a humility of perception, which allows no sense of the meaning of life beyond what is underwritten by the dogmas of a church; at the other end is a brisk individualism which simply asserts the adequacy of emotional states to serve as ethical answers. It is one of the fascinations of the Tudor/Stuart period that it allows us to see these polarities in historical as well as ethical terms. At the beginning of the Tudors we are close to the humble aesthetic of a Christian

viewpoint; by 1642 we are at least within sight of individual responsibility for individual fate. The "great period" (say 1585–1625)
is marked by a tension that runs between the two positions and
allows each to brace the other. It is probably only under this kind of
tension that a fiction can be written which is at once resolutely
secular (and so "real") yet at the same time capable of energizing the
deepest emotional levels of engagement with the Unknown.

Tudor drama begins with perceptions rather remote from
tragedy. The biblical cycles, still in full swing in 1485, showed
human potential in terms of one single ideal, the life of Christ.
Faith and infidelity, belief and disbelief are here the basic forms of
good and evil that generate the specific behavior we are asked to
approve or abhor in Satan, Cain, Abraham, Noah, Herod, the
Magi, Paul, and many others such. Secular behavior, that is, has to
be understood as a means of expressing religious status. Even in the
morality plays and hybrid moralities that followed, individual
motives were continually infringed by spiritual standards, whether
the case be that of Sir Jonathas and his disbelief in the True Body of
the Eucharist (in *The Play of the Sacrament*) or the prodigal son's
revolt against his father's benevolence (in such plays as *The Glass of
Government, Nice Wanton, Youth, Hickscorner*). Even when the subject matter of these early Tudor plays was political and social rather
than private and particular the same infringing shadow lay across
the image of the secular world. The duty the king owes to his
country is judged valid because it is a picture of the duty owed to
God. "Good" or "bad" political actions are still seen to be dependent on supernatural norms even when the relationship of good
government to good conduct remains inexplicit or mysterious, as in
Gorboduc or Pickering's *Horestes.*

In terms of an understanding of history as relentlessly progressive one may explain the presence of these secular elements in early
Tudor plays as part of a developing dialectic: dramatic art emerges
from the Middle Ages, we might say, by setting an eventually
triumphant secularism and individuality against the pietism and
external authority of the past. The shaky chronology of the plays I
am talking about does not entirely support the Whig (alias Marxist)

view of progress, but it is also too shaky to refute it. It is fortunate therefore that I raise the issue only to point out its irrelevance to the argument I am conducting. What I am concerned with here is not the way in which different values rub against each other (secularism/spirituality, individualism/belief) to ignite the future, but rather the extent to which the same values, the same emotional patterns, survive across historical discontinuity, taking on a new face, adopting a new language, preserving meanings even though the forms that seemed to embody them disappear or are destroyed.

Our response to literature as a representation of human values is shown perhaps most clearly in our reaction to those value-bearing central characters we call heroes. I wish to consider some fashions in heroism in the drama of the Tudor period, fashions that drift from religious to secular norms. In speaking of such fashions I must of course indicate the ways in which different heroic values reflect the cultural assumptions of different historical periods. But, as I have indicated above, my aim is not to follow the process of historical change but rather to indicate the power of metamorphosis that lies within these values, allowing them to be reinterpreted and so to survive from one age into another. An age in which Jesus Christ is the dominant hero of the culture demands literary heroism of a particular kind. Of course no time since Homer's, or probably before, has been insensitive to the dazzle of military heroism. But the magnetism of Christ in an age of Christian faith was bound to pull military prowess in one particular direction, as is obvious (to stay with English examples) in such a work as *Gawain and the Green Knight,* where patience, loyalty, courtesy, and other such un-Achillean qualities are at the center of knightly virtue. Chaucer's great gallery of human types in *The Canterbury Tales* shows his knight likewise assimilated to a Christian ethic. The values that he follows are described as "chivalrye / Trouthe and honour, fredom and curteisye": in his port he is "as meke as is a mayde." The power of the ethic is measured precisely by the difficulty of belief in a *meke* warrior: *credo quia impossibile.* Elsewhere Chaucer can show the prevailing values with less strain. Clerk, Persoun, and Plowman are his most unambiguously praised characters because they are the most unambiguously Christlike, humble, meek, patient and—in a word—selfless. The word is useful: it reminds us of the gap between virtue and character, especially important if we are thinking of character as a principal part of theatrical effect. In narrative, particularly as mediated and moralized by a "right-thinking" narrator, the local representative of our Christian values, a hero who merely suffers can be supported by a framework of assumptions and accorded special privileges above the hurly-burly of competitive action and reaction. But in the theater there are no such privileges. In fact as well as etymology drama is essentially a representation of *doings* and its characters must be doers (Aristotle's *prattontes*). A passive hero creates a blank space in the center of the action, and this normally means that the spectator will look elsewhere for his interest. A protagonist who is *selfless* directs our attention to the compensating *selves,* the strongly marked individual characters who are needed to bring the whole design into equilibrium.

The clearest examples of this point appear in the visual arts. The various versions of Jerome Bosch's *Carrying of the Cross,* and particularly that in the Musée des Beaux Arts in Ghent, shows us the canvas crowded with faces of lurid intensity. In the middle of this apparently random swirl of violence and (in the Ghent picture) marked out as central by its position on the diagonal beams of the cross, is a face of complete inexpressiveness, passive, shut away, with the eyes closed. The positioning of Christ's face and our knowledge of the subject tells us that this unanimated figure is the source of the frenzied animation elsewhere. This is what they are all talking about, what "character" is responding to, the eye of the storm, the "still point of the turning world." The inexpressive blank at the heart of Bosch's painting is given its power by its formal placing and by the force of the antagonisms it balances and holds together. The strength of the victim is measured by the energy of the victimizers, the hidden radiance of the protagonist made visible only in the mirror of antagonism, the negative known only by the positives it releases. In the more dynamic terms of the theater one may say that this martyr demands these tyrants.

In the biblical cycles of the late Middle Ages Christ is, of course, the center of the story; but He is a center round whom the action moves rather than one whose character controls or takes overt responsibility for the way the plot advances. The important function of character-as-cause has to be carried by other figures in the story. Professor Arnold Williams in *The Characterization of Pilate in the Towneley Plays* notes the degree to which the extant cycles are dominated by the antagonist figures, Pharaoh, Augustus, Pilate, Herod.[3] These are the persons with whom we can have an immediate theatrical rapport, whom we love to hate and enjoy fearing. The famous stage direction in the (true) Coventry plays, "Here Erod rages in the pagond and in the strete also"[4] indicates how deeply ingrained is the response that late-night horror movies appeal to, and how adaptable to different cultural matrices are the appropriate emotions. The Coventry accounts give another measurement of the relative importance of different characters and again it is one that speaks directly to modern sensibilities. The sums paid to various actors are listed:[5] the top salaries go to Pilate, and then to Herod and Caiaphas; God (or Christ) is in these terms a comparatively marginal figure. The payments reflect practicalities; the tyrant characters in the cycles possess all the qualities that leap from stage to audience and demand our immediate engagement. In play as in life the spectacle of aggression, dominance, power-hunger, self-advertisement, commands our response, whether willing or unwilling; in a context which assures us that brilliant short-term success is dearly bought we are especially willing to enjoy the quick thrill of unrestricted power, safe in the knowledge that reality is different and that our own mediocrity will be justified. The pressure of Christ the protagonist on the whole design is of course the main reason why the authors of the cycles can give so much freedom to the bullies and atheists. We understand all the time that brilliance and aggression must fail; but we must notice that the ethic that tells us this does not reach us through action but rather through the overall design, as in the Bosch picture.

Tyrant drama is an important part of early Elizabethan tragedy.[6] In the predominantly political context in which good and bad were represented on the stage of this period the antagonist tends to exercise his malign power against our representative the body politic rather than our representative the individual martyr; but the distinction sounds more basic than it is. Outside the allegorical drama the body politic is always embodied in individuals. Such individuals, it is true, come and go rather quickly as the tyrant exercises his capacity for murder, so that a wide range of political existences can be exemplified. But each victim is shown in terms that tend to repeat the mode of religious martyrdom. When we see Cambyses victimize Praxaspes, Appius exploit Virginia, Richard of Gloucester betray Clarence, we see tyranny as one expression of a more basic opposition between bad and good, so that it need not surprise us to find that the tyrant is inevitably also the sadist, the ravisher, the infidel or atheist. The effect of this assimilation is most often discussed in macrocosmic terms: the tyrant is explained as the "scourge" or soiled instrument that God uses to cleanse the world and then puts into the fire.[7] The "scourge" concept is, however, more relevant to thoughts about tragedy than to the experience of tragedies. My concern here is rather with the specific ways in which political antagonist figures are set against traditional Christian protagonists. How can these fully realized representatives of political success be judged, in the context of the apolitical virtue of their passive victims? Certainly the traditional contrast between flesh and spirit, damned and blessed remains important; but new concentration on the reality of the political world, the arguable self-sufficiency of its values, brings new perspectives into existence. What I wish to consider is the extent to which such political treatments are capable of carrying forward the older judgments, how far the new reality simply contradicts the Christian values of the former age.

The flamboyant but brief trajectory of the tyrant figure as he cuts his path across the tragic scene, when set against the passive but inextinguishable ethos of his martyr-victim, shows us a traditional mixture; but it is one which becomes unstable as soon as political values show independence from religious good. At this point two incompatible value systems (one judging by fixed norms and punishments, the other by the relativities of survival) begin to grate against each other. Under these circumstances the dramatist who does not wish to get snared in the ethical confusions of a *Cambyses,* a *Horestes,* an *Appius and Virginia,* must be tempted to escape from the clash in the middle of the system by concentrating the drama on one extreme or the other, tyrant or martyr. The play that is often thought to be the first example of mature Elizabethan tragedy—Marlowe's *Tamburlaine*—gives a clear picture of the advantages and limitations that attach to such an escape (the point is particularly clear if we consider only the original conception of the play, found in Part I). In this extraordinary and indeed unique work the martyr-victims project no serious values; the aesthetic indulgence of the antagonist-hero is carried by poetry of such brilliance that it virtually succeeds in blanking-out the moral outrage of the action. But Tamburlaine not only stunned Marlowe's generation; he also numbed its power of creative imitation. One can see why. The pressures of the time can be understood most succinctly as pressures toward individuation; but the tyrant figure keeps attention fixed on the external rather than the internal, on success rather than achievement, on power over others rather than self-realization. In *Tamburlaine,* one might say, tyrant tragedy is liberated into a spectacular dead end. To move, I argue, Elizabethan tragedy had to reach out to the other side of the medieval inheritance and take up the potential of the martyr as tragic hero.

The drama of the late Middle Ages in western Europe offered not only the prototype martyr in Christ but also the legends of the saints, surrogates for their Master in careers of similar structure.[8] At first sight the secular importance of such stories seems strange. The tyrant belongs to the secular world by his very profession; but the saint can be understood only by those who intuit the invisible spiritual meaning he perceives in his own destiny, even though the secular world around him denies it. On the other hand the wildly romantic stories of saints and martyrs (as told in *The Golden Legend,* for example) show us how easily hagiography shades into the mode of the ever popular Greek romance. The Christian martyr struggles to preserve virtue and keep faith with the Lord; the romance hero and heroine endure (successfully) the continual assault on virginity and integrity, and keep faith with one another. And so in European romantic fiction inner vision is exalted even in the face of public disaster. The definition of the *self* which must be preserved from assault provides, of course, the essential distinction between hagiography and romantic fiction. In Greek romance the central self seems to be that which is held by love and contract to the constant service of the beloved. The Saint's life makes the beloved a spiritual ideal rather than a person and so requires the relationship between inner vision and outer experience to be one that stresses the former as the source of all meaning in the latter. And so the form tends to give a quality of transparency and unreality to the human plane. Such epithets ("unreal," "transparent") are normally pejorative; however, if one is concentrating on the power of a value-bearing system to survive out of one culture and into another one, preserving its structure though losing its content, then such transparency may be judged an advantage. Certainly the next historical transition, to the secular inwardness of those saints of passive virtue, persecuted wives,[9] is accomplished with remarkable ease. Patient Griselda endures every indignity the Marquis can devise. Her patience may be allowed to have a spiritual basis but it is also valid in purely secular terms. She is female and poor, while he is princely and male. Not only her sense of herself but also our sense of how things must be in this milieu point her toward the triumphs of passive virtue, and we accept her reasons for acting as she does as entirely appropriate to the space left open to her by her social relations.

To define the nature of this inner life more vividly without drawing on the external correlatives provided by the spiritual sphere requires, however, more capacity for self-assertion than Griselda shows. Stories of female martyrs have always been immensely popular, for they offer a particularly poignant model of helplessness and defeat turned into acceptance and victory by an external intervention. But the individuality of the inner life that achieves such victory tends to be played down. To achieve the paradox of an inner life creating its own external definition of being, in positive defiance of political and external pressures, probably demands, under Renaissance conditions at least, a male protagonist—someone who can combine integrity of soul with a power of self-projection that had

hitherto been the prerogative of the villain. I have suggested that
Marlowe's Tamburlaine shows us the glamour of the tyrant detached
from the judgment that the feelings of the victim focus for us. The
other tragedy normally thought of as the herald of the great age of
Elizabethan drama—Kyd's *The Spanish Tragedy*—provides a natural
complement to this, for if *Tamburlaine* is a tyrant play without a
martyr, *The Spanish Tragedy* is a martyr play without a tyrant.
Hieronimo, the martyr-hero of Kyd's play, offers us an illuminating
insight into some of the problems that arise when we try to give the
martyr a sufficient and positive dramatic force. The religious martyr
bears witness (*martyria*) to a truth that is only objectively valid for
believers, only confirmed in the invisible world above. He can
afford to be wholly passive in the compensating knowledge that
God is active. In the twelfth chapter of the Epistle to the Romans
Paul exhorts his brethren to Christian passivity: "Bless them which
persecute you. . . . Recompense to no man evil for evil." The payoff
becomes clear at the end of the chapter: "avenge not your selves, but
rather give place unto wrath: for it is written,[10] Vengeance is mine:
I will repay, saith the Lord. Therefore if thine enemy hunger, feed
him; if he thirst, give him drink: for in so doing thou shalt heap
coals of fire on his head." Clearly enough Hieronimo and Kyd's
audience know this rule of conduct. But even for believers the wrath
to come is too far away to be dramatic. Hieronimo quotes from
Paul: *Vindicta mihi* (*mihi vindicta, ego retribuam, dicit Dominus*), but
the requirements of drama forbid him to live by the maxim. He
finds it too far away to be usable:

> *Vindicta mihi!*
> Ay, heaven will be reveng'd of every ill,
> Nor will they suffer murder unrepaid:
> Then stay, Hieronimo, attend their will,
> For mortal men may not appoint their time.
> *Per scelus semper tutum est sceleribus iter.*
> Strike, and strike home, where wrong is offer'd thee,
> For evils until ills conductors be,
> And death's the worst of resolution:
> For he that thinks with patience to contend
> To quiet life, his life shall easily end.
> [3.13.1–11]

Against the imperative of religious patience Hieronimo sets the more theatrical imperative of a life span made meaningful by what it can be seen to achieve, retreating from religion to pragmatism. Yet the one ethic does not simply overcome the other. In the first half of the play, while Hieronimo is sane, he seeks to realize this passive good inside the framework of a just and well-ordered Christian society. If God has delegated his vengeance to the king and the king to the magistrates (as standard doctrine alleged), then the Christian who sought revenge could rely on Paul's advice. But this system does not work for Hieronimo and he is driven to other exigents. Yet the second half of the play is not simply a substitution of individual action for religious passivity; it is also a judgment on secularity and individualism. The religious pressures on Hieronimo do not clear away. They take a new and distorted form, especially relevant to the world of intense Calvinism in which Kyd and his original audience lived. It was well known that the oracles had ceased; the only place where God's voice could still be heard was inside the human heart. But when is the claim to special inspiration a truth and when a delusion? Hieronimo's flight from the standard processes of a Christian society leads him to claim that he bears a special destiny to act as God's immediate surrogate (*"I* will repay"). But an inner voice presenting demands that society can neither understand nor fulfill is as much the mark of madness as of election. Within the capacious sense of self that madness allows, Hieronimo must reconcile the parts of both tyrant and martyr, be the betrayer and murderer (of the innocent Castile no less than the guilty Lorenzo), yet still be in command of the rhetoric of the suffering victim of undeserved wrongs. Kyd establishes a new relationship between tyrant and victim, presenting them as quasi-psychological polarities set up by a single mind rather than social polarities or religious opposites. Hieronimo the victim is rebuffed by the social world and its conventional processes; he retreats into his inner vision of the good, but all he finds there is a false apotheosis speciously representing his mental suffering as a religious license for tyranny. We can see here rather clearly the process by which Elizabethan spirituality became dramatic psychology. The inner voice commands him not to abandon but to cleanse the world, setting him up as a ghastly parody of the divine logos. In terms of the vocabulary that Fredson Bowers[11] has so tellingly applied to *Hamlet* Hieronimo becomes the scourge of God, not His minister, as he is driven to (highly dramatic) action by impulses that the play cannot endorse. The final act of martyrdom is presented as a willed holocaust in which the cleansing fire, or tide of blood, is accepted as valid not because of any signs of higher approval but because of the emotional grip the individual will of the protagonist imposes on the audience; and the justice of it pleases us because Hieronimo is seen as mainly anxious to secure an even-handed justice that condemns himself as well as his enemies. Beyond the tyranny and the murders lies the necessity to bear witness (here conflated with the theatrical device of anagnorisis) and to die as victim rather than victimizer. At the end of the play the stage is a bloody shambles, but clearly we are meant to remember, behind the uncontrolled horror, the personal loyalty, the unswerving purpose and commitment that drove Hieronimo outside the proper and allowed social remedies for wrong and into a nightmare world where he could no longer care about means or about himself and could make sense of his experience only by clinging to the fulfillment of mission, at whatever cost. It seems as if we must condemn means (villainous) but allow motives (self-sacrificing) and so achieve the paradox of an appropriate Christian catharsis.

In such a story the martyr has become, in some sense, a martyr to himself, and in these terms the play might be considered a study in psychology rather than ethos. Yet Elizabethan tragic heroes are seldom if ever satisfactory as objects of psychological investigation. The mode of their poetry, the largeness of their world view, the presence of the supernatural, coupled to the weakness of realistic constraints (in continuity of time, place, narrative) all press our attention toward a sense that human destiny is only explicable at some level beyond the personal. *The Spanish Tragedy* is typical in that it does not even hint how we could describe this spiritual power to which personal life is properly sacrificed. One can argue, of course, that the plays are evasive only because the state required it.

The proclamation of May 1559 ordered that magistrates in charge of plays "permit none to be played wherein either matters of religion or of the governance of the estate of the common weal shall be handled or treated."[12] It goes against the modern grain to agree with the censors; yet the demand that secular drama should use secular terms was surely right aesthetically. The secular worlds of Elizabethan tragedy show religious intuitions about human destiny embodied in forms that belong to general human experience and that therefore cannot be dismissed as merely doctrinal or historical. By presenting its action in terms of the undogmatic daily business of life this drama has been able to draw its deepest intuitions out of one culture and through several others.

It is this survival of religious perceptions into secular expressions that is my central concern here and in pursuing this I choose to pass rather rapidly over *Titus Andronicus* and *Hamlet,* the Shakespeare tragedies that most obviously pick up developments of Christian martyrdom appearing in *The Spanish Tragedy.* Titus closely follows Hieronimo as a second martyr to the social or political ideal of justice, pursuing a similar line from petitions to legal authority and into a mad assumption of avenging godhead. *Hamlet,* more resolutely secular and intently personal, blurs the external signs of the stages the hero must pass through. We do not see Hamlet attempting to use the social machinery of justice; and indeed his social position makes that almost impossible. But the play retains a strong sense of the good secular individual who is caught up by the demand that he act on principles outside the secular range, indeed that he deny all the good ordinariness of life— reasonableness, social and family trust, established political order, national loyalty—and embrace a course of action clearly damnable, so that some unknown and indeed unknowable Higher Good be fulfilled. And again our sense of necessary martyrdom is made valid not by understanding what the martyrdom is for but by learning to share the martyr's belief that it is necessary.

The tragedies of the so-called revenge tradition are the obvious secular derivatives from the religious past: they keep their heroes blatantly in touch with promptings from a supernatural source that requires their deaths as witness for its importance. But the resting place of the brief story I have told would show a more telling survival of the pattern of tyrant and martyr if the pattern could be found to survive into worlds whose surface is wholly secular and whose promptings seem to be derived only from the individual, worlds such as that of *Othello,* set as close to domestic life as is feasible in poetry. This is sometimes thought to be the quality in *Othello* that keeps it from truly mystical resonance. A. C. Bradley finds its "confinement" or lack of the "symbolic" highly damaging: "We seem to be aware of . . . a certain limitation, a partial suppression of that element in Shakespeare's mind which unites him with the mystical poets and with the great musicians and philosophers."[13] One certainly must allow that *Othello* avoids unambiguous reference to the supernatural; if there is a theological strand to the play it must be so woven into the ordinariness of the experience that it can be seen only as a coloring of ordinary human feeling, a range of expectations and assumptions that any modern man might be expected to possess. The action, of course, does take place in a Christian community, moreover in one that is largely defined by the threat of an anti-Christian enemy—the Turk. But this quasi-historical framework only serves to underpin perceptions that depend for their truth and their development on private human responses and relationships. The central issue of the Othello-Desdemona-Iago triangle could be displayed under any creed and it would still, I believe, if handled with the same inwardness, evoke at its deepest levels of humanity the same traditionally religious feelings.

"I look down towards his feet" says Othello of Iago at the end of the play. He looks for the cloven hooves of the incarnate devil. He does not see them and dismisses the idea: "but that's a fable." The moment illustrates poignantly the point I seek to make. The devil does not appear in such a real world as Othello's (or ours) in the form of a creature with horns, goat's feet, and a tail. He appears as your friendly neighbourhood realist, "honest Iago," who does you a bluff good turn by telling you where your wife goes in the afternoon. We have all met Iagos and most of us have learned to accommodate our

ideals to his cynicism, allowing that to be a natural part of the
human scene, with its own truth and usefulness. We would feel
foolish if we spent our time looking for cloven hooves. And yet we
must allow that if the idea of evil means something in human life,
even the most down-to-earth human life, then it can be expected to
have its greatest power in some such form as Iago's. The unspectacular
quality of the appearance should not lead us to discount the principle behind it, for if principles are to have any continuous influence
on reality they must operate not with a panoply of theological
symbols, warning us that Good and Evil are holiday pageants, but
as scarcely perceptible intensifications of ordinary experience, drawing on the potential of what is always there, dissolved in ordinariness.

That Shakespeare's conception of the *Othello* story involved some
sense of the theological devil behind the ordinary Iago is made
probable by a number of references, perhaps most interestingly in
the background to Othello's speech (4.2.48ff.), where, the feelings
almost burned away, he looks back over the irreversible change that
has occurred:

> Had it pleas'd heaven
> To try me with affliction; had they rain'd
> All kinds of sores and shames on my bare head,
> Steep'd me in poverty to the very lips,
> Given to captivity me and my utmost hopes,
> I should have found in some place of my soul
> A drop of patience . . .
> But there, where I have garner'd up my heart . . .
> Turn thy complexion there,
> Patience, thou young and rose-lipp'd cherubin
> Ay, here, look grim as hell.

There seems to be little doubt that the figure Shakespeare here
remembers, afflicted with sores and shames, steeped in poverty, is
Job, not only in a technical sense the type of Christ but a character
model for all patient heroes, the martyr to his own passive goodness.
It is presumably important to remember how Job came to his unfor-
tunate condition. Chapter 1 of the book tells us that "When the

children of God came and stood before the Lord, Satan came also among them"; God points to Job as a man perfect in his ways, but Satan observes that it is easy to be perfect when everything goes right for you:

> Doth Job fear God for naught? Has thou not made an hedge about him and about his house, and about all that he hath on every side? thou hast blessed the work of his hands, and his substance is increased in the land. [1:10][14]

And so Job has to be given over to the temptation of Satan, to shave his head, to be covered with boils, to live in poverty in the affliction that scripture retrospectively calls "captivity" (42:10), and all for reasons that are wholly beyond reason and yet are profoundly resonant of what we may suspect to be the basic human condition.

The analogy I am pointing to is not a simple one. Certainly I do not seek to present *Job* as a key to the meaning of *Othello;* I am not suggesting that *Othello* is an allegory covering a religious truth more nakedly expressed in *Job.* All I do allege is that *Othello* raises in minds attuned to secular harmonies a set of feelings and perceptions of human destiny analogous (in some respects at least) to those raised in a religious context by the contemplation of *Job.* The obvious differences of mode rule out any relationship beyond analogy. The realistic framework of *Othello* makes the martyr status of its protagonist and his eventual condemnation and death seem matters wholly psychological and social. It requires critical legerdemain of a high order to change our concern with the story of *Othello* into the mode of attention required by *Job*—waiting for the voice of God to abolish all human explanation. In its power to show us that the voice of the absolute does not simply obliterate humanity but gradually carries us through its transformation, as local truth is eaten away by loyalty to principles, *Othello* is much closer to *The Spanish Tragedy* than to *Job.* But Hieronimo's sacrifice of humanity to principles, his confusion of minister with scourge, is realistically acceptable only because he has "gone mad"—madness being a socially allowed mode of escape from restrictions of ordinary behaviour, in terms of which a man like us can be conceived to "imagine" himself a divine agent called upon to cleanse the body politic. In *Othello* Shakespeare turns the realistic screws too tight to allow this. The protagonist is required to move between the polarities of tyrant and martyr, judge and victim, without invoking supernatural sanctions and without even moving outside our sense of what it is like to be sane.

Othello kills Desdemona not convinced in madness that he is a divine agent but persuaded in sanity that he is a righteous judge. The reduction in metaphysical scope has some disadvantages. "Yet she must die, else she'll betray more men" seems a police court kind of argument when set against the hieratic ritual of Hieronimo's mad rationalizations of murder:

> Here lay my hope, and here my hope hath end;
> Here lay my heart, and here my heart was slain;
> Here lay my treasure, here my treasure lost;
> Here lay my bliss, and here my bliss bereft;
> But hope, heart, treasure, joy, and bliss,
> All fled, fail'd, died, yea, all decay'd with this
>
> [4.4.90–95]

Hieronimo's *here* is specific: he refers to the body of his son which at this point he draws out from behind the arras. His emotions are referred to a palpable object, a presence that speaks his loss and for which he is only a commentator. But when Othello, in the 4.2 speech which I have already quoted in part, tells us of "there, where I have garner'd up my heart, / Where either I must live or bear no life" there is no palpable *there* to set before an audience. All is within the mind of the speaker and we must understand his mind before we can make any sense of what he is saying. The small-scale inwardness, the minimal gesturing outward in Othello's presentation of his destiny, requires us to attend to his mode of speech as one that draws only on the invisible shapes by which the mind creates meaning for itself. The mode is intensely personal and poignant, and yet (perhaps for this very reason) the nature of the moral judgments made becomes essentially indeterminable. When, at the end of the play, Shakespeare makes his hero reach out to a political and objective world so that he can place his suicide in a generalizing

context we cannot tell if the Aleppo incident he recounts is to be
taken as an essential turning point in Othello's moral history, a
chance memory or an invented pretext, or even an *illumination,* such
as dying men are often credited with. It hardly matters; the function
of the episode is not to rank with true or false but to be acted on as if
it were true. It is significant because Othello thinks it significant,
and it has true meaning for us only inside our sense of character.

Shakespeare sets up Iago as the antagonist to the suffering hero
of his play, as the Book of Job sets up Satan as the enemy of *that*
suffering hero. But the final action in such a play cannot be resolved
by the mere disproof of Satan's ethic. The secular drama of self-
responsible individuals cannot allow that individuality is ever completely in the grip of forces outside itself. Only if the enemy is also
the self can the battle for the individual soul be fought in terms to
which we are wholly responsive, however doctrinally distanced. The
sustaining invisible order which gives the martyr his power to defeat
the strength of his enemy the tyrant is now the protagonist's grasp
on some (equally invisible) essential core of selfhood. This is sold
into the captivity of the self which belongs to society, but eventually it understands, recants, and throws itself into the refining fire.
It seems virtually impossible to talk about such experience without
drawing on the language of religion, and it is easy, in any such
historical survey as the present, to argue why this should be so. In
the actual experience of the play, however, we seem to be given
understanding not so much of a point of view outside human nature
as of the essential movements of our own inner beings.

NOTES

1. An earlier version of the substance of this essay was delivered at
Cornell University in May 1980 as the first Paul Gottschalk Memorial
Lecture.
2. See L. L. Martz, "The Saint as Tragic Hero: *St Joan* and *Murder in
the Cathedral,*" in *Tragic Themes in Western Literature,* ed. Cleanth Brooks
(New Haven: Yale University Press, 1955), pp. 150–78. J. A. Bryant,
Jr., *Hippolyta's View: Some Christian Aspects of Shakespeare's Plays*

(Lexington: University of Kentucky Press, 1961), pp. 109–15. One might also refer to Butcher on Aristotle—S. H. Butcher, *Aristotle's Theory of Poetry and Fine Art* (London: Macmillan, 1895), p. 289, and Corneille's second *Discours* ("De la Tragedie") (*Corneille Critique et son temps*) (Paris: Buchet-Castel, 1964), p. 206.

3. Arnold Williams, *The Characterization of Pilate in the Towneley Plays* (East Lansing: Michigan State College Press, 1950), p. 37.

4. Thomas Sharp, *A Dissertation on the Pageants or Dramatic Mysteries Anciently Performed at Coventry* (Coventry: Merridew, 1825), p. 107.

5. Williams, *The Characterization of Pilate*, p. 14, citing Sharp, *A Dissertation,* p. 16.

6. See W. A. Armstrong, "The Elizabethan Conception of the Tyrant," *RES* 22 (1946), 161–81.

7. See Roy W. Battenhouse, *Marlowe's "Tamburlaine": A Study in Renaissance Moral Philosophy* (New Haven: Yale University Press, 1938).

8. For the spread of these in England see J. M. Manly, "The Miracle Play in England," *Essays by Divers Hands* 7 (1927), 133–53.

9. See Ortgies Siefkin, *Das geduldige Weib in der englischen Literatur bis auf Shakespeare* (Rathenow: Buckdruckerei von M. Babenzien, 1903).

10. "It is written" in Deuteronomy 32:35 and Psalms 94:1. St. Paul repeats the point in the Epistle to the Hebrews 10:30.

11. Fredson Bowers, "Hamlet as Scourge and Minister," *PMLA* 70 (1955), 740–49.

12. Quoted from E. K. Chambers, *The Elizabethan Stage,* 4:263.

13. A. C. Bradley, *Shakespearean Tragedy* (London: Macmillan, 1905), p. 185.

14. Quoted in the Geneva version.

ALVIN B. KERNAN

Courtly Servants and Public Players: Shakespeare's Image of Theater in the Court at Elsinore and Whitehall

Across Europe from the fourteenth to the late seventeenth century, poetry and theater, like the other arts, were primarily in the service of the court and its aristocratic political and social values.[1] The dominant social characteristics of poetry in this time—production by a gentleman amateur, involvement in patronage, control by censorship, address to a small select audience, and avoidance of print in favor of circulation in manuscript—all reflect the courtly ethos. The primary aesthetic principles of poetry during this same time—mimesis, moral teaching, imitation of the ancients, obedience to the rules, decorum, high style—express in poetic terms such essential courtly values as service, obedience to tradition and authority, good manners, and elegant artfulness.

The place of poetry and its function in the courtly world are perfectly imaged in Castiglione's *The Courtier,* where the ideal courtier is expected in the service of his prince to be, among other things, a poet who displays in his writing the same civility, manners, control, and perfection of the self that he also realized in dancing, dress, horsemanship, relations with the other sex, soldiership, and counselling of the ruler. Poetry is assigned an important place in the perfection toward which the courtly life strives— "writing is simply a form of speaking which endures even after it is uttered, the image, as it were, or better, the soul of our words"[2]— but as there is only one acknowledged poet, the occasional poet Bernardo Accolti, known as Unico Aretino, present among the many courtiers at Urbino, so poetry is but one of the many arts

seeking civilization through beauty, grace, clarity, harmony, and
that studied nonchalance called *sprezzatura*.

If in Urbino in 1528 we are somewhere near the beginning of
the long tradition of literary art in the service of the court, we are
close to its end in the royal library in the Queen's House in London
in February 1767, when George III leaves his own work and comes
to visit the monarch of literature, Doctor Johnson, who was "in a
profound study" in the library. Johnson is properly respectful of his
king, even though he professed to be something of a Jacobite, but
the writer now rules in the palace of literature, the library, and the
king asks deferentially to be instructed by him in such literary
matters as the comparative size of the Oxford and Cambridge libraries, the state of Johnson's own writings, and the merits of
various publications. "During the whole of this interview," Boswell
tells us,

> Johnson talked to his Majesty with profound respect, but still in his
> firm manly manner, with a sonorous voice, and never in that subdued
> tone which is commonly used at the levee and in the drawing-room.
> After the King withdrew, Johnson shewed himself highly pleased
> with his Majesty's conversation and gracious behaviour.[3]

Print, with the free marketplace, author's copyright, and the
public audience it created, made Johnson a Grub Street hack, but it
also freed him and literature from courtly service, constructed the
library in which the writer rules, and enabled Johnson to write the
famous letter to Lord Chesterfield that announced the emancipation
of the poet from courtly patronage. Print was not the only force
working to free literature from dependence upon the court during
the four centuries when poetry in the service of the state remained
the norm. The appearance of professional writers such as Spenser
and Shakespeare in the late sixteenth century; religious upheaval,
which found in poetry a vehicle for the expression of deeply personal
feelings (a tradition that Louis Martz has traced so carefully and
profoundly in many of his writings); and the appearance of the novel
all called into question, though they did not quite destroy, the
dominant image of the courtly amateur poet, using poetry in the
patronage game, circulating his poems among a small group of

friends of similar tastes, and writing in the service of the dominant aristocratic order.

The concept of art in the service of the court and the established order was challenged during this time most overtly, however, by the English public theater between the years 1576, when the first theater was built in London, and 1642, when Parliament finally closed the theaters in the interest of the new commonwealth of the saints. It is this entertainment business, with its public audience, writing for pay, venture capital, and marketplace economy, on which modern criticism and literary history have chosen to concentrate almost exclusively, partly because it is the primary theatrical fact of the period, and partly because it allows us to think of Shakespeare and his fellow playwrights as Romantic artists making great art out of the free creative play of the imagination, unlimited by the constraints of service and patronage. The emphasis is not misplaced, for the public theater was unquestionably the center of London playing and it obviously did provide, as the plays of writers like Marlowe and Shakespeare testify, a kind of freedom for the playwright which was most unusual in this period and did not become the literary norm again until the eighteenth century.

But the importance of the public theater has tended to blind us to a number of obvious facts that, taken together, suggest that while the players may have made most of their money and done most of their work on the Bankside, their established social identity may have continued to be the traditional one of servants of the court and the aristocratic social order which centered there. This much seems guaranteed by the players continuing to wear the livery of great nobles, the lord chamberlain, or the king; serving their aristocratic masters not only by providing them with entertainment but, as we know from various documents, marching in funeral processions, serving as guides to distinguished visitors, providing the speaking parts for masques and other occasional court performances; and, in the largest sense of service, bearing testimony to the wealth and artistic cultivation of their patrons in the great peers' struggle for preeminence at court. As Lawrence Stone says, "The players were travelling advertisements for the greater glory of their patrons and it became a question of status to have a company to one's name."[4] At the same time the court maintained control of all performances, public and at court, through censorship and operated a large and expensive revels office charged with providing royal entertainment. The court did not ignore the fact that the players worked most regularly in the city, or at least on the edges of it, but there was a very neat way of explaining these public performances of the royal servants in courtly terms. On several occasions when the court intervened, as it often did, to protect the actors from having their playhouses "plucked down" by irate aldermen, or to free some obstreperous actor from prison, the Privy Council explained that the companies were to be allowed "to use and practise stage playes, whereby they might be the better enhabled and prepared to shew such plaies before her Majestie as they shalbe required at tymes meete and accustomed, to which ende they have bin cheefelie licensed and tollerated. . . ."[5] In other words, public playing was treated as merely rehearsal for courtly performance. In closing the theaters, the Puritans were not then merely engaging in some fanatical Platonic hatred of imitation and pretense, or biblical zeal against transvestism, but proceeding in good political fashion to eliminate what was in their view one of the instruments of the king they were on their way to beheading.

There seems, in view of these and other facts, little doubt about how court and country regarded the players, they were in title and in fact the King's Men; but the more interesting question is how the players, and chiefly William Shakespeare, saw themselves in relation to the court. We might open this question with what seems, to me at least, a rather startling fact. By a conservative count, using the court calendar E. K. Chambers provides in volume 4 of *The Elizabethan Stage,* between 1594 and 1612—years in which Shakespeare was surely actively involved with these companies—the Chamberlain's Men and King's Men performed at court 245 times, or an average of thirteen-plus times a year.[6] Shakespeare, we must conclude, was at court very frequently, and as a sharer he must have derived a good deal of income from this source, since the payment for a court performance was six or ten pounds, usually the latter, plus a number of outright gifts from James, though not from the parsimonious Elizabeth. This, in addition to the other evidence discussed, puts, I suggest, the Shakespearean dramatic subject matter in a rather different light from what we have been accustomed to. That he wrote almost exclusively about courtly and aristocratic life, with only occasional pictures of the common world in the Boarshead Tavern or the sheepfarms of Bohemia, has long been recognized, but we have traditionally assumed that this parade of kings, peers, and gentry with their aristocratic politics, courtly views of love, and fashionable wordplay was designed to satisfy the desires of the public audience for an inside view of what their betters did in the palace. It may well be, however, that we should consider the aristocratic Shakespearean subject matter as satisfying the court interests it was designed to serve in the same way that Inigo Jones built the kinds of buildings the aristocracy wanted and Van Dyck and Rubens painted the kinds of pictures considered suitable. In this regard it might also be profitable to reconsider the many speculations about different plays being written to order for particular courtly occasions: *Macbeth* as a tribute to King James' noble Scottish ancestry and his interest in demonology; *A Midsummer Night's Dream* as an epithalamium for a great wedding; *Henry VIII* as a return to the theater to provide something suitable to celebrate the marriage of the Princess Elizabeth to the Elector Palatine in 1613; *Troilus* as a special production for the legal and philosophical tastes of the Inns of Court; and *Twelfth Night* as an oblique comment on court affairs and the theme of epiphany at a great Twelfth Night feast in 1601 honoring Italian and Russian ambassadors. These are only a few of the many arguments made for particular plays as tailored to court interests, and probably the only one which seems entirely convincing is that for *Macbeth*. Yet taken in the aggregate, they suggest, even if they do not prove, how closely the Shakespearean plays conform to the kind of theater that serves an aristocratic audience by talking about its main interests and supporting its values, mirroring the courtly world in action, taking part in its festivals and great ritual occasions, and providing graceful compliments to its patrons.[7]

The plays mentioned above as examples of courtly theater are complex enough to warn us away from any too-easy identification of Shakespeare with such a straightforward playwright-servant as John Lyly, who spent his theatrical life providing almost exactly what the court wanted and vainly seeking as his reward the reversion of the office of Master of the Revels.[8] We can perhaps get a glimpse of Shakespeare's own much more complicated relationship with the court in his major internal plays, which always take the form of courtly entertainments presented in an aristocratic setting: the great house of a noble lord in *The Taming of the Shrew,* the park of the king of Navarre in *Love's Labour's Lost,* the banqueting hall of Duke Theseus in *A Midsummer Night's Dream,* the great hall or presence chamber of Elsinore in *Hamlet,* and the wedding masque presented in a magical theater by a duke for his daughter and her betrothed in *The Tempest.* The plays presented on these occasions tend to be old-fashioned in style—*The Pageant of the Nine Worthies, Pyramus and Thisbe,* and *The Murder of Gonzago.* The players are either lower-class, frequently inept amateurs or, in the cases of *The Shrew* and *Hamlet,* politely subservient traveling companies of professional players. Even those remarkable actors in *The Tempest,* "Ariel and all his quality,"[9] those "meaner fellows" who are able "to fly, To swim, to dive into the fire, to ride On the curled clouds" (1.2.190–92), are treated contemptuously as mere instruments of policy by the duke they serve. The audiences at the internal plays are as distinctly upper-class as the players are lower-class—even Christopher Sly thinks he is a lord while he watches the "comonty" of the Shrew— and with the notable exceptions of Ferdinand and Miranda at *The Masque of Juno and Ceres* these aristocratic audiences are poor audiences, mocking the players out of their parts in *The Pageant of the Nine Worthies,* commenting loudly on the ineptitudes of *Pyramus and Thisbe,* talking during the performance and baiting the actors in *The Murder of Gonzago.* Even in that idealized theater of *The Tempest* where the playwright is a magician, the actors spirits, the theater a magical island, and the "audience" literally entranced by the spectacles, some nobles like Sebastian and Antonio remain cynical and unmoved by the spectacles they are shown. This same aristocratic scorn for the common players appears also in the Boarshead playlet where Hal dislikes the way Falstaff plays the monarch "in King Cambyses vein," and in Cleopatra's queenly disdain for "the quick comedians" who will squeak and boy her "greatness I' th' posture of a whore."

Nothing is quite right whenever Shakespeare shows a play being staged in an aristocratic setting before a noble audience, and as a result the plays never quite succeed in achieving their proposed ends—not even in *The Shrew* and *The Tempest,* where they come closest to success. This characteristic structure of the internal plays as an antagonistic relationship—between lower-class, old-fashioned players and self-centered, impolite, and scornful aristocratic audiences—suggests that Shakespeare the professional playwright was persistently uneasy about the relationship of his theatrical art to the court it so frequently served. This view of the relationship was not peculiar to Shakespeare, for the same tension is present in such other internal plays of the period as those of *The Spanish Tragedy, Doctor Faustus,* and *The Roman Actor,* and it is voiced openly by Ben Jonson in his attempts to establish the importance of his poetry in the masques he wrote for the court.

It is, however, in *The Murder of Gonzago* in *Hamlet* that we come closest, extraordinarily close, to the actual situation of the Lord Chamberlain's Men and the King's Men and their playwright performing in the banqueting house or great chamber at Whitehall before the royal court. In one respect the circumstances of playing in Elsinore do not accord exactly with the usual arrangements at Whitehall. The "tragedians of the city" are not commanded to appear and perform on a particular night, as would normally be the case in courtly performances, but simply appear at the palace during a tour of the country forced on them by the loss of their accustomed "estimation" or popularity in the city to the children's companies and their satirical plays in which "the poet and the player" go "to cuffs in the question." The way in which a sudden command performance might be arranged, as well as some flavor of the aristocratic attitude to the players and the use of them in the courtly game of favor, appears in a letter written in 1604–05 to Robert Cecil, then the king's secretary, by Sir Walter Cope, who had apparently been asked to arrange a play for Queen Anne on short notice at Southampton House:

> Sir,—I have sent and bene all thys morning huntyng for players Juglers & such kinde of Creaturs, but fynde them harde to finde, wherfore Leavinge notes for them to seeke me, burbage ys come, & Sayes ther ys no new playe that the quene hath not seene, but they have Revyved an olde one, Cawled *Loves Labore lost,* which for wytt and mirthe he sayes will please her excedingly. And Thys ys apointed to be playd to Morowe night at my Lord of Sowthamptons, unless yow send a wrytt to Remove the Corpus Cum Causa to your howse in the strande. Burbage ys my messenger Ready attendyng your pleasure.
> Yours most humbly,
>   Walter Cope[10]

Court performances were, however, usually arranged well ahead of time by the master of the revels, who operated out of his office in Blackfriars in the City; he auditioned the players, selected plays from their repertory that would be suitable for court performance, made necessary changes in them, and gave orders for the production. In *Hamlet* it is the prince himself, interestingly enough, who takes on most of the functions of master of the revels and performs his traditional duties. He welcomes the players and, familiar with the company and its repertory, jokes with them, auditions the leading player in a speech describing the death of Priam, instructs them in their art, selects a play, *The Murder of Gonzago,* from their repertory, adjusts the play for royal performance by adding the famous "dozen or sixteen lines," arranges for the actors to be "well bestowed," signals the beginning of the performance before the court, and assures the uneasy king during the performance that he has heard the argument of the play and that there is "no offense" in it.

There is something very odd of course in a prince of the blood playing the part of master of the revels (Dramatic economy? A suggestion of the power of royalty over the players? Another Elsinorean maimed rite?), but the other arrangements conform exactly to courtly practice as we know it. *The Murder of Gonzago* was probably presented between Christmas and Lent,[11] the usual period of the most intense theatrical activity in court, and it was played at night—"There is a play tonight before the king" (3.2.75)—when the public players, having performed in the city in the afternoon, acted before the court. The arrangement of the audience in the banqueting hall of the palace also conforms to what we know of court practice.

It is clear that Claudius, with Gertrude beside him, has to be seated in some very prominent place where Hamlet can "observe his looks. . . . If 'a do blench" (2.2.603–04), can "rivet" his eyes "to his face" (3.2.85), and where Horatio, as he says, can give the king such "heedful note" that "If 'a steal aught the whilst this play is playing, And scape detecting, I will pay the theft" (3.2.88–89). The king's place of central visibility is further emphasized at the beginning of the performance when the queen asks Hamlet to sit by her, presumably in the "state," the canopied seat of the royal party, and Hamlet refuses, withdrawing to sit by Ophelia in a place sufficiently distant to allow the monarchs to appear clearly in perspective. "Look you," says Hamlet to Ophelia, "how cheerfully my mother looks" (3.2.127–28). All these hints about the prominent placement and visibility of the king and queen become clear when we realize that at court performances the monarchs, attended on occasion by certain favored courtiers, did not simply occupy the best seats in the audience but were placed in a position where they were visible to everyone in the hall as they watched the play. The evidence suggests that the state in which the king sat could be placed at the back of the stage, on one side of it, or could be isolated in front of the stage at the ideal point for viewing and being seen. Being seen seems to have been more important than seeing, for in 1605 in preparation for a royal performance in the hall at Christ Church, "we hear," says E. K. Chambers,

> of a dispute between the academic functionaries and those of the Household as to the placing of the King's chair. The latter complained that it was fixed so low that only His Majesty's cheek would be visible to the auditory; the latter [sic] attempted to explain that, by the laws of perspective, the King would have a much better view

than if he sat higher. There was a solemn debate in the council chamber, resulting in the decision that a King must not merely see, but be seen, and the state was moved to the middle of the hall, twenty-eight feet from the stage, which in fact proved too far, as he could not well hear or understand the long speeches. The Queen and Prince shared the state with the King; in front, but on a lower level, were seats for ladies; the state itself was ringed with lights; on either side were placed nobles; and the populace thronged around the walls.[12]

I forbear from remarking on the extraordinary applicability of these details to the performance of *The Murder of Gonzago,* but Stephen Orgel catches exactly the meaning of these same arrangements in the hall at Elsinore when he tells us that at court performances "what the rest of the spectators watched was not a play but the queen [Elizabeth] at a play, and their response would have been not simply to the drama, but to the relationship between the drama and its primary audience, the royal spectator."[13]

This characteristic placement of the royal party at court performances realizes in space the social relationship between a monarch and his servant players. The play was not the thing, but merely a part of the setting for the real center of attention at a performance, the king and his power. That Shakespeare was sensitive to this reality there can be no doubt, for the relationship implicit in the arrangement of the theater is specifically enacted in *Hamlet.* The class differences of common players and noble audience, usual in Shakespeare, are obvious here in the deference with which the actors treat Hamlet and the patience with which these professionals accept the instructions of an amateur; and the social gap widens when Polonius, charged with the bestowal of the players, perhaps resenting that the king's principal secretary should be asked to perform so menial a task, remarks that he will "use them according to their desert." But the most meaningful difference between the court and the players is in their conception of the nature of theater. The players, for all their former high standing in the city and the presence in their repertory of a play which is "caviary to the general," are a standard public repertory company with a king, an "adventurous knight," a lover, a "humorous man," a clown, and a boy playing a lady. The old-fashioned play they perform is, as Howard Felperin says, "a substantial fragment of a primitive Elizabethan revenge tragedy, its morality affiliations—dumb-show, emblematic setting, generalizing rhetoric, virtue figures, and a highly theatrical Vice—intact."[14] Their acting is equally old-style, rhetorical and melodramatic. The players and the play they perform in Elsinore are part of that long tradition of popular playing that came down from the mystery and morality plays; traveled in small companies across England for three centuries; and played for hire in town halls, great houses, market squares, and inn yards until in the late sixteenth century it settled in London. There its popularity built public theaters, and its players became the tragedians of the city for whom Shakespeare wrote. But if this was an old-fashioned folk-theater, it was also, paradoxically, in its financial arrangements and the attitudes they encouraged, an extremely modern venture-capital business which struggled against censorship, competed for customers in a free marketplace, rewarded its successful authors and players with large returns, encouraged artistic freedom, and gave independent importance to the art of player and playwright. Even as this theater looked back to an almost timeless way of playing, so it also anticipated the social situation of art in the future. How much of this Shakespeare could have known is problematical, to say the least, but to the modern eye the public theater stretching far into the past and extending on into the future has a universality which makes courtly theater seem "momentary as a sound," and this sense of an endless theater surrounding the courtly moment is enacted very powerfully in the dialogue of the player king and player queen in *The Murder of Gonzago*.

In Whitehall, as in Elsinore, a very different "idea of a theater," courtly, humanistic, and neoclassic, had developed during the Renaissance. We smell the lamp and hear the inkhorn terms of this courtly humanism when Polonius, who had, during his humanist education, learned to play in classical drama at the university, categorizes theater by genres—"tragedy, comedy, history, and pastoral"—differentiates between Seneca and Plautus, refers to the unities—"scene individable" and "the law of writ"—and waxes enthusiastic over an unusual piece of diction—"That's good. 'Mobled queen' is good" (2.2.511). We hear a nobler, more imaginative version of this same humanistic, neoclassical ideal when Hamlet speaks approvingly of plays "well digested in the scenes, set down with as much modesty as cunning" (2.2.446–47), of a verbal style "more handsome than fine," of lines pronounced "trippingly on the tongue," and stage action managed with "a temperance that may give it smoothness." Sidney himself seems to be speaking when Hamlet voices his dislike of the jigs, the bawdry, the clowns, and the strutting, bellowing actors of the popular theater. The courtly disdain of this critical tradition for the public theater can be heard openly in Hamlet's dislike "of the groundlings, who for the most part are capable of nothing but inexplicable dumb shows and noise" (3.2.10–12), and the aristocratic bias sounds unmistakably in Hamlet's statement that the censure of one "judicious" critic must "o'erweigh a whole theater of others" (3.2.28).

The antagonism between courtly artistic values and the practices of the public playhouse becomes overt in the performance of *The Murder of Gonzago,* where after a very explicable dumb show, of the kind for which Hamlet has already expressed his scorn, Hamlet audibly interprets the play in a critical way for the spectators, comments cynically on the brief prologue, engages in loud conversation with the king, the queen, and Ophelia during the performance, and mocks the melodramatic acting style of the villain—"Begin, murderer. Leave thy damnable faces and begin. Come, the croaking raven doth bellow for revenge" (3.2.256–58). This may well have been the way in which aristocratic audiences acted at the court performance of public plays, and it is the way the courtly audiences respond in such other Shakespearean plays as *A Midsummer Night's Dream* and *Love's Labour's Lost.* After all, here in the court, not the play, but the court which the play is serving, is the thing. All eyes are on the king watching, not the play being performed.

The humanistic neoclassical view of theater expressed in *Hamlet* accorded perfectly with the courtly world of which humanism was the intellectual expression. Dramatic poetry, like all other art, was believed properly to serve the aristocratic social order: conferring fame by serving as "the abstract and brief chronicles of the time" (2.2.531); imaging the world of which it was a part by holding "the mirror up to nature"; teaching the appropriate morality by showing "virtue her own feature, scorn her own image" (3.2.22–23); and even participating in great affairs of state by catching "the conscience of the king" in tragedy that, as Sidney puts it, in words that come very close to the disease imagery of *Hamlet,* "openeth the greatest wounds, and sheweth forth the Ulcers that are covered with Tissue; . . . maketh Kinges feare to be Tyrants, and Tyrants manifest their tirannical humors."[15]

In arranging for *The Murder of Gonzago* to be performed at court, Hamlet is testing the ability of playing to perform the very highest moral and political services claimed for it by humanism:

> I have heard that guilty creatures sitting at a play
> Have by the very cunning of the scene
> Been struck so to the soul that presently
> They have proclaimed their malefactions.
> [2.2.596–99]

The more ordinary services expected of court plays are suggested by the instructions of the lord chamberlain for a great Twelfth Night festival in 1601 at which several plays were a part of an elaborate entertainment, including banquets, dancing, receptions, and church services, for Italian and Muscovite ambassadors. The master of the revels, the lord chamberlain writes, should take

> order generally with the players to make choyse of [a] play that shalbe best furnished with rich apparell, have greate variety and change of Musicke and daunces, and of a Subiect that may be most pleasing to her Maiestie."[16]

The Murder of Gonzago was not most pleasing to King Claudius, but, in either Hamlet's or the lord chamberlain's version, it is assumed that the play serves the court. Shakespeare contrives, however, by the cunning of *his* scene, to shift the dramatic focus from the court to the play itself, revealing, as Marion Jones points out, "a self-consciousness about the function of drama on an entirely different level from the sententiousness of Hamlet's advice to the players or his topical gossip with Rosencrantz and Guildenstern."[17] *The Murder of Gonzago* is gradually centered on stage by managing the responses of the courtly audience to the play in such a way that their adequacy begins to be judged by the play, rather than the value of the play by the audience. The power of the play and its moral priority are established by showing each of the major characters in *Hamlet* responding to the internal play in exactly the same way that they have previously responded to the events in Elsinore, but now in a fashion that utterly reveals and brings out the meaning of their standard attitudes. Ophelia remains, as always, utterly innocent of what is going on—"Belike this show imports the argument of the play" (3.2.142–43), she says of the dumb-show. Gertrude, again as always, cannot understand the applicability to herself of the events of the play—"The lady doth protest too much, methinks" (3.2.234). Claudius is, as the many conflicting interpretations of his actions at the play demonstrate, more difficult to understand in his reactions to the play, but we know for certain that the play's obvious message does reach him—though we do not know at what point in the performance he begins to understand—and it not only tells him for the first time that Hamlet knows the truth but also releases in him the qualms of conscience which humanist theories of the moral effect of theater so confidently assumed, "O, my offense is rank, it smells to heaven" (3.3.36). His understanding of what is going on is characteristic of him, but so is his response, for before he tries to pray in the chapel he has already arranged for Hamlet to be sent to England where he will be murdered, and the momentary struggle with his conscience brings about no reformation of his character.

Hamlet's response to the play is equally characteristic and revealing of him, for while it confirms his suspicions about the king, the discovery gives rise only to a manic moment which passes without the taking of revenge. It would also appear that Hamlet himself does not fully comprehend the play. The central section of *The Murder of Gonzago* is a long, old-fashioned moral dialogue between the player king and the player queen about the inevitable mutability of human

purposes in time, the necessary failure of men and women to live up
to their own ideals:

> Our wills and fates do so contrary run
> That our devices still are overthrown;
> Our thoughts are ours, their ends none of our own.
>
> {3.2.215–17}

From our position in the audience outside the play *Hamlet*, these
lines seem as applicable to Hamlet, whose vowed purpose of revenge
has failed in time, as they do from Hamlet's position in the audience
of *The Murder of Gonzago* to Gertrude, whose failed faith to Old
Hamlet is directly represented by the internal play. But Gertrude's
failure to understand the literal sense of the play reflects Hamlet's
failure to understand its deeper and more general moral sense,
which corresponds very closely to what he does finally learn in his
own play about all men being only momentary actors in a world
where "the readiness is all."

If I am interpreting the internal play in the court of Elsinore
correctly, it shows us not only how the public players performed at
and served the court but suggests a very complex view of the nature
and value of that service. Hamlet feels that the play has been a real
coup de théâtre which could earn *him* "a fellowship in a cry of players"
(3.2.281–82), and there is no question that for all of its old-
fashioned style the internal play has held the mirror up to nature, at
least to some natures, and achieved, at least for the moment, the
social effectiveness that humanism posited for theater. But the effects
are transitory since Claudius fails to reform, Hamlet fails to act on
the knowledge the play provides, and the rest of the audience seems
to have no idea at all of what was shown or why. The court,
disliking the old-fashioned style of the play, prove to be a poor
audience both in their theatrical manners and in their understanding of the play. In the end the play is broken off with a call for
lights, and the characters of *Hamlet* return to their own elaborate
theatricals in Elsinore, almost entirely unenlightened by the
glimpse the internal play has given them of the status of all men

including themselves as actors in a larger play where "our thoughts are ours, their ends none of our own."

Shakespeare is, I believe, in a subtle way here giving priority to the players and their play over the court in which they are, as theater and the other arts were expected to be, his majesty's servants. He does not hide the fact, here or elsewhere, that the public theater for which he wrote was crude in its effects, melodramatic in style, and old-fashioned in its structure. Although *The Murder of Gonzago* is not as sophisticated as Shakespeare's own plays, it is a somewhat sad acknowledgment on his part that the public theater, even at its best, retained a good deal of the popular tradition from which it came. But for all its crudeness and grimaces, its dumb-show and prologue, the old play and its players tell the court truths about itself which it is incapable of recognizing. The players do "tell all," but the court cannot hear what they say, and *The Murder of Gonzago* provides us with a most unusual and remarkable image of theater in the court and of the playwright governed by patronage. For all of its old-fashioned qualities, *The Murder of Gonzago* could not be more totally theatrical: a player king and queen playing before a player king and queen (Claudius and Gertrude) playing, if the performance is in court, before other kings and queens (Elizabeth, James and Anne) playing out their royal roles, each mirroring the situation of the other. And what the player king says to the player queen comes from as deep within the theater as the play itself, for his voice, speaking calmly, measuredly, about the inevitable transformations of human purpose and human life in the course of the changes in time, is the essential voice of the theater, telling us what every play, regardless of its surface events, tells us about all the world being a stage. *The Murder of Gonzago* is not just a play but *the* play, the idea of theater, at least as Shakespeare conceived it, whose essential meaning is contained in its unchanging mode of theatrical pretense. But the courtly audience understand the play not at all or only in terms of its relevance to their own immediate problems and intrigues. And so Hamlet hurries off to stab Polonius, and Claudius exits to plan Hamlet's death, both moving unknown toward ends which are none of their own:

carnal, bloody, and unnatural acts,
... accidental judgments, casual slaughters,
... deaths put on by cunning and forced cause,
And, in this upshot, purposes mistook
Fall'n on th' inventors' heads.

[5.2.383–87]

We do not know that *Hamlet* was played at court before 1636–37, though it is almost certain that it was played in the early 1600s when it was first written; but whenever it was performed, it must have been a remarkable scene at Whitehall as a real ruler, Elizabeth, James, or Charles, those absolute monarchs, watched Claudius, sitting in the same isolated position the actual ruler occupied in the hall, watching a player king talking to his queen about the impossibility of monarchs maintaining their sworn vows.

We know the titles of fourteen Shakespeare plays presented before the court, and though the records are incomplete it is more than probable that most of the others were also played there in circumstances very close to those in which *The Murder of Gonzago* is performed in Elsinore, and with something like the same effect. The King's Men too told all to their noble audiences, who rose and called for lights after seeing plays that bore so closely on their own circumstances as *Richard II*, *Hamlet*, *King Lear*, *Macbeth* and *Coriolanus*, and then moved on not to where their wills but to where their fates ran. Eventually they ran to an end which Shakespeare anticipated but on which he could not have improved—to the stage where Charles I was beheaded, outside the window of the banqueting house at Whitehall, built by Inigo Jones for the performance of plays and masques at court.

NOTES

1. An excellent description of the European court and its use of art as a symbol of the power and values of the state is to be found in *The Courts of Europe, Politics, Patronage and Royalty 1400–1800,* ed. A. G. Dickens (London: Thames and Hudson, 1977). For discussions of the use of theater in the court see Roy Strong, *Splendor at Court: Renaissance Spectacle and the*

Theater of Power (Boston: Houghton Mifflin, 1973): and Stephen Orgel, *The Illusion of Power, Political Theater in the English Renaissance* (Berkeley: University of California Press, 1975).

2. Baldesar Castiglione, *The Book of the Courtier*, trans. Charles S. Singleton (New York: Doubleday, 1959), p. 48.

3. *Life of Johnson*, ed. R. W. Chapman, corrected by J. D. Fleeman (London: Oxford University Press, 1970), p. 384.

4. Lawrence Stone, *The Crisis of the Aristocracy, 1558–1641*, abridged ed. (Oxford: Oxford University Press, 1967), pp. 321–22. J. Leeds Barroll, "Drama and the Court", in *The Revels History of Drama in English* (London: Methuen, 1975), ed. Clifford Leech and T. W. Craik, 3:3–27, offers a number of interesting details about the ways in which companies were used at court to achieve favor for the patron.

5. Privy Council Minutes, Feb. 19, 1598, printed in E. K. Chambers, *The Elizabethan Stage* (Oxford: Oxford University Press, 1923), 4:325.

6. The occasions of playing at court and relevant information are also conveniently collected and listed in chronological order in Mary S. Steele, *Plays and Masques at Court During the Reigns of Elizabeth, James and Charles* (New Haven: Yale University Press, 1926).

7. R. Chris Hassel, Jr., *Renaissance Drama and the English Church Year* (Lincoln: University of Nebraska Press, 1979), argues persuasively that there were seven principal church feast days on which plays were presented at court and that an effort was made by the Office of the Revels to correlate the plays with the leading liturgical themes of the days on which they were presented. The effect of this argument is to suggest additional ways in which the theater was used to further not its own ends but the religious and social functions of court life. Leslie Hotson, *The First Night of "Twelfth Night"* (New York: Macmillan, 1954), presents a remarkable collection of evidence suggesting the way in which plays at court were but one part of elaborate entertainments involving feasting, dances, church services, the entertainment of ambassadors, and the conduct of matters of state.

8. G. K. Hunter, *John Lyly, The Humanist as Courtier* (Cambridge: Harvard University Press, 1962), provides a fine description of the life of a courtly writer who worked almost entirely under patronage and an analysis of the nature of fully successful courtly theater.

9. All citations of Shakespeare are to *The Complete Signet Classic Shakespeare*, ed. Sylvan Barnet (New York: Harcourt Brace, 1972).

10. Steele, *Plays and Masques at Court*, p. 141.

11. I take Rosencrantz's line, "if you delight not in man, what lenten entertainment the players shall receive from you" (2.2.323–24), to refer obliquely to the fact that the players would not have performed at court in

Lent, and since they are welcomed it would seem to follow that the season is not Lent. That it is winter, but after Christmas, is established in 1.1.

12. Chambers, *The Elizabethan Stage,* 1:228.

13. Orgel, *The Illusion of Power: Political Theater in the English Renaissance,* p. 9.

14. *Shakespearean Representation* (Princeton: Princeton University Press, 1977), p. 48.

15. Sir Philip Sidney, "Apology for Poetry," in *Elizabethan Critical Essays,* ed. G. Gregory Smith (Oxford: Oxford University Press, 1904), 1:177. Details of the relationship of *Hamlet* and the "Apology" are to be found in William A. Ringler, Jr., "Hamlet's Defense of the Players," in *Essays on Shakespeare and Elizabethan Drama in Honor of Hardin Craig,* ed. Richard Hosley (Columbia: University of Missouri Press, 1962) pp. 201–11. Ringler notes that the historical example Sidney offers for the moral effectiveness of theater describes a performance of Euripides' *Trojan Women,* a play on the same subject, the sorrows of Hecuba, as the play from which Hamlet requests speeches when the players first arrive in Elsinore.

16. Hotson, *The First Night of "Twelfth Night",* p. 15.

17. "The Court and the Dramatists," in *Elizabethan Theatre,* Stratford-Upon-Avon Studies 9, ed. J. R. Brown and Bernard Harris (New York: St. Martin's Press, 1967), p. 188.

LOWRY NELSON, JR.

The Matter of Rime: Sonnets of Sidney, Daniel, and Shakespeare

To rhyme or not to rhyme
is not the question—
The perfect poem
is a perfect crime.
—*Aleksis Rannit*

Poets may be born but poems are made. As even poetasters know, the ring of a word, the aptness of a phrase, the interlacement of motifs, the shaping of a form, are achieved at some expense of labor and feeling. Writing in meter and rime is a subjection to discipline and also an exploitation of constraints. In crude terms, the sonnet may well have been such a common form since the late Middle Ages for the very reason that the rimes suggest collocations and continuities and endings that throw up a challenge to ingenuity which may seem very much like inspiration. A sonnet or any other rimed lyric form is a pattern that requires fulfilment in words rhythmically set in grammatical idiom and words that rime at appropriate places. Often if the pattern is adequately fulfilled it is simply taken for granted and neglected. In English a breach of pattern or form often goes unrecognized or more often tolerated as a peccadillo, perhaps, or as a puzzle for the workaday prosodist. One should now be more precise and say *poetic* prosodist, since linguists have taken to using the word "prosody" to refer to suprasegmental features (such as intonation, juncture, and stress) in *any* use of

language. The poetic prosodist, then, will describe the passage or
line in terms of a vocabulary that includes words like feet, caesura,
hypermetrical, stress, trochee, and all the rest. Let us assume he has
a proper notion of what he is about. For one thing, he must distinguish between meter and rhythm. He must recognize that "regular"
and "irregular" are neutral terms and that it is the poet's business to
vary and avoid monotony. In describing rime, he must be aware of
historically changing pronunciation and of regional variation. He
must have some criteria of exactness and approximation. Above all,
any poetic effect depends on some kind of performance, from silent
reading to recitation, that evokes the text as an aesthetic entity in
sounds and meanings.

   Performance in the sense of reading that is aesthetic or artistically
aware, whether silent or aloud, was assumed by Renaissance poets
and should—though it often is not—be assumed by us. Not much
is known, beyond the poetic texts themselves, and their occasional
musical settings, of the manner or manners of performance. Yet it
seems within reason to posit modalities of success and go beyond
description to arrive at some judgment of quality. I confine myself
to rime, an obvious phonic feature of much poetry and one that
often either goes unheard or unremarked. My sampling is from
three English poets over a period of about thirty years. The norma-
tive poetics I assume is, I think, congenial to their own. Rime is
most closely associated with rhythm, but not without reason.

   In the Western world rime fairly exploded into vernacular being
with the first troubadours around 1100. It does have a prehistory,
but that is not my concern here. From the troubadours the vogue of
rime spread quickly to France, England, and the Germanic lands.
But for the English Renaissance (not to mention the high English
Middle Ages) the line of rime went by way of Sicily to Emilia and
Tuscany, and, with Boccaccio and, most clearly, with Petrarch and
his followers in Europe, it came to England along with many other
conventions that went native. Until this century normal verse was
rimed, and perhaps only now can one say that rime is no longer the
normal expectation in poetry, and that "unrimed verse" may, at
least for a time, be as obsolete an expression in English as "the

talkies." Of course in previous centuries unrimed Latin poetry was written, experiments were made in quantitative vernacular poetry, and in England blank verse since Surrey has had great vogue and great success almost always in larger compositions than the lyric.

My brief account of the riming practice of three outstanding poets does not set out to prove anything definitive or establish rules of thumb or examine all instances. Nor can it rely on a compilation of statistics whose upshot could well be depressingly fractional and characterless. What remains is to attempt some characterization of riming practice based upon the range of possibilities. It will be assumed that variety, contrast, and novelty, as well as evenness, likeness, and familiarity, are essential to the modulations of art. The main criteria I have in mind are: (1) rime between monosyllables; (2) rime between a monosyllable and a polysyllable; (3) rime between polysyllables (withal/befall); (4) rime between two-word phrases (to all/through all); (5) rime between the same or different grammatical categories and forms; (6) masculine or feminine rime; (7) eye-rime; (8) slant rime; and (9) archaic or historical rime. Then there is of course botched or even absent rime. But no issue should hinge upon dogmatic declarations of how a word was then pronounced or should now be pronounced: it is reasonable to suppose that "love" and "move" rimed for many English ears then; but it is improbable that "eye" and "enmity" ever did after 1500, though both final vowels may have been more rounded than now. Conventional eye-rimes or slant-rimes are often "explained" otiosely as conventional. My notion, however, is that a poet would prefer a true rime and has, for whatever reason, settled for less. A poet must, of course, settle for the rimes existent in his language. English is not notably rich in rimes, and often striking rimes can simply manufacture the subject matter: heart, dart, smart, part (not to mention amore, cuore, dolore, furore or amour, jour, tour, séjour). Nearly "obligatory" or at least very common words such as the forms of the verb "to be" or the pronouns or words with marked endings like "-ness" or "-ly" can be used in rime. Even in English, as well as in highly inflected languages, such obligatory words and endings can quickly become blemishes if overused. Yet when singling out rime to observe one must naturally be mindful that the whole line, indeed poem, gives space to prepare the fleeting though essential effect. Roughly speaking, two stratagems are special emphasis and special deemphasis, with a whole gamut in between.

As prolegomena to an intrinsic and aesthetic study of rime in the English Renaissance, I briefly consider Sir Philip Sidney's *Astrophel and Stella*, Samuel Daniel's *Delia* and William Shakespeare's *Sonnets*.

Sidney was the first modern English virtuoso of letters. His poetry shows far more of a schooling in Italian and French practice than his most noteworthy, though halting, forerunners, Wyatt and Surrey. He can be quite free in his variations on the Petrarchan sonnet form, though for the most part in *Astrophel and Stella* he conforms to it. As with later English poetry, his staple of rime-words is monosyllabic and disyllabic nouns and verbs: show/pain/know/obtain/woe/entertain/flow/brain/stay/blows/way/throws/spite/write (Sonnet 1). To fit in "entertaine" he is put on his mettle. Two syntactical inversions in the line cast the rhythm first adrift and then press toward the final stress: "Studying inventions fine, her wits to entertaine," where the "expanded" trochee (or more pedantically, substitute dactyl) is compensated for by the unusual stress on "fine" and on the final syllable of "entertaine" (itself an unusual word in this meaning for the time). Elsewhere in this sonnet the rhythm is varied most skilfully to keep the twelve-syllable line from plodding or breaking. In general the rimes in this sonnet are what might be uninvidiously called conventional. Their placement shows skill: in particular the one run-over line ("to see if thence would flow/Some fresh and fruitful showers") keeps its shape and the rime-word "braine" is neatly set off by the striking epithet "sunne-burn'd."

One of Sidney's great virtues in his sonnets is his ability to convey a sense of the sweep and wholeness of a colloquial utterance. He takes risks. In Sonnet 55 he renounces the muses' eloquence in favor of simply crying Stella's name, and at the end the eloquence collapses (perhaps by design?):

> For let me but name her whom I do love,
>> So sweete sounds straight mine eare and heart do hit,
>> That I well find no eloquence like it.

His hope to find something better than "eloquence" seems belied by the rather awkward rhythm of the first line quoted, by the monotonous monosyllables, and by the graceless use of "hit" (sweet sounds *hit?*) and the riming combination hit/it. Oddly, only the word "eloquence" mitigates the failure. The sonnet had begun fairly well. In contrast, to my ear, the next sonnet (56) is quite generally strained and inferior:

> Fy, schoole of Patience, Fy, your lesson is
>> Far far too long to learne it without booke:
>> What, a whole weeke without one peece of looke,
> And thinke I should not your large precepts misse?
> When I might read those letters faire of blisse,
>> Which in her face teach vertue, I could brooke
>> Somewhat thy lead'n counsels, which I tooke
> As of a friend that meant not much amisse:
>> But now that I, alas, do want her sight,
> What, dost thou thinke that I can ever take
> In thy cold stuffe a flegmatike delight?
> No Patience, if thou wilt my good, then make
>> Her come, and heare with patience my desire,
>> And then with patience bid me beare my fire.

The spoken flair and the wholeness of utterance found elsewhere in *Astrophel and Stella* are here compromised by uncertain rhythm and by rimes which, though in themselves unexceptionable, are ill-used. Patience's book too long to memorize is a good conceit undermined by the wilful phrase "peece of looke" (which others may defend as a schoolboy colloquialism). "Is" riming with "misse," "blisse," and "amisse," we may accept as either a common conventional off-rime or as an authentic pronunciation. Yet the strained sense of "misse" in line 4 is simply compounded by the awkward sound, rhythm, and inversion of the line—surely one of the ungainliest. By this time the reader's own patience is tried and he may not indulge "letters faire of blisse" or the uninteresting use of the remaining conventional rimes. In a better setting the eighth line could have shown, in its rhythmical looseness, an effective colloquial litotes: in this sonnet it seems merely lame and ill-fashioned simply for the rime-word. Others may disagree and cite, point for point, some occurrence registered in the *OED,* but it seems to me that Sidney is bending idiom to the breaking point for the sake of rime, which then becomes egregiously prominent and loses its subtle structural value.

It would be easy to catalogue at length Sidney's fine use of ordinary rime (as in Sonnets 39 or 94 or in "Leave me ô Love, which reachest but to dust"): some of his best poems make no more than skilful unobtrusive use of rime. There are instances, though, of unusual inventiveness in finding rimes and in setting them off. In Sonnet 13 we encounter a good conclusive use of monosyllable riming with polysyllable: "then / . . . Gentlemen"; and in 29 an especially effective use is made of noun ending in "-ity" and pronoun:

> So *Stella's* heart, finding what power *Love* brings,
> > To keepe it selfe in life and liberty,
> > Doth willing graunt, that in the frontiers he
> Use all to help his other conquerings.

The word "he" requires pause and emphasis, but also fulfilment in the next line. Both this heightening and also the very sense of the passage deliver great stress on the word "all" and, contrastively, some emphasis on "other." One good result is that the weak rime brings/conquerings seems more natural as part of colloquial intonation. A similar example occurs in the striking sonnet on two negatives making a positive (63). Stella has "twise said, No, No," and the poet exults:

> Sing then my Muse, now *Io Paen* sing,
> Heav'ns envy not at my high triumphing . . .

Modern readers at least must often pause to consider how the lines are to be read. According to Latin grammar one would describe "envy not" as optative subjunctive. But the rime sing/triumphing may seem awkward till one determines to lay the otherwise wavering stress fully upon the syllable "tri." As if to prepare for that and to solemnize the phrase, thus drawing out all the syllables of "triumphing," including the final riming one, this word is preceded by the same diphthong [ai] in "my" and "high." For full effect the line also requires that the word "not" receive careful emphasis. The finish of the sonnet is indeed a fine triumphing flourish:

> But Grammer's force with sweet successe confirme,
>   For Grammar sayes (ô this deare *Stella* weighe,)
>   For Grammar sayes (to Grammer who sayes nay)
> That in one speech two Negatives affirme.

The concluding rimes have a stable and measured authority that proclaims quod erat demonstrandum.

More unstable in rhythm and rime is Sonnet 31 ("With how sad steps, ô Moone, thou climb'st the skies"). The rimes are commonplace (wit/yet was not then substandard), though the word "descries" in the sense of "cries out" or "proclaims" needs a modern gloss. But they are freshened in several ways. In the first three lines the ambiguous distribution of stress holds movement back noticeably and thus does not make prominent the commonness of the rimes. Then the movement begins to surge forward as we find that even the first proposition is a question and will soon know that the whole poem is pitched interrogatively. The audacious epithet in line 5 propels us to its end and into the following lines:

> Sure, if that long with *Love* acquainted eyes
>   Can judge of *Love,* thou feel'st a Lover's case;
>   I read it in thy lookes[;] thy languisht grace,
> To me that felt the like, thy state descries.

Even the rime-word so weakly intonable in "Then ev'n of fellowship, ô Moone, tell me" is justified or naturalized rhythmically as the line spills over into the next. And the final rime-word of the poem, polysyllabic and commonplace in its substantive suffix, gains, by the forward sweep, a potential force that nonetheless requires a sudden, careful, and questioning articulation:

> Do they above love to be lov'd, and yet
>   Those Lovers scorne whom that *Love* doth possesse?
>   Do they call *Vertue* there ungratefulnesse?

Indeed that forward rush almost compels us to take "possesse" in the sense of being possessed by a god. "Love," italicized in the text, comes into full personification. The internal monorime of "love-" is also, of course, part of the phonic echoing (as in "above"), along with end-rime and, for that matter, the notable alliteration and assonance. Besides, "love-," in its various occurrences here, takes varying stress and so partakes of the hesitant interrogative mode.

Sidney's master was Petrarch, whom he clearly read with far more comprehension of language and understanding of technique than did any of his English predecessors. It was Petrarch who gave the universal example of rime in vernacular poetry. That there should be some attempt to imitate quantitative unrimed Latin poetry in English is not surprising. Practically everyone learned Latin and read not only classical poetry but also the vastly cultivated Neo-Latin verse written by Pontanus, Politian, Buchanan, and a host of others, including many poets in English who wrote in Latin as well, from More to Milton and Marvell. Perhaps rime did need a defense, which Samuel Daniel elegantly supplied on provocation of Thomas Campion's lightweight challenge, in order to repel the threat "to overthrow the whole state of Ryme in this Kingdom." Rime, for Daniel, gives "both to the Eare an Eccho of a delightfull report & to the Memorie a deeper impression of what is delivered therein." It provides a "knowne frame" for "those due staies for the minde, those incounters of touch as makes the motion certaine, though the varietie be infinite." In general, Daniel's principles and strictures are sensible, and his committed earnestness is at times even moving. One feels almost invited into the poet's workroom to hear him talk of his indispensable tools. We might presume, then, to inspect the jointure of his artifacts.

Most of Daniel's sonnets are in fact workmanlike, fashioned well, conventional in conceit, and smooth. Rather too insistently the poet plays the theme of the "cruel fair" who opposes her immobile disdain to his modulating praise and complaint. Only occasionally does Daniel succeed in working out an original or skilful conceit as Sidney could: it would seem that he tried, as with the notion of "reining in" in Sonnet 25. He attempts a whole sonnet in correlative verses in Sonnet 11, but the crucial last lines are poorly rimed:

> Yet will I weepe, vowe, pray to cruell Shee;
> Flint, frost, Disdaine, weares, melts, and yeelds we see.

The potentially striking ungrammatical "Shee" entirely misses being clinched and thus "justified" by a powerful rime-pair. In Sonnet 15 he again tries for effect and fails to join his fine phrases:

> And if a brow with cares caracters painted,
> Bewraies my loue, with broken words halfe spoken,
> To her that sits in my thoughts Temple sainted,
> And layes to view my Vultur-gnawne hart open . . .

The "carácters" or broken words traced on his brow are strikingly half-spoken, but the brow lays bare his heart in a phrase that ends in the daring off-rime "open" spoiled by odd idiom, lame rhythm, and the ineffective sound of the ambitious phrase "vultur-gnawne."

Not to say that some of his rimes are not enterprising. Apart from possible dialectal exact rimes (thoughts/notes in Sonnet 9 and thoughts/dotes in 20), there are such unusual rimes as: horror/for her (20), Lady/made I (26), merit/were it (26), speedy/need I (27), fire/nye her (28), honor/uppon her (31), t'inwoman/assomon (37), and theaters/waters (48). Though they are not too ingeniously muted into place and though they require extraordinary tact in performance, nonetheless they deserve a sort of experimental honor. They show the earnestness, even doggedness, of Daniel's artisanry, since, though he tinkered with his poetry from edition to edition, he did not change them. His use of feminine rimes in such sonnets as 16 (sestet), 17 (throughout), and 27 (all but the last two lines), is clearly another mode of experiment. Some fine effects are achieved in Sonnet 34:

> When Winter snowes upon thy golden heares,
> And frost of age hath nipt thy flowers neere:
> When darke shall seeme thy day that neuer cleares,
> And all lyes withred that was held so deere.
>   Then take this picture which I heere present thee,
> Limned with a Pensill not all vnworthy:

Heere see the giftes that God and nature lent thee;
Heere read thy selfe, and what I suffred for thee.
   This may remaine thy lasting monument,
Which happily posteritie may cherish:
These collours with thy fading are not spent;
These may remaine, when thou and I shall perish.
   If they remaine, then thou shalt liue thereby;
   They will remaine, and so thou canst not dye.

The rimes in the first quatrain are commonplace, but in their end-stopped similarity they help convey a tone of solemn sobriety. Line 3 interestingly holds back from merely saying "thy day shall be thy night," yet the delicacy is marred by the echoing relative clause in the next line which has the flatness of filler unredeemed by its rime: "that was held so deere." Interest is enhanced in the second quatrain by a freshening of the conceit of the lady's portrait done in words. The portrait is indeed to be read, as the poem says with admirable succinctness: "Heere read thy selfe." Rime helps greatly in conveying meaning and nuance. "Which I heere present thee" has in its feminine ending, a pathetic formality. Its rime-pair, "that God and nature lent thee," economically heightens the pathos in expressing the transitoriness of her beauty in the word "lent." It is also a *good* instance of this sort of relative clause which can often seem mere filler to plaster in the rime, as happens, I think, in line 4 of this sonnet. The other set of rimes is even more unusual phonically and successful conceptually. "Not all vnworthy" is an appropriately muted, rather latinate boast which enhances the almost casual but moving "and what I suffred for thee." The "picture" will convey not only her youthful beauty but also his suffering or the reason for his suffering. In the sestet the poem gains force from the polysyllabic rime-word "monument," which raises expectations that are then fulfilled in its riming line: "These collours with thy fading are not spent." She fades, but the colors of her picture, his art, do not. And those colors, we need not be told, are also the colors of rhetoric: the poet's pen-pencil is "not all vnworthy" because it expresses communal and universal language. With mingled boast and humility the poet, after including himself in mortality ("when thou and I shall perish"), gradually rises from "These may remaine" to "If they remaine" (propositional) to "They will remaine"—all in an impressive echoing iteration. The final couplet has a quiet and simple definitiveness that makes this sonnet an outstanding example of the plain Petrarchan mode in which Daniel took such pains to do well.

His two most famous sonnets, "Care-charmer sleepe, sonne of the Sable night" (45) and "Let others sing of Knights and Palladines" (46), should of course be acknowledged in any account of his work. In this context of rime they do not, despite their almost Sidnean virtues, contain striking novelties. A proper discussion would have to go into the textual problems for which there is no time. I should, however, like to express my preference for the earlier version of the last lines of Sonnet 46. Daniel's preference seems to have differed; in the last printings (1601–11) during his lifetime the lines read:

> Though th'error of my youth in them appeare,
> Suffice they shew I liv'd and lov'd thee deare.

("Them" refers to his verses as "the Arkes, the Tropheis I erect.") Their smooth triteness is unexceptionable: they are straight from the supply house of sonneteering. For nearly the whole previous decade (1591–98), they were printed thus:

> Though th'error of my youth they shall discouer,
> Suffice they shew I liu'd and was thy louer.

It is not so much the use of the word "lover" as a general term that surprises; it is the direct and particular first-person assertion "I . . . was thy louer" that, in its conclusiveness and singular outspokenness, startles as it rimes in final place.

The perils of the sonnet lie not so much in its high technical demands as in its challenge to proliferation. It is like an addicting puzzle with confines, rules, and infinite fulfilment by hook or crook: many a collection in the Petrarchan vein may deserve the collective "a surfeit of sonnets." But the practicing sonneteer may have a special affection even for his least successful "solutions," an affection that may not attach to freer forms that can be amended or

improved or shaped by discursive addition. Among the many things
we do not and shall not know about *Shakes-speares /Sonnets/ Neuer
before Imprinted* (1609) is whether Shakespeare would have published
them all as they now stand. Apart from matters of order, many of
the 154 sonnets seem poor or mediocre or merely tolerable. Apart
from matters of psychobiography (a good use here for that parlous
word), the printed order seems to indicate that Shakespeare took up
a theme and elaborated it in a run of sonnets and then went on to
another theme. That the vague scheme is so unpredictable and so
resistant to our making a full story out of it invites the conjecture
that in reading the sonnets we are in Shakespeare's workshop. Surely
all the poets of short poems work differently, but they are all makers
as well as self-expressers and what they make is a technical feat, an
artifact. Whatever Shakespeare's project may have been—whether
to publish a set of sonnets with a title and perhaps a plot or whether
not to publish any sonnets at all—we are free to imagine that
someone purloined a sheaf of working papers which then George Eld
printed for the publisher Thomas Thorpe. For some reason we do
not know, they were not reprinted until 1640. Short of wishing to
write yet another scenario for the *Sonnets,* I advance the supposition
that what we have is a sheaf of poems from a poet's workshop.

Like any sonneteer, Shakespeare had to choose his rimes and
take artistic chances with the rhythm and the sense. Indeed an
intimation of rime is an intimation of possible meaning, and with
several sets of rimes (and provisional alternatives) the range of meaning becomes more defined and at the same time more complex.
Accommodating rime to its place in the poem entails, then, the
dynamic triad of rime, rhythm, and sense. For the most part
Shakespeare's rimes are not unusual, but rather part of the stock
familiar from reading such of his immediate predecessors as Sidney
and Daniel. In Sonnet 76 he concludes, for the nonce, "So all my
best is dressing old words new, / Spending again what is already
spent," on the grounds that his theme and "addressee" also remain
the same. On more general grounds there is truth in this. Most
often he rimes familiar English monosyllables, at times based on
now-archaic pronunciation but occasionally forced, and perhaps

too often [ai] and [i] as in die/memory (1) and eye/majesty (7). All
told, this "eye-rime" occurs thirteen times, though trisyllabic
nouns ending in "-y" are sometimes loosely but interestingly rimed
as in flattery/alchemy (114), memory/eternity (122), or husbandry/
posterity (3). In Sonnet 55 there is a finer use that is even flaunted
by the two contrasting pairs, masonry/memory and enmity/
posterity, which have the *force* of riming in two syllables. On rare
occasions Shakespeare rimes inexactly, as in field/held (2), fleet'st/
sweets (19), o'erread/dead (81), and open/broken (61). But almost
always, even in the poor sonnets (of which there are too many for a
great poet), the rimes are good and serviceable, as rime in the main
ought to be.

As a conscientious poet Shakespeare had the conviction of his
rimes, and in some clear cases was put to shifts to make the sense
and rhythm come out at least acceptably. A common fault in rimed
poetry—which Shakespeare in his best sonnets worked to avoid—is,
as I have noted, the lame relative clause or descriptive phrase that
could better have been a single word. It is, of course, difficult to
distinguish padding from convincing colloquial prolixity; besides,
extreme compression can well be a fault, as it is in quite a few of
Shakespeare's sonnets that have to many seemed obscure. In this
regard it is interesting to compare Sonnets 55 and 116, the first in
the *exegi monumentum* vein, the second on the constancy of love. In
55 we read, as the poem exaltedly and rather verbosely flows,

> . . . your praise shall still find room
> Even in the eyes of all posterity
> That wear this world out to the ending doom.

The rime and the notion are accommodated. Yet the last line given
here seems rhythmically weak and too long as an enjambed descriptive clause, lamely and otiosely modifying "doom" with "ending."
In 116, which perhaps begins less strikingly, we find "doom"
(which I take to be a true rime here in Shakespeare's pronunciation)
again in the same position at the end of the twelfth line:

> Love's not Time's fool, though rosy lips and cheeks
> Within his bending sickle's compass come;

Love alters not with his brief hours and weeks,
But bears it out even to the edge of doom.

Here, to begin with, the clause is independent and the verb-phrase "bears it out" is not weakened by a long object ("it" vs. "this world"). The trochaic stress on "even" tilts the line toward a strong conclusion with two climactic stresses on "edge" and "doom." Thus the word "doom," resonant in both sound and sense, can express its full and elemental import. Incidentally the rhythmic force, to my ear, shortens "even" to "evn." These two passages are clearly related, not so much in subject matter or sense as in sound and technique. We are in Shakespeare's ear.

Such experiments in sound, and more particularly in the potency of rime words in different contexts, are naturally part of a poet's activity. Other instances could be adduced—for example, the rime hope/scope in sonnets 52 and 29: in the first it is used in the concluding couplet with the then ordinary meaning of "scope" as "purpose" or "means"; in the second ("Desiring this man's art and that man's scope") these forceful words are tensionally separated in the second quatrain and "scope" takes on what was then a new meaning of "range." There are numerous other instances in which it could be argued that Shakespeare might have been thinking in rime-pairs and testing them out. One must, however, be wary and aware that some of his best sonnets show no remarkable inventiveness in rime and that some of his virtuoso rimes (as well as wordplay and conceits) occur in faulty and lightweight poems.

In larger terms of technique it is fascinating to observe the sequences, however brief, of poems on more or less the same theme, such as love-servitude, time, flattery, praise, demise, and poetry, not to mention procreation, beauty, blackness, and triangular passion. Some sonnets seem closely matched in theme, though different in quality, to the point that, fancifully, one may imagine a poor sonnet to be an acknowledged botch and a good one to be a more finely achieved response to the "same" challenge of expression. Thus I think of Sonnets 50 and 51, both dealing with a journey on horseback away from the beloved; of 80, 85, 86, all three concern-

ing the poet's failing craft and the notorious Rival Poet; and 64 and
65, which, along with 63, are most interesting to compare. It
would be foolhardy to claim that, in irrecoverable reality, Sonnet 65
was a rewriting of 64: whichever one was written first, my claim is
only that they are intimately related and that 65 is far better. Sonnet
63 may less plausibly be considered the botched start of the series.

A glance shows that they share no rime-words or even rime-
sounds except decay/decays:

64

When I have seen by Time's fell hand defaced
The rich proud cost of outworn buried age,
When sometime lofty towers I see down-rased
And brass eternal slave to mortal rage;
When I have seen the hungry ocean gain
Advantage on the kingdom of the shore,
And the firm soil win of the wat'ry main,
Increasing store with loss and loss with store;
When I have seen such interchange of state,
Or state itself confounded to decay,
Ruin hath taught me thus to ruminate,
That Time will come and take my love away.
　　This thought is as a death, which cannot choose
　　But weep to have that which it fears to lose.

65

Since brass, nor stone, nor earth, nor boundless sea,
But sad mortality o'ersways their power,
How with this rage shall beauty hold a plea,
Whose action is no stronger than a flower?
O, how shall summer's honey breath hold out
Against the wrackful siege of batt'ring days,
When rocks impregnable are not so stout,
Nor gates of steel so strong but Time decays?
O fearful meditation: where, alack,
Shall Time's best jewel from Time's chest lie hid?
Or what strong hand can hold his swift foot back,
Or who his spoil of beauty can forbid?
　　O, none, unless this miracle have might,
　　That in black ink my love may still shine bright.

Both poems are meditations on the theme of time's destructiveness. The rimes of 64 seem appropriate and pregnant with suggestion, especially age/rage, shore/store (in Shakespeare's favorite sense of abundance in reserve), and decay/away. "Kingdom of the shore" prepares for "state" in the sense of high or assured position. "State" makes a good rime for "meditate," and that word certainly would have fitted. But instead we find the less usual word "ruminate," not itself very elevated but making an obvious local effect in alliteration with the strong and emphatic "Ruin." But a rime for "decay" may have suggested the next disappointingly trite line, "That Time will come and take my love away," which would have been all right in a different context, but not as a climax to a somber and even violent thought. Now Time "comes" and "takes away" rather weakly, though at the beginning "Time's fell hand" more powerfully "defaced." Choose/lose is certainly as effective a couplet-rime as any, but the conceit of the thought as "a death" that cannot help weeping over future loss seems ordinary. The remaining rimes, defaced/down-rased and gain/main, would in this context seem fertile in suggestiveness to the practicing sonneteer. Defaced/rased may have been an off-rime for Shakespeare; at any rate, he has to insure the less common meaning of "rased" by adding "down." That is in keeping with the other redundancies of the poem, as is also the riming phrasal pair: the hungry ocean gain/of the wat'ry main. Over such rimes a supersensitive poet might weep in his watery beer.

Sonnet 65 makes use of some of the same words (brass, rage, hand, love) and more or less specific notions, but it proceeds and culminates far more impressively. The first magnificent line ends in the emphatic word "sea," which, when defined by so rhythmically and phonically effective an epithet as "boundless," is surely richer than "ocean" (especially "hungry ocean"). "Mortality" is stronger when not rivaling Time for space and when not tied up in a phrase like "mortal rage" (meaning "ravages of mortality") which is, however, characteristically Shakespearean, one must grant, and concise. If there is some loss in not using "rage" as rime-word, it gains in Sonnet 65 by being directed lawlessly against beauty's lawful innocence: the simple legal terminology humanizes the geodetic landscape. Summer also will succumb. The interrogative mode is a skilful way of avoiding platitudinous assertion. Besides, there is a climax of mortality's destructiveness when even "gates of steel" are not "so strong but Time decays." Indeed it is, finally, inhuman Time that destroys; the verb "decays" used transitively has the convincing force of "destroy," while as a noun in 64 it comes as anticlimactic filler in the line "Or state itself confounded to decay." With the exclamation "O fearful meditation" the poem takes itself seriously, indeed desperately so in the questions that follow. It also takes itself seriously in answering the questions in an honest conditional. By a miracle, mere ink may survive what seemingly solid substances could not. Again, the rime-words of this final couplet could serve as well as any other: might/bright is certainly a common rime. Yet the emphatic, trisyllabic and necessary word "miracle" alliterates with "might" and the whole line rushes in rhythm to the last word. Thereby the following, final line becomes, in its consistent, mostly closed monosyllables, solemn and deliberate: "black ink" is truly climactic; "my love," only now mentioned, may have some chance of permanence both somber and bright.

It can be as useful to discuss rime in poetry as to discuss any other constituent of art: one may talk statistically or mensurally of the incidence of patterning of rime just as in painting one may note the angle and curvature of a line or the saturation of colors. But rimes and lines and colors are found in contexts that possess value and somehow confer value on all their constitutive parts. So it is that in discussing a relatively nonconceptual element in the language-art of poetry like rime, one may easily falter in trying plausibly to encompass rime-in-the-abstract, a particular set or use of rime, and a single value-laden context—a particular poem. One reason I confine myself to the sonnet is that it reduces the variables of comparison. My three authors are convenient temporally and aesthetically in that they are the great English masters of the sonnet before Donne and Milton. I know of only a few attempts to discuss the use of rime in this period (or any other in English literature) as both a technical and an aesthetic means of poetry. The subject to some may seem pat, to others unimportant or antiquarian. As to its place in English poetry, we cannot help recalling what Milton said on rejecting rime for the "Heroic Verse" of *Paradise Lost:* rime was the "Invention of a barbarous age, to set off wretched matter with lame Meter; grac't indeed since by the use of some famous modern Poets, carried away by Custom, but much to their own vexation, hindrance, and constraint to express many things otherwise, and for the most part worse than else they would have exprest them." The whole prefatory paragraph is a fine spate of special pleading, a veritable "example set . . . of ancient liberty recover'd to Heroic Poem from the troublesome and modern bondage of Riming." Even under Charles' son Charles, the aged Areopagite proclaims yet another "ancient liberty." Of course pugnacity is understandable in a great and masterful poet, but we can be grateful that Milton did not carry his reverence for free unriming Homer so far as to turn quantitative.

No revolutions in literature are permanent. We are now in a time when the most prestigious poetry is rimeless and often meterless, however rhythmical it may be. At the same time the loudest criticism currently mocks what it calls formalism (using, perhaps unwittingly, Leon Trotsky's opprobrious term) or New Criticism (caricaturing a supposedly unified doctrine of form in isolation), and instead often reduces poetry to language in general or to "discourse" subject to further but equal discourse in a tropological and ideological vein or to simply the flow and froth of words in their capricious suggestiveness. The technicality, the formality, the art of poetry are at best taken for granted. Indeed most critics, of whatever persuasion, write about poetry as if it could just as well have been prose. But even in an unrimed age, aesthetically successful rime can hold its own. As Modernism and its eddies continue to recede and stagnate in repetition, perhaps we can look for a renewed cultivation of craft and for a renewed formal mastery, not to mention fresh transformations of reality in art. Historically, rime since the troubadours has been a potent poetic resource and remains so still potentially. In rimed poetry, rime, as part of the matter, matters.

NOTES

The standard editions I have used are: Sir Philip Sidney, *The Poems,* ed. William A. Ringler, Jr. (Oxford: Oxford University Press, Clarendon Press, 1962); Samuel Daniel, *Poems and A Defence of Ryme,* ed. Arthur Colby Sprague (Chicago: University of Chicago Press, 1965; corrected from the first edition of 1930); and William Shakespeare, *The Sonnets,* ed. Douglas Bush and Alfred Harbage (New York: Penguin, 1970). The first two are properly old-spelling editions, the Shakespeare follows the convention of modernization and I have checked it against the facsimile reproduction of the 1609 edition published by the Scolar Press (Menston, England, 1968).

The best account of rime is Viktor Zhirmunskij, *Rifma, eë istorija i teorija* (Petrograd: Voprosy Poètiki, 1923), reprinted now definitively in his *Teorija stikha* (Leningrad: Sovetskij Pisatel', 1975). Of equal importance are the many studies of Roman Jakobson, as collected in volume 5 of his *Selected Writings: On Verse, its Masters and Explorers,* ed. Stephen Rudy and Martha Taylor (The Hague: Mouton, 1979). Other important studies, including collaborative exegeses, are conveniently collected in *Questions de poétique* (Paris: Editions du Seuil, 1973). The recent *Shakespeare's Verbal Art in Th'expence of Spirit* by Roman Jakobson and Lawrence G. Jones (The Hague: Mouton, 1970) is a particularly apposite instance of Jakobson's method of practical criticism.

George Saintsbury's *A History of English Prosody from the Twelfth Century to the Present Day* in 3 vols. (London: Macmillan, 1906–10) is leisurely, chatty, and not very helpful. Much more trustworthy is the linguistically informed treatise of John Thompson, *The Founding of English Metre* (New York: Columbia University Press, 1961), which culminates in celebrating Sidney as the first poet in modern English to reach metrical "perfection"; but almost nothing is said of rime. The best essay in English on rime is William K. Wimsatt, "One Relation of Rhyme to Reason," in *The Verbal Icon; Studies in the Meaning of Poetry* (Lexington: University of Kentucky Press, 1954), pp. 153–66; originally published in 1944. For reliable discussions of the relation between rhythm and meter the most useful volume of reference is W. K. Wimsatt, ed., *Versification: Major Language Types* (New York: Modern Language Association/New York University Press, 1972); in my contribution, "Spanish Versification," I state my own general views on pp. 169–70. Currently the best historically minded and aesthetically perceptive analyst of the relation between sound and sense, including rime, is John Hollander, *Vision and Resonance: Two Senses of Poetic Form* (New York: Oxford University Press, 1975).

It is not to my immediate purpose to cite any of the stylistic analyses of Sidney, Daniel, and Shakespeare. I am not aware of any direct indebtedness to such studies in questions of rime.

THOMAS M. GREENE

Anti-hermeneutics: The Case of Shakespeare's Sonnet 129

A scholarly contention has recently re-arisen over the editing of Shakespeare's *Sonnets* that focuses conveniently a complex of perennial problems, not only affecting the editing of Shakespeare or any other author but also adumbrating vaster questions of historical understanding. In his useful, important, and exhaustive edition with commentary on the *Sonnets*, Stephen Booth takes vigorous issue with a well-known essay by Robert Graves and Laura Riding, "A Study in Original Punctuation and Spelling." This essay, published in its original form over fifty years ago, argues against the modernization of Shakespeare by comparing the original and re-edited texts of a single sonnet, 129, "Th'expense of Spirit in a waste of shame." By explicating the allegedly richer, more open, more polysemous quarto version and by showing the reductive flatness imposed by modernization, Graves and Riding call into question what they call the "perversely stupid" habits of most modern editors. Professor Booth, no mean polemicist himself, labels this essay "an exercise in irresponsible editorial restraint" and devotes more than five large pages to disposing of its arguments. His basic position is that "an editor distorts the sonnet more for a modern reader by maintaining the 1609 text than he would if he modernized its spelling and punctuation."[1]

No one can deny the enduring importance of this contention between, on the one hand, two practicing poets writing a long time ago as radical critics beyond the pale of the scholarly guild and on the other hand a gifted contemporary member of the guild, not lacking in professional independence and even irreverence, but in this dispute adopting something close to a hard-line conservative position. But in describing Booth as the conservative one may already falsify the issue, since Graves and Riding would argue that they are the true conservatives, preserving Shakespeare's original words and meanings against the tendentious contaminators of the intervening centuries. Perhaps one useful step toward resolving the quarrel would be to ask which side has the better right to be called conservative in the best, most positive sense.

Clearly this inexhaustible question will not be settled simply by an appeal to Sonnet 129, but a glance at the two versions competing for our attention could be instructive. Booth provides both the quarto text and, facing it throughout, a compromise modernization that represents what he calls a "mid-point" between the punctuation and spelling of the original and modern directive adaptations.

> Th'expence of Spirit in a waste of shame
> Is lust in action, and till action, lust   2
> Is periurd, murdrous, blouddy full of blame,
> Sauage, extreame, rude, cruell, not to trust,   4
> Inioy'd no sooner but dispised straight,
> Past reason hunted, and no sooner had   6
> Past reason hated as a swollowed bayt,
> On purpose layd to make the taker mad.   8
> Made In pursut and in possession so,
> Had, having, and in quest, to have extreame,   10
> A blisse in proofe and proud and very wo,
> Before a ioy proposd behind a dreame,   12
>   All this the world well knowes yet none knowes well,
>   To shun the heaven that leads men to this hell.   14
>
> Th'expense of spirit in a waste of shame
> Is lust in action, and till action lust   2
> Is perjured, murd'rous, bloody, full of blame,
> Savage, extreme, rude, cruel, not to trust,   4
> Enjoyed no sooner but despisèd straight,
> Past reason hunted, and no sooner had,   6
> Past reason hated as a swallowed bait,
> On purpose laid to make the taker mad;   8
> Mad in pursuit, and in possession so,
> Had, having, and in quest to have, extreme,   10

A bliss in proof, and proved, a very woe,
Before, a joy proposed, behind, a dream.   12
    All this the world well knows, yet none knows well
    To shun the heav'n that leads men to this hell.   14

What are the main differences? Booth supplies a comma after
"bloudy" in line 3 and another at the end of line 6 where the
quarto has nothing; at the end of line 8 he substitutes a semicolon
for the quarto's period; together with virtually all editors he emends
the first word of line 9 from "Made" to "Mad," adds a comma after
"pursut" in line 9, and shifts the third comma in line 10. In lines
11 and 12 the surgery is radical: in 11 two commas are added and
"a" is substituted for "and"; in 12 three commas are added and a
period at the end replaces the quarto's only comma. Finally in line
13, a comma is shifted from the end to the middle. The spelling is
modernized, with apostrophes inserted in "murdrous" and
"heaven." If this text does represent a midpoint in editorial tact,
we're left to wonder what further changes are possible, but in fact
the text from *The Oxford Book of English Verse* quoted by Graves and
Riding is still more freely repunctuated.

    This is not the occasion to analyze thoroughly the semantic
transformations, some subtle and some obtrusive, effected by the
modern version. But if one stands back and contemplates the two
texts as a set, a few impressions emerge immediately. The revised
version is undeniably more accessible. Assuming with Booth that
the Jacobean reader found few obstacles to reading the poem and
that the modern reader should be assisted to enjoy a similar facility
so far as possible, then unquestionably the revised version does
extend us that assistance. It smoothes over almost all the superficial
perplexities in this poem of anguish and despair, this terrible sonnet. For example it attaches the third quatrain to the first two, thus
allowing all three to form one coherent sentence, rather than attach-
ing the third quatrain to the couplet as the quarto does, a little
mysteriously. The new version helps us to understand the first word
of line 9, which here simply echoes the last word of the previous
line—"mad"; in the quarto version one's eye has to move further
back in line 8 to the verb "to make" and then understand "Made" in

the next line as an altered form of it. "Mad" clearly assists the reader, as does the substitution of "a" for "and"; the line in its old version *could* mean, as Graves and Riding point out, that lust is both bliss and woe at once, both "in proof" and "provd," during its gratification and afterwards. But that meaning has to be worked for. The revised line 12 imposes a reassuring tidiness on the puzzling original, where we have to struggle to see how lust could be a joy which is "proposd," envisioned, behind a dream. Again the original *could* make sense, but not easily. Throughout the modern version supplies us with the *facilior lectio,* and if that is what it takes for our reading to approach the Jacobeans', then undoubtedly the quarto text can only be regarded as unsuitable. "In 129," writes Booth, "modern punctuation gains 'sheer facility in reading' and denies a modern reader nothing that Shakespeare's contemporaries would have perceived."[2]

Surely for better or worse the modernization does more than that. It really acts as a shield for the modern reader, a shield extended to protect him from the problematic contingencies of the original. It protects him from worrying whether the punctuation in front of him corresponds to Shakespeare's actual intent or only his compositor's—whether in fact it corresponds to any knowledgeable intent rather than an ignorant man's caprice. The altered text does certainly correspond to a knowledgeable intent, its editor's, and in this certainty we take comfort. We're protected as well from the strenuous effort of groping unassisted for those shifting, floating, ambiguous relations of clause to clause, phrase to phrase, that constitute one of the outstanding rhetorical features of the *Sonnets* and which Booth himself stresses. Thus in the altered text we don't have to grope for the elusive, possibly nonexistent connection between the third quatrain and the couplet that would justify their separation by a mere comma after line 12. But should we really have this protection? Do we truly want it? Don't we ultimately want, or shouldn't we want, the actual mysterious artifact history has handed down to us with all its built-in puzzlements and uncertainties? Some of these surely the Jacobean reader wrestled with also. What *did* he do with that "Made" in line 9? Why should we be spared his perplexities if his experience is the norm we're expected to approach?

Most decisively and significantly the altered text shields us from that curious Renaissance sense of grammar that fails to isolate a self-contained sentence from its successor. Take one of the most assertive and distinct and self-enclosed affirmations in the *Sonnets:* "Let me not to the marriage of true mindes / Admit impediments." That affirmation is denied in the quarto the full stop it deserves according to our logic: ". . . Admit impediments, love is not love . . ." Here at least the practice is too common to blame only on the compositor, and even if it were the compositor's alone, we have no reason to believe that it troubled the Jacobean reader. We are forced to recognize that the sense of syntactic closure, the sense of declarative completeness, the very status of the affirmation during the Jacobean period violate our grammar and our logic. This troubling recognition would also be spared us if we confined our reading to the altered text. Even if it were true that modern punctuation denies us nothing a Jacobean would have *perceived,* it does deny us something crucial about the presuppositions he brought to the printed page: it denies us something about his mind-set. Modernization in this respect is less conservative because it fails to preserve an important element of Shakespeare's semiotic world. It not only conceals the mysteries, the contingencies, the authentic riddles truly present for us in the original; it conceals those offenses to our logic that historical distance will always impose.

That distance makes itself felt equally in the puzzles posed by individual words. In Sonnet 129 the opening phrase immediately presents a kind of hermeneutic hurdle. The expression "expence of Spirit" sustains the fundamental metaphor of the sequence linking economics with emotion and sexuality. The constant concern with husbandry, with cost-accounting, with thrift and profligacy, with a friendship too dear for one's possessing, with bonds and terms and leases—this repetitive series of analogies organizes the *Sonnets,* and there is nothing a priori in this figural pattern that is necessarily inaccessible to a twentieth-century reader. The metaphor begins to lose us only when the economic implications of "expence" are taken literally at the physiological level. The sexual act is really impoverishing only if one holds the medieval and Renaissance belief that it shortens a man's life. If, in place of the restorative, therapeutic release our post-Freudian society perceives, one attributes to sex a literal expenditure of vitality, then the struggle between the sexes takes on a crude economic reality, and we begin to understand the linkage made by the Wyf of Bath. She ends her tale by praying for "housebondes meeke, yonge, and fressh abedde" while calling down a plague on "olde and angry niggardes of dispence."[3] In Sonnets 1–126 of Shakespeare's sequence, the bourgeois poet speaks for the values of husbandry, as befits his class, in order prudently to correct the failures of this art assigned to that social class of "unthrifts" which includes the friend. It is true that the conduct associated with good husbandry shifts radically; if in Sonnets 1–17 it means marriage, and solitude is "unprovident," by Sonnet 95 ("They that haue powre to hurt . . .") only the solitary can "husband natures ritches from expence," with a stinginess not calculated to please the Wyf of Bath. In Sonnet 129 the young man's profligacy is less at issue than, one presumes, the bourgeois speaker's among others. The phrase "th'expence of Spirit" means several things, including the implication that the speaker has been *unclassed* by lust, that he is now guilty of that aristocratic waste he had attempted in so many preceding poems to moderate. In yielding to lust he is yielding to a literally self-destructive extravagance, which heretofore he has followed tradition in charging to his social superiors.[4] This biological as well as sociological undoing of the self, implicit in Shakespeare's word "expence," remains an abstraction for us even if we catch its resonance. We might begin to recapture that reference to personal ontology by taking seriously the lost implications of such words as "dissolute" and "dissipated."

Modernized spelling also helps to conceal the different status of the word itself in a prelexicographical culture. The quarto calls attention to the word "Spirit" by capitalizing it, a stress modern editors tend to drop. The word is not easily defined in any case. Glosses for "Spirit" suggested by Booth and other editors include "physical vigor," "mental energy," "spiritual essence," "life force," "bodily fluid," "penis erectus," and "the subtle vapor supposed to be contained in the heart and needed for generation." This gives seven distinct glosses which the modern reader experiences as a supersaturated plethora of competing meanings. But it is unlikely that the prelexicographical reader felt this kind of division and subdivision; it is more likely that he or she read the word "Spirit" as a multifaceted unity we can only try to imagine. The polyvalent word before the era of dictionaries could not simply be felt as the sum of an indefinite series of parallel definitions; it must have been apprehended as a veined monolith. It was not yet reducible to a vertical list of semidiscrete equivalents. It must have remained somehow a simultaneous whole which nonetheless presented multiple aspects to be perceived as context indicated. Not only do the lost meanings of a word elude us but the very process of their fusion within a single signifier.

One peculiarly elusive word appears at the openings of lines 2 and 3. One of the most deceptive signifiers in the code of any remote text is the copula: deceptive because to the naked eye it looks to be the most unchanging and the most transparent of all parts of speech. But in fact the copula, underlying implicitly or explicitly most metaphorization and predication, is the part of speech most sensitive to historically shifting intuitions of relationship and reality. It is rooted in each culture's, each era's metaphysical and epistemological assumptions—not necessarily the assumptions spelt out discursively but those silently shared and invoked in poetry as in ordinary speech. Fully to understand the force of a copula in a given text is to understand a good deal of the text and the semiotic universe that nourished it. Shakespeare's Sonnet 129 is largely controlled by those two copulas appearing at the opening of the second and third lines. The second of these is the more important, since so much of what follows depends on it; it is also the more mysterious. To begin to understand the force of "is" in line 3, we have to decide whether its subject, "lust," the last word in line 2, is passion working within a given individual; or rather the lustful individual himself; or rather a partially allegorized Lust, a sort of personification out of Spenser, or rather the experience of gratification. If we

read "this hell," the last words of the sonnet, to summarize all that
has been predicated about lust, then we have to extend the meaning
of that word to the object of male desire, since the word "hell" in
subsequent sonnets will clearly acquire a specific anatomical reference.[5] "Lust" thus has four or five potential meanings that fade in
and out or reinforce each other a little confusingly as the reader
moves through the series of participles, nouns, and clauses that
maintain the predication apparently through line 12. All the rich,
disturbing intricacy of meaning hangs upon that "is." Is lust "murdrous" because it destroys the individual who feels it, or is he led to
feel murderous toward the person he desires? Or toward himself? Is
lust "cruell" toward other feelings and traits, virtues and vices, in a
kind of shadowy psychomachia, or toward human beings? Are we
dimly invited to half-imagine some hypostasized embodiment,
some furious naked "salvage man" spotted with gore, both hunted
and hated? How does that potential predication jibe with lust as
bliss and woe in line 11? There the "salvage man" disappears and
lust "is" the feelings stemming from the end of its quest. Is it
possible for so many alternative predications to be jammed into one
uncertain copula? As we read we have to keep revision or recombin-
ing our notions of just how the signifier "lust is," can be something.
We strain to grasp the mysterious equations implied in that deceptively innocent bridge. Only if we are puzzled by it will we begin to
unravel its secrets. Booth's argument against distortion obscures the
need for puzzlement. We need to register the actual warping, which
from our perspective is there, before we can set out to deal with it.
The distortion in the case of the copula is particularly insidious
because modernization leaves it untouched.

"No editor," Booth writes, "is likely to succeed perfectly in
accommodating a modern reader and a Renaissance text to one
another, but that is no reason to do nothing."[6] The question is what
one *can* do if one measures the full distance between the two. To do
what Booth and most editors do risks a sham accommodation with
the past which in fact increases our estrangement from it. How does
the editor avoid that trap? To begin to answer this question satisfac-
torily one really needs a theory of understanding; one has to ask how
a reader would evade the trap. One has to bracket the editorial

problem and consider the larger problems of hermeneutic theory; one has to reflect on the process of understanding any remote text. The growing body of hermeneutic speculation is by no means irrelevant to the practical decisions of editors, just as the consequences of their decisions are not irrelevant to theory. The crucial question focused by Booth's polemic is not whether we want original or altered texts—both are necessary for different purposes—but rather how and to what degree a modern reader's experience might resemble that of its first readers.

No linguist would dissent from Sapir's formulation.

> Language moves down time in a current of its own making. It has a drift. . . . Nothing is perfectly static. Every word, every grammatical element, every locution, every sound and accent is a slowly changing configuration, moulded by the invisible and impersonal drift that is the life of language.[7]

This drift was first discovered for the modern world by Dante and the philologists of the Italian Renaissance. Lorenzo Valla insisted on the central dilemma of anachronistic reading with all the energy of his ferocious intelligence. Changing referents require changing terms: *nova res novum vocabulum flagitat.* But referents and words change at varying rates of speed. Language ideally requires a continuity which neither words nor things possess.

The fact of historical estrangement, historical solitude, is doubtless most fully grasped by those like Valla who spend their careers contending with it. The pathos of estrangement has never been evoked more beautifully than by one of the heroes of modern philology, Wilamowitz.

> The tradition yields us only ruins. The more closely we test and examine them, the more clearly we see how ruinous they are; and out of ruins no whole can be built. The tradition is dead; our task is to revivify life that has passed away. We know that ghosts cannot speak until they have drunk blood; and the spirits which we evoke demand the blood of our hearts. We give it to them gladly; but if they then abide our question, something from us has entered into them.[8]

A little of ourselves will always enter into the ghosts we force to speak. If, as Heidegger suggests, we are what we understand to be, then what we understand to be will already be a part of us. The conversation with our classics will always be partial; we can never altogether escape interpretive anachronism. "Which of your Hesterdays Mean Ye to Morra?": that Joycean song haunts the historian of meanings. It haunted Theodore Adorno: "Nothing more is given to philosophy than fleeting, disappearing traces in the riddle-figures of that which exists and their astonishing entwinings."[9] We can love from the past only that which we have begun by misunderstanding and continue to understand gropingly. Perhaps this is why we love the shard, the ruin, the blurred hieroglyph as we love those broken, discolored, weather-beaten statues, hieratic and withdrawn, standing at the portal of a cathedral.

One can approach the central hermeneutic problem through the experience of the classroom. The teacher is compelled by his role to perform a kind of activity analogous to textual modernization. He is obliged to translate, to find contemporary equivalents and glosses for his students in order to make a remote text "accessible." He can only present a literary work to them in their terms or in terms they can follow. In doing this the teacher has literally no choice. But if he is at all self-conscious, he knows that his glosses and his explanations are subtly or palpably inaccurate. How will he gloss the word "Spirit" at the opening of Sonnet 129? He has no means of conveying the different feeling for syntactic closure of the English Renaissance. And what happens in the classroom is only a heightened imitation of what happens to the solitary reader in his study; he too inevitably translates into his own dialect. He appropriates, anachronizes, no matter how deep his historical consciousness. If we read Sonnet 129 in its quarto version, we try to organize its apparent disorder and soften its offences to our mind set. To begin to read any unfamiliar text is to try to make it less strange, make it new. In Norman N. Holland's Freudian vocabulary, the act of reading involves " a kind of fusion or introjection based on oral wishes to incorporate."[10]

The act of appropriation has been described more than once in hermeneutic theory. Hans-Georg Gadamer calls it *Aneignung,* and Paul Ricoeur uses the French word *appropriation.* In the thought of each it has a positive resonance; ideally for each it leads to self-knowledge. For Ricoeur appropriation occurs when "the interpretation of a text is completed by the self-interpretation of a subject who henceforth understands himself better or differently or even begins to understand himself."[11] Gadamer quotes with approval Hegel's statement that *Aneignung*—appropriation or assimilation—"is the fundamental fact of being alive." But his own hermeneutics invests the term with a somewhat different significance. Gadamer's analysis of the entire process of understanding is very rich and sometimes profound. His perception of its historicity, its "situatedness," his critique of nineteenth-century historicism, his analysis of the mutual questioning between reader and text, his quest for a dialogue across time—these and other contributions to hermeneutic thought are welcome and valuable. But other elements of his theory raise doubts about its viability as a whole system.

According to Gadamer, understanding begins when something other, something outside addresses us. Something, such as a text from the past, asserts its own validity, which is distant from our own. In responding to this stimulus we are led properly to an awareness of our own prejudices and can correct our own preunderstandings through a circular process which is not vicious but productive. The proper goal of the hermeneutic encounter for Gadamer is a blending or fusion of horizons, a *horizontverschmelzung*. This occurs when the interpreter widens his own horizon of experience to include that of the text, reaches an intuitive understanding of the questions the text poses and answers through the common medium of language; he thus enlarges his own personal horizon, perceives it afresh, and gains insight into both worlds now blended into one. This experience is possible because both interpreter and text belong to a single continuous tradition.

> Historical consciousness is aware of its own otherness and hence distinguishes the horizon of tradition from its own. On the other hand, it is itself... only something laid over a continuing tradition, and hence it immediately recombines what it has distinguished in order, in the unity of the historical horizon that it thus acquires, to become again one with itself.[12]

This act of combining followed by a reassuring return to selfhood is so smooth because the tradition for Gadamer is in fact so "continuing"; it seems to be free of all revolts, gaps, leaps, and disjunctures. The concept of tradition becomes an instrument to tame, sweeten, and abstract history, which now appears purely unbroken and unalienating. It is true that Gadamer speaks of a tension between the two horizons. But functionally this tension counts for less than the blending mediation. Distance in time, Gadamer writes, is "not a yawning abyss, but is filled with the continuity of custom and tradition, in the light of which all that is handed down presents itself to us." Elsewhere he speaks of tradition as "an unbroken stream."[13] But tradition as we know it may not be a healing, sacred river but a polluting Love Canal which carries dangerous flotsam. Tradition as a stream has many tributaries, falls, and blockages. It runs less smoothly than this account suggests, and the history of interpretation as we know it reveals the defenses interpreters have had to raise against the threat of tradition. What if the tension between horizons proves to be intolerable? Allegoresis developed partly as one defense against unwelcome meanings suspected in past texts; we in our day have abandoned allegoresis for a more economical defense, ironization. If a given text, say More's *Utopia*, asserts too emphatically its estrangement from us, we shield ourselves by reading it ironically. Frank Kermode has recently shown the affinities of interpretation not with a fresh openness but with an enclosing institutionalism, with a group of insiders reluctant to open their gateway and reveal their arcane knowledge.[14] Graves and Riding, we remember, wrote very consciously as outsiders against one form of institutional protectionism.

The actual status of the original text emerges from Gadamer's formulation a little blurred.

> The true historical object is not an object at all, but the unity of the one [the object] and the other [true historical thinking taking account of its own historicality], a relationship in which exist both the reality of history and the reality of historical understanding.[15]

If the true object is not an object, then it is difficult to see how it can form half of a higher unity. What seems to emerge from this

sentence as actually real is a historical understanding lacking a solid
thing to understand. For Gadamer the text has no existence independent of the tradition in which it is understood; in effect he
denies the text an original historical situatedness such as he claims
for the interpreter. This denial calls into question the equality of the
dialogue as well as the tension between horizons. Essentially the
text is robbed of its own particular horizon. The supposed dialogue
lacks symmetry because only the interpreter's governing assumptions are called into play, not those of the text. The context of each
work is not its original, living semiotic matrix but rather a series of
posthumous readings. Gadamer in his own way wants to protect us
from our solitude. The resulting concept of appropriation fails to
isolate its potential self-deception. His account of understanding
blurs a little the central problem of interpretation: language
changes, modes of experience change, texts become estranged, and
yet the contact with texts in their authentic otherness would provide
precious knowledge and self-knowledge, would save us from hermeneutic narcissism.

My own plea would be for a moment in the process of understanding which no hermeneutics has authorized. I would ask for a
moment which deliberately tries to frustrate appropriation, which
tries to restore the work to its own world of meanings perceived in
all their distant strangeness. Simply to draw the work to ourselves,
wilfully, voraciously, is to dim that clarification which contact with
otherness does truly bring. Let us for a moment refuse to appropriate; let us try, however unsuccessfully, to return the work to its
own mysterious alienation. Instead of clutching it too quickly, we
should recognize its isolation and vulnerability, recognize what de-
ceives our expectations, offends our proprieties, refuses dialogue,
will not abide our questions. We need to measure without blinking
the pathos of estrangement, the ruptures of history, the blockages of
tradition.[16] It is true that this act of distancing the work is itself
subject to the distortions of our historical moment. But if our
distortions are to be progressively corrected, they will not be affected by a bland tradition but by perceived interuptions of tradition. Let us try for a moment to overcome that force which Heidegger calls "averageness" (*Durchschnittlichkeit*) and which, he says,

smoothly suppresses every kind of spiritual priority. "Overnight," he writes, "everything that is primordial gets glossed over as something that has long been well known. . . . Every secret loses its force."[17] Let us try to recover that sense of the work's forceful secrecy. Let us for a moment refuse to understand.

The response to that moment can take one of two directions. One alternative would be to find a kind of freedom in this impasse, call the rupture radical and total, and play with the flotsam of the past as context-free, neutral counters to be juggled at will. This response would free the interpreter from any responsibility to a vestige of original meaning, which, according to Jacques Derrida, will undergo a loss inherent in the character of all utterances. One can then appropriate with a vengeance, liberated from all constraints; one might even hope with Derrida to take a kind of Nietzschean joy in an endless innocent game of free associations. The one thing excluded from such play would of course be the stimulus of contact as well as the risk; there could be no dangerous impact which would challenge and conceivably clarify. The work interpreted would be an ink-blot test in which the interpreter would reveal over and over only his own obsessions without understanding them, lacking any transcendental key to make sense of his private musings. Derrida's own discussions of texts by Plato, Descartes, Leibniz, Rousseau, Hegel, and others do not in fact play with them freely and "innocently," but tend rather to subject these texts to precise and often brilliant analysis which assumes personal time-bound authorship.[18] Everyone doubtless has a right to his own avocations, but some will be moved to ask, as Shakespeare asks his friend: "Why dost thou spend, upon thy selfe thy beauties legacy?" For some, the pleasure of the "profitless usurer" quickly loses its charm.

The alternative to this hermeneutic play with free associations would be much more austere. This course would try to avoid that self-indulgence as it avoided the opposite mirror indulgence that denies the work's estrangement. This hermeneutic would accept estrangement as a given and then search out patiently some bridge, some passage, some common term which might help to mitigate it. On this basis one would suspect all modernized versions and easy assimilations, one would settle for less than full understanding, but one would accept a responsibility for a partial interpretive correspondence to an intrinsic meaning or complex of meanings. One would think not of appropriating but of working out a reading appropriate to those intrinsic meanings. One would conceive of a text coming to us bearing its own intentionality—not the intentionality of its creator but simply its own patent design for a certain kind of use. A chair exists to be sat on; a text exists to be read and read *appropriately*, within certain limits of potential response. It carries with it coded directions or provocations to the mind, and certain types of mental responses befit a given text more closely than others. The task of the reader is to ascertain the experience or the activity most perfectly corresponding to the text's coded instigations. In the case of a remote text—and no formula can specify how remote is "remote"—the directions or instigations will always be blurred, but one accepts a need to begin deciphering them. In the case of a mathematical equation one can think of the directions to the mind as *commands* to perform certain operations; in the case of a poem one can think of the directions rather as *orientations*. To interpret, Ricoeur writes suggestively, is to set out toward the *orient* of the text. To think of interpreting as an appropriate response to coded but blurred directions is not to limit the potential wealth of suggestion of a literary work, but it is to rule out the expense of spirit in self-indulgent anachronism. The wealth of significance has to stem from the work's concrete historical situation as we can best divine it.[19] If it does this, then we may gain a small accretion of self-knowledge. In the case of Shakespeare's sonnets, this would include—what can be gathered from most Renaissance poems—the limiting regularity, the hypertrophy of logic in our assumptions about words and syntax; in the case of Sonnet 129, this might include an altered view of the pallid, therapeutic sexuality of our post-Freudian era, Eliot's "natural, life-giving, cheery automatism,"[20] which is not of course to be found in Freud. But these crude indications of acquired self-consciousness badly approximate the gradual, profound growth of understanding whereby we slowly and fumblingly come to situate ourselves in history.[21]

The first, simple, and difficult act of reading is to see the remote text as truly remote. To begin to measure its removal from us, to intuit its privacy and specificity, to make out the density of its aura, one has to restore it to its original silence. The text comes to us as a shard, out of its own quietude and distance; by disencumbering it of its secular impediments, by stripping it of its false modernity, we release it to withdraw from us back into its own universe of meanings, cruelly and beautifully back where we can gauge its strangeness. In that strangeness begins true knowledge, the true partial knowledge that history allows us. We can begin to read only after granting the text the seclusion and the particularity of its unique inflection.

NOTES

1. The essay by Graves and Riding first appeared under the title "William Shakespeare and E. E. Cummings" in *A Survey of Modernist Poetry* (London: Heinemann, 1927) and in revised form was later included in Graves's *The Common Asphodel* (London: Hamilton, 1949) under the title "A Study in Original Punctuation and Spelling." The reply to Graves and Riding appears on pp. 447–52 of *Shakespeare's Sonnets,* edited with analytic commentary by Stephen Booth (New Haven: Yale University Press, 1980). The passages quoted appear on p. 447.

2. Booth, *Sonnets*, p. 450. Booth explains and defends his editorial policy on p. ix of his preface as follows:

> My primary purpose in the present edition is to provide a text that will give a modern reader as much as I can resurrect of a Renaissance reader's experience of the 1609 Quarto; it is, after all, the sonnets we have and not some hypothetical originals that we value. I have adopted no editorial principle beyond that of trying to adapt a modern reader—with his assumptions about idiom, spelling, and punctuation—and the 1609 text to one another.... Both my text and my commentary are determined by what I think a Renaissance reader would have thought as he moved from line to line and sonnet to sonnet in the Quarto. I make no major substantial emendations and few minor ones. It might therefore seem reasonable to reprint the Quarto text alone and simply comment on that, but the effects of almost four centuries are such that a modern reader faced with the

Quarto text sees something that is effectively very different from what a seventeenth-century reader saw.

In modernizing spelling and punctuation I have taken each poem individually and tried to find a mid-point between following the punctuation and spelling of the Quarto text (which modern readers, accustomed to logically and semantically directive punctuation and spelling, are inclined to misinterpret) and modern directive spelling and punctuation (which often pays for its clarity by sacrificing a considerable amount of a poem's substance and energy). In each case I have tried to find the least distorting available compromise. Sometimes no compromise is satisfactory, and I describe the probable operation of a line or quatrain in a note.

3. Lines 1258–63. See also "The Shipman's Tale," 7.170 ff.

4. The considerable reality behind the nobility's reputation for extravagance is detailed in chapter 10 of Lawrence Stone's *Crisis of the Aristocracy, 1558–1641* (Oxford: Oxford University Press, Clarendon Press, 1965).

5. See, e.g., Sonnet 144, line 12.

6. Booth, *Sonnets,* p. 448.

7. Edward Sapir, *Language* (New York: Harcourt, Brace and World, 1949), pp. 150, 171.

8. Ulrich von Wilamowitz-Moellendorff, *Greek Historical Writing and Apollo,* trans. G. Murray (Oxford: Oxford University Press, Clarendon Press, 1908), p. 26.

9. T. W. Adorno, *Moments Musicaux* (1930), quoted by Susan Buck-Morss, *The Origins of Negative Dialectics* (New York: The Free Press, 1977), p. 52.

10. Norman N. Holland, *The Dynamics of Literary Response* (New York: Norton, 1975), p. 104.

11. French text in Paul Ricoeur, "Qu'est-ce-qu'un texte?" in *Hermeneutik und Dialektik,* ed. R. Bubner et al. (Tübingen: Mohr, 1970), 2:194–95.

12. Hans-Georg Gadamer, *Truth and Method* (New York: Seabury, 1975), p. 273. German text in Gadamer, *Wahrheit und Methode* (Tübingen: Mohr, 1960), p. 290:

Das historische Bewusstsein ist sich seiner eigenen Andersheit bewusst und hebt daher den Horizont der Überlieferung von dem eigenen Horizont ab. Andererseits aber ist es selbst nur... wie eine Überlagerung über einer fortwirkenden Tradition, und daher nimmt es das voneinander Abgehobene sogleich weider zusammen, um in der

Einheit des geschichtlichen Horizontes, den es sich so erwirbt, sich
mit sich selbst zu vermitteln.

13. Gadamer, *Truth and Method,* pp. 264–65, 262.

14. Frank Kermode, *The Genesis of Secrecy: On the Interpretation of Narrative* (Cambridge: Harvard University Press, 1979).

15. *Truth and Method,* p. 267. German text in *Wahrheit und Methode.*
p. 283: "Der wahre historische Gegenstand ist kein Gegenstand, sondern
die Einheit dieses Einen und Anderen, ein Verhältnis, in dem die
Wirklichkeit der Geschichte ebenso wie die Wirklichkeit des geschichtlichen Verstehens besteht."

16. Maurice Blanchot evokes the danger to the literary work judged to
be good; it is likely to be "made useful" and exploited. The work judged
to be bad on the other hand is preserved by its lack of esteem: ". . . set aside,
relegated to the inferno by libraries, burned, forgotten: but this exile, this
disappearance into the heat of the fire or the tepidness of oblivion, *prolongs
in a certain way the just distance of the work. . . .* The work does not endure;
it is" (my italics). French text in *L'espace littéraire* (Paris: Gallimard, 1955),
p. 270.

17. Martin Heidegger, *Being and Time,* trans. J. Macquarrie and E.
Robinson (New York: Harper and Row, 1962), p. 165.

18. "This structuralist thematic of broken immediacy is therefore the
saddened, *negative,* nostalgic, guilty Rousseauistic side of the thinking of
play, whose other side would be the Nietzschean *affirmation,* that is the
joyous affirmation of the play of the world and of the innocence of becoming, the affirmation of a world of signs without fault, without truth, and
without origin which is offered to an active interpretation" (Jacques Derrida, *Writing and Difference,* trans. A. Bass [Chicago: University of Chicago
Press, 1978], p. 272; French text in *L'écriture et la différence* [Paris: Seuil,
1967], p. 427). The very allusions to Rousseau and Nietzsche in the
sentence quoted imply a knowable, traceable continuity, an identifiable
determinacy inherent in the ideas of these two thinkers and resistant to the
misunderstandings of history. The "immediacy" of their work would
appear not to have been broken. It is unclear finally just how much
Derrida concedes to history.

19. It is true, as Stanley Fish has argued, that interpretation is guided
by context, but to deny the text (with Fish) *any* priority to interpretation
is to be excessively rigid. The literary text when read as literature is
precisely of that kind which invites a series of circular adjustments between itself and its interpretive context. This series never ends; it never
fully succeeds; but a fitting interpretive context possesses a flexible capacity for revision which Fish is unwilling to recognize. The fact is that

interpreters can meaningfully discuss a text, persuade one another, and revise their interpretations without surrendering an entire "set of interpretive assumptions." Revised interpretations within a single "context" are possible because a prior text does exist. See Stanley Fish, "Normal Circumstances, Literal Language, Direct Speech Acts, the Ordinary, the Everyday, the Obvious, What Goes without Saying, and Other Special Cases," *Critical Inquiry* 4 (1978), 625–44.

20. T. S. Eliot, *Selected Essays* (London: Faber and Faber, 1956), p. 429.

21. Wolfgang Iser writes suggestively of the reading process: "The production of the meaning of literary texts . . . does not merely entail the discovery of the unformulated . . .; it also entails the possibility that we may formulate ourselves and so discover what had previously seemed to elude our consciousness," (*The Implied Reader* [Baltimore: Johns Hopkins Press, 1974], p. 294). But I would not agree that "the convergence of text and reader brings the literary work into existence" (p. 275). To split the text and the work is to court a potentially narcissistic subjectivism.

ALASTAIR FOWLER

The Silva Tradition in Jonson's *The Forrest*

When Ben Jonson put together the fifteen poems of *The Forrest,*
he did something more original and yet at the same time more
bound up with tradition than readily appears. We take for granted
the idea of a collection of short poems in loose thematic sequence,
but it is not at all an obvious idea: coherence is far from easy in a
volume of short poems. In the sixteenth century, volumes of verse
were mostly anthologies or manuscript miscellanies of single or
group authorship. Sonnet "sequences" might have a quasi-narrative
order, and there were Continental collections with a more
monolithic unity, such as *Les blasons anatomiques du corps féminin* and
Johannes Secundus' *Basia.* But a collection of different sorts of
poems, composed into a sequence, if not a structure—what kind of
writing would that be?

Jonson's title helps answer this. It is not only a voguish but also
an ancient title. In one of the earliest extant discussions of titling,
Aulus Gellius speaks of writers who, since they "had laboriously
gathered varied, manifold, and as it were indiscriminate learning,
invented ingenious titles accordingly, to correspond with that idea.
Thus some called their books *The Muses*, others *Woods* [*Silvarum*]."[1]
Here *silva* (like the Greek *hylē*) means raw material, stuff in a rough
form. That is also the sense of *Timber,* the title Jonson gave to his
own laboriously gathered critical *loci.*[2] But in *The Forrest* he seems
to mean something a little different—"rough drafts," perhaps, or "a
crowded mass, abundance or quantity."[3]

This is the sense in which Statius' collection of silvery *pièces
d'occasion* is called *Silvae.* Its five books gather poems of various

genres, commissioned by patron-friends. Description, consolation, encomium, birthday ode, and epigram: all these and more are among the "crowded mass" of kinds. Their roughness, however, is more problematic. The prefaces make much of the extempore, spontaneous occasionality. The Stella epithalamium was composed in two days; the description of Manilius Vopiscus' villa took one; the praise of Claudius Etruscus' baths was dashed off during dinner; and the Glaucias epicede was "written in distress" (*a confuso scriptum*). David Vessey takes this *sprezzatura* pretty well at face value.[4] But Statius protests altogether too much; in actuality the *Silvae* are distinguished by an art that is contrived to the last manneristic degree.[5]

They certainly need to be read in the light of Quintilian's remarks on the vogue for publishing a rough draft, or *silva*. Costive perfectionism is bad, he says, but there is a precisely opposite fault, of those

> who insist on first making a rapid draft of their subject as fast as their pen is able, and write in the heat and impulse of the moment. They call this their rough copy [*hanc silvam vocant*]. They then revise what they have written, and arrange their hasty outpourings. But while the words and rhythm may be corrected, the matter is still marked by the superficiality with which it was crowded together. The more correct method, then, is to exercise care from the very beginning, and so to form the work that it only needs to be chiselled, not remade from scratch. Sometimes, however, we must follow the stream of our emotions, since their warmth will achieve more than any diligence.[6]

Quintilian advocates a mean: a right method of artful spontaneity, of warm art.

During the Middle Ages little seems to have been written about the form, in spite of Statius' great influence; for his *Silvae* was lost and only rediscovered in the fifteenth century by Poggio Bracciolini. It was the Renaissance genre theorist Julius Caesar Scaliger who took the new step of treating the silva as a conventional genre. Scaliger describes it as a collection form, characterized by variety. Dismissing other explanations of the term (such as that wood can be used for almost countless purposes),[7] he promotes Quintilian's. Silvae are poems expressed spontaneously and with warmth (*subito excussa calore*). They derive their name from the multifarious matter, the crowd of things treated, or else from their roughness—for poets "used to pour out effusions in an unpolished form and correct them afterwards." In theory, any subject will do; as Scaliger says, you can meditate on anything and express this as a silva. But in practice, it seems, certain topics "are suitable as materials for *silvae.*" He instances praises, whether of a place or a person or an action or a fortuitous event. Accordingly, the succeeding chapters give disposition rules for occasional kinds: epithalamium, genethliacon, propempticon; for panegyric; for *consolatio,* which conceals praise; for hymn, lyric, elegy, epigram, invocation (*evocatorii, siue invocatorii*), and others. He covers, in fact, all the kinds in Jonson's *The Forrest.* Nevertheless, although the *Poetices* is of the utmost value in interpreting Renaissance silvae, I do not mean to suggest that Jonson wrote to fill Scaliger's prescriptions.

Apart from anything else, he had a model of great brilliance in Ronsard's *Bocage.*[8] Ronsard's two books—each with about the same number of poems as Jonson's one—had given the form a new turn, making it more elevated and less limited by occasion. His praises aimed high: *Bocage* 1 opens with panegyrics addressed to Henri III, and 1.5 is a satiric dialogue with the muses, of interest in connection with *The Forrest* 10. Jonson's knowledge of Ronsard has been doubted: Drummond records him as having said "that the best pieces of Ronsard were his Odes," but adds the dismissive judgment, "All this was to no purpose, for he neither doth understand French nor Italian." This, however, like Jonson's own remark about Shakespeare's small Latin, needs to be put in context. Drummond was an excellent modern linguist whose formidable annual program of reading in French, Italian, and Spanish (carefully recorded)[9] would make any ordinary comparatist blanch. What he probably means is that he tried to chat in French and Jonson could not keep up.

The mannerist vogue for metaphorical genre labels planted quite a thicket of silvae: besides Jonson's and Ronsard's, there were Phineas Fletcher's *Sylva poetica* (1633), George Herbert's *Lucus,* Robert Herrick's *Hesperides* (1648), and John Dryden's *Sylvae: or,*

The Second Part of poetical miscellanies (1685).[10] Jonson's titles *The Forrest* and *Underwoods* would be enough in themselves to indicate the genre. But in case they were not, he added a preface "To the Reader" before *Underwoods,* which bears by implication on the earlier volume:

> With the same leave, the Ancients called that kind of body *Sylva,* or [Hylē] in which there were workes of divers nature, and matter congested; as the multitude call Timber-trees, promiscuously growing, a *Wood,* or *Forrest:* so am I bold to entitle these lesser Poems, of later growth, by this of *Under-wood,* out of the Analogie they hold to the *Forrest,* in my former booke, and no otherwise.[11]

The expectation of spontaneous *pièces d'occasion* is further heightened by such individual titles as 4, "To the World: A Farewell for a Gentlewoman, Virtuous and Noble." In the event, as we shall see, the expectation is only in part fulfilled, but there is all the diversity of silva, so far as genre is concerned. Besides praises of place (2, 3) and person (12, 13), we find genethliac ode (14), palinode (1, 10), epode (11), epistle (12, 13), valediction (4), invocation (10), song (5, 6, 7, 9), and hymn (15). Several could be construed as epigrams, including 1, 10 and even 7 ("Song: That Women Are But Mens Shaddowes"). Then, the matter is so compact ("prest") that it certainly gives the correct impression of being "congested" or crowded. George Parfitt has argued with some truth that Jonson's achievement depends upon "exclusion of important aspects of human experience" and "the reduction of moral complexity to simplified clarity." But the reader's actual impression from *The Forrest* is of things put in rather than left out. "To Penshurst" and "To Sir Robert Wroth," in particular, are so full of a great number of things that there seems only just room for them and not quite enough for their description. Things are crowded very much indeed like trees in a wood:

> The early cherry, with the later plum,
> Fig, grape and quince, each in his time doth come;
> The blushing apricot and wooly peach
> Hang on thy walls that every child may reach.

Jonson achieves the extemporary effect of silvae through a plain style, as Wesley Trimpi's able study has shown. It is a style devised for *sermo* ("speech") or epistle, without elaborate or noticeable figures and without rounded periods—without, in fact, many left-branching word groups. *The Forrest* has even some direct speech, as in the opening poem: "Away (quoth hee)/Can Poets hope to fetter mee?" The style too is direct—and seems simple. But it is a resonant style, which as Lester Beaurline says "implies more than it includes." It has it ambiguities, although the *doubles ententes* more often than not are mutually reinforcing. They say the same thing twice over—"how blest are thou, canst love the country, Wroth, / Whether by choice, or fate, or both." Wroth's blessedness is a matter of fate (or choice and fate), as well as his ability to love the country. The complexity of election is rendered by the intricately unsearchable syntax. One can see what Parfitt means by Jonson's simplifying omissions, achieved by "a use of language in which association and paradox are reduced to a minimum, in favour of precision and local meaning."[12] But passages come to mind whose clarity goes with poetic logic and with meanings large enough to elude critical sensors adjusted for small conceit-sized objects.

Forrest 3, "To Sir Robert Wroth," may serve as a fair example; not so powerful as "To Penshurst" but underrated nevertheless.[13] Ostensibly encomium of Durrants, Wroth's estate, it emerges as encomium of the country life—an ancient genre, and one later to be developed on Jonsonian lines by Herrick, Randolph, and Fane. This good life is contrasted with London life, Wroth's modest contentment with ambitious striving for preferment and wealth. Jonson begins with a jaundiced glance at city occupations Wroth chooses not to waste his time with (although Durrants is so conveniently near to London that he could if he wanted to). The satire is almost ostentatiously monocular: even masques, which at other times Jonson did not disdain too much to write, are treated dismissively as "the short braverie of the night." The scenes that follow make up one of the warmest portrayals of rural life in our literature. It has a marvellous completeness: its high degree of order requires selection and generalization, yet it succeeds in being authentically specific. The contrast of town and country is often called pastoral, but there is little pastoral about a description in which hunting and seasons and work have such large parts. "Thou," says Jonson to Wroth,

> canst, at home, in thy securer rest,
>   Live, with un-bought provision blest;
> Free from proud porches, or their guilded roofes,
>   'Mongst loughing heards, and solide hoofes:
> Along'st the curled woods, and painted meades,
>   Through which a serpent river leades
> To some coole, courteous shade, which he calls his,
>   And makes sleepe softer than it is!
> Or, if thou list the night in watch to breake,
>   A-bed canst heare the loud stag speake,
> In spring, oft roused for thy masters sport. . . .

The crisp Hesiodic details have an immediate appeal. That stag audibly "speake[s]," those "solide hoofes" palpably thud. But it is less obvious how Jonson achieves such confident rightness. For example he may have been led to "solide hoofes" from the biblical injunction against animals with divided hoofs (many such allusions have been noted in "To Penshurst" by Paul Cubeta and Gayle Wilson), or from a wish to set solid contentment against superficial ambition (the proud porches' roofs are only "guilded" but the hoofs are solid through and through). There may even be a visual confrontation: hoofs are not wholly unlike apse roofs. The mutually confirming senses give a resonant impression, convincing in its rightness.

There are subtler effects in the passage beginning "Along'st the curled woods, and painted meades." Presentation of nature as artificial is common enough in Jacobean poetry; but in Jonson's silva it has special force. Since at Durrants nature is so ordered, there can be no material exactly raw. The landscape is just that—composed and "painted" landscape—in which Jonson achieves depth of field, just as a landscape artist does, by interposing a winding stream.[14] In context, the "serpent river" seems to have something of the ambivalent effect of "mazy error" and similar phrases in Milton's unfallen paradise.[15] This impression is marked in the verse "And makes sleepe softer then it is!" Can it be innocent to make things seem what they are not?—but then we see how the line must be construed: the river in a sense really makes sleep softer than the river itself (or its lulling sound). It is one of the most beautiful effects in Jonson even if its syntax does not quite obey Parfitt's rules. Ambivalence culminates in the river's pretension to own the shade. Like the "high swolne Medway" in "To Penshurst," this serves as an unobtrusive reminder of evil: the paradise of Durrants is complete even to the point of offering a temptation. The temptation is to regard the retired shade complacently as a possession. Wroth may be like a king beneath the state or canopy of the grove, but he has a duty to his master. So the "courteous shade" turns out to be a lead-in to the king's spring progress (lines 23–24), when James makes Durrants "his court."

The "loud stag" in spring begins a catalogue of the year's varied pleasures: hunting deer, partridge, and hare; hawking; shooting. Another seasonal cycle follows this, of occupations. Here again there are pleasures but also (and it is a Jonsonian emphasis) several particularized labors. In summer "The mowed meadowes, with the fleeced sheepe, / And feasts that either shearers keepe,"—the quiet metaphor that Wallace Stevens brings into the limelight in his "shearsman of sorts." And in winter, after "The hogs return'd home fat from mast," Wroth sees "The trees cut out in log; and those boughes made / A fire now, that lent a shade!" Then, as Orgel finely remarks, "the masque is summoned up again" as "Comus puts in, for new delights." Wroth does not need London masques, since he has the gods themselves at Durrants. He lives close to nature, but has art too: "Nor are the Muses strangers found."

We notice three things characteristic of many of the poems in *The Forrest:* the crowded variety of the things mentioned; their ordered arrangement, as in the calendrical passages; and their repeated moral contrasts (town and country, contentment and ambition).

If *The Forrest* has the crowded variety of silvae, it does not often give a very strong sense of extemporal spontaneity. Several of the poems, especially the praises and the concluding hymn, give an altogether bigger and less fortuitous impression. Moreover, a few readers have sensed articulation of the poems into a single structure. "It may be," Hugh Maclean suggests, "that the arrangement of these fifteen poems is deliberate; certainly it is of interest that the first poem bids a sad farewell to Cupid while the last affirms the poet's love of God."[16] We may suppose that Jonson gave full attention to Scaliger's emphasis on the silva's crowded variety, but even more to his disposition rules for component genres. He seems to have shared Quintilian's suspicion of the silva's informality and casual arrangement. Perhaps he saw in it an "attempt to escape . . . responsibility" (as Trimpi has suggested) "for the conceptual and formal control of statement by pleading the ephemeral nature of the genres."[17] A poet who drafted his poems in prose is not likely to have embraced the idea of random spontaneity.

Nevertheless, the formal coherence of *The Forrest* is not easy to grasp. What structure could it have? Classical theory of the silva gives no hint. In any case, most readers have felt the collection's miscellaneousness more than its order. To see the force of this point of view, just consider its contradictory stances: the sequence begins with a farewell to love poetry—but goes on to include three love poems, and how are the songs to be reconciled with the stoicism of "To the World"?—or either of these with the intense religious feeling of "To Heaven"? To glimpse the Scaligerian diversity of it all, we have only to review the subjects and themes. Or so it seems, until we look at their sequence more closely:

1. "Why I Write Not Of Love"
2. "To Penshurst"
3. "To Sir Robert Wroth"
4. "To the World: A Farewell for a Gentle-woman, Vertuous and Noble"
5. "Song: To Celia"
6. "To the Same"
7. "Song: That Women Are But Mens Shaddowes"
8. "To Sicknesse"

9. "Song: To Celia"
10. "[Praeludium]"
11. "Epode"
12. "Epistle: To Elizabeth, Countesse of Rutland"
13. "Epistle: To Katherine, Lady Aubigny"
14. "Ode: To Sir William Sydney, on His Birthday"
15. "To Heaven"

On reflection one can see that many of the poems are in fact connected by themes of retirement and religious aspiration. A corresponding inward movement runs through much of the sequence.

From this point of view, *Forrest* 1 appears as a serious palinode. "I thought to bind him in my verse" has been taken to mean that Jonson tried to write love poetry. But it means, I think, something rather more specific: that he thought to restrain Cupid, which is to say, to make him virtuous. At all events, Cupid eluded him; and it is not until the second part of the sequence, after a new introduction, that he treats chaste love. Jonson has contrived a liminal poem that is sincerely confessional. The second and third silvae form an obvious pair as epigram-epistles and estate poems. They also form a sequence. Thus, the point of "To Penshurst" depends on the king's unexpected visit when the family was from home, but in *Forrest* 3 Durrants' lord "dwells" in every sense—"when man's state is well, / 'Tis better, if he there can dwell" (93–94). Within the estate he can further retire to the cool shade, where the temptation is only to sleep. Like its companion poem, 3 leads up to prayer: Wroth's morning's and "evening's vow" is to be for health and a life of service—and that when life is over he may think it "a thing but lent." The clash of action and withdrawal, and of good and evil, is sharper, more obvious.[18] In *Forrest* 4 farewell to life comes closer still; retirement is now the explicit subject. It is an intimate poem: the farewell to the "false world" is for an unnamed gentlewoman; but the persona is almost bypassed by such details as "My part is ended on thy stage" (line 4). Unlike the estate poems, which were full of sharp visual images, 4 turns to a more abstract style. Its *contemptus mundi* moves inside what were merely outward symbols of retirement in "To Sir Robert Wroth"; and the "bird, or beast" tamed or hunted before is now identified with "tasting air and freedom" (lines 29–31). The retirement stops unexpectedly short of rejection of the world. Instead the speaker makes a choice of private life, well within the world in one sense—"Here in my bosame, and at home." It is a stance of sombre bold independent stoicism; but the moment marks a turn to a more inward orientation.

The songs, together with the satiric epigram on loose women (*Forrest* 8), seem at first to interrupt the sequence. On reflection we might see them as bringing the world's evil into further promi- nence. In several, the standpoint is captured by a cynicism that belongs to the world that was rejected in *Forrest* 4, thus inviting discrimination on the reader's part. But the inward sequence does not resume until the untitled *Forrest* 10. This reinvocation is a liminal poem marking a new beginning. True, it proudly refuses to invoke seven of the pagan gods and the nine muses.[19] But it does in fact beg something of Cupid: "His absence in my verse, is all I aske." Is this petition an anti-invocation of Eros or an invocation of Anteros? It has the same riddling quality as the treatment of love in *Forrest* 1. In any event, *Forrest* 10 rises above libertine passion and the pantheon of antiquity, claiming to bring the poet's "owne true fire." The poetry to follow will be on a higher plane: "my thought takes wing, / And now an Epode to deepe eares I sing" (line 29).

Forrest 11 is a serious praise of chaste love, as its generic descrip- tion partly announces. It celebrates true love with burning sincerity as "an essence . . . divine" and a "golden chain let down from heaven" (lines 45–47), preserving community in "godlike unity" (line 53). There follow a pair of epistles to ladies, of which 12 rises in a still more visionary flight. It asserts ideas of poetic immortality—"It is the Muse alone [*scilicet,* not riches] can raise to heaven"—and of stellification. This has been represented as a "rather uncongenial doctrine" dragged in to fill the need for a unifying principle,[20] but it is an almost inevitable part of the sequence of thought we are tracing. *Forrest* 14 rises again, at least generically: it is a genethliac ode. (The form is realized stanzaically, with "stand still" punningly at the center.) It encourages Sydney to strive and aspire: "The Birth-day shines, when logs not burne, but men" (line 60). Finally, *Forrest* 15, "To Heaven," addresses God in prayer and so has the "highest" subject of all. Yet its diction is as plain and intimately spoken as any in the sequence. William Kerrigan's fine discussion has dismissed the notion of Jonson as a "public" writer by tracing the poem's inwardness and its turns of strong religious feeling.[21] This is a significant change from my point of view; for it was probably the mistaken idea that Jonson had "little involvement with a personal god"[22] that obscured the strategic position of *Forrest* 15. The poem is a fitting climax to the honest striving of the whole sequence. But it also reveals the goal that that striving has tended toward. *The Forrest* is a ladder of love, ascending to God.

The inner structure of ascent is matched by an external structure; for fifteen (the number of poems) conventionally signified ascent to heaven. For more than 500 years, from St. Bernard of Clairvaux and Durandus to Dryden and Shadwell, this was one of the most familiar of number symbolisms. Based on the fifteen steps to the temple and the fifteen gradual psalms, it was later connected with Jacob's ladder and with the scale of music—the double octave containing fifteen notes. It might take the form of a homiletic *scala humilitatis* or of the practical scale of meditation discussed by Louis Martz in *The Poetry of Meditation,* numbering decades of aves in the Dominican rosary.[23] About the time when *The Forrest* was written, Cardinal Bellarmino's *De ascensione mentis per scalam rerum creaturarum* (1615) explicitly announced its own division according to the same symbolism.[24] But fifteen was also an aspiring number because it belonged to the series of pyramidal numbers (1, 4, 10, 15, . . .), and it is to this form that Jonson likens his "strange poems": "Like a rich and golden pyramid / Borne up by statues, shall I rear your head."[25]

Thinking of the *scala mentis* as a theme for silvae, one recalls the ancient symbolism of the *selva oscura,* the entangling forest of error.[26] This is the unfavorable meaning that informs the forest in "*Praeludium*", the version of *Forrest* 10 written for *Love's Martyr* (1601): "Such, as in lustes wilde forrest love to rainge" (line 9). It is striking how Jonson overgoes Statius in the device of taking up various senses of silva and making them generate topic after topic for the sequence.[27] In "To Penshurst," trees provide "writhed barke" for the confessions of love of "many a Sylvane," Gamage Copse serves deer, Ashore's and Sidney's copses are fertile with wood and game, and the orchard yields fruit "that every child may reach." In "To Sir Robert Wroth," as we have seen, there are "curled woods" for shade and perhaps a paradise, "cop'ces green," an "apple-harvest," and wood for fuel. Behind these estate trees are family trees, and physical trees symbolic of them: Lady Leicester's oak and "That taller tree, which of a nut was set" to mark Sir Philip Sidney's birth. Elsewhere, we come on the Clifton-Aubigny "noble stem"—"Grow, grow, faire tree, and as thy branches shoote" (8.99); and repeatedly the idea of silva as congested multiplicity appears in crowded, overlapping enumerations. The things and people of *The Forrest* are far from giving an overpolished *raffiné* impression, yet they certainly seem highly organized. Recalling the potential meaning of silva as formless chaos, hylē waiting to be formed, one is inclined to think that this forest by contrast is rather "cut out in log" and "curled." We may even, perhaps, see the whole progression of the sequence as an aspiration above the entanglements of matter to form and spirit.

A use of the word "silva" in Cicero's *De Oratore*—where he speaks of "material furnished by virtues and vices" (*virtutum et vitiorum . . . silva*)[28]—may serve to turn our attention to another ordering principle of *The Forrest*. I mean by this the embattling of contrasted images of virtues and vices, praised and dispraised, higher and lower: it is a common and much-discussed feature of Jonson's work. Here, Penshurst is set against the prodigy houses, L'Isle's liberal hospitality against a certain peer's arrogance, Wroth's happy country life against the ambitious pursuit of honor, and so forth. Such paired images are diametrically opposed to one another; and by implication each baser term impedes the ascent through the world's entangling forest. At the same time, Jonson appreciates the internalized nature of the conflict: the contrast is not allowed to be an external one merely, between good and bad people. Instead he tries to take in the mind's whole forest, the variety of morals, the divided man. So his encomia of L'Isle and Wroth are balanced by long passages taken up with inferior forms of life—which, he hints, subsist at least to some degree within the walls of the praised estates. And the epistle to Lady Aubigny balances praise of her virtue with satire on a whole nation of false-seemers, extravagant livers, loose women, and users of cosmetics. The praise of virtue is not to get above itself or drift into unrooted idealism.

An apparent exception is the epode. It develops an ideal of chaste love that is not obviously balanced by any less ideal view— unless we count the quickly overborne opinion of "some vicious fool" who "swears there's no such thing" (lines 66–67). But although there is no internal contrast, the epode as a whole can be seen as balancing the less than ideal presentation of love in the songs (*Forrest* 5–7), in the satiric *Forrest* 8, and even in the exquisite "Song to Celia," *Forrest* 9. This correspondence may possibly be underlined by the external form; for the line-total of *Forrest* 5–9 is exactly equal to the line-total of the epode: namely, 116.

We are now in a position to understand the place of *The Forrest*'s songs. They treat forms of love lower in the scale than the epode's virtuous love, and among themselves they compose a subsequence of increasing aspiration.[29] It may seem improbably calculating on Jonson's part to write love songs expressing emotions he rejected. But, after all, *Forrest* 5 and 6 were used in *Volpone* in a courtship less than ideal. Enough has been written about the songs as imitations to show how unspontaneous Jonson could be in that regard.[30] *Forrest* 5, "Come, my Celia, let us prove," is partly *imitatio* of Catullus' persuasion to love. But its carpe diem sentiment (the seducer's standby) is firmly placed, as Joseph Summers has remarked, by the addition of the unpagan words "sin" and "crimes." *Forrest* 6 is the expression of a libertine, a "warie lover." *Forrest* 7, "That Women Are But Mens Shaddowes," although labeled song is a paradox or epigram defending an outrageous position playfully; but even it contrives to bring in the serious thought of inconstant love's shadowy insubstantiality.[31] *Forrest* 8, an unpleasant satiric epigram, gives rein to a mood of cynical disgust at women's eagerness to sin, and then *Forrest* 9 answers with an equally serious devotion whose elevated sentiment partly restores wholeness.

Forrest 9 is Jonson's most popular poem, read by many as a perfect lyric of pure love. Others who know more have discovered (again and again)[32] its complicated construction as a *cento* of phrases and images from Philostratos' *Love Letters* (some of them homosexual). Jonson's thefts are rigorously exhaustive (none at all of the material is Jonson's own, is "raw"). The stolen goods are raw in another sense, however: as Richard Cumberland put it, they were "calculated to disgust a man of Jonson's classic taste." Nevertheless the common view of the poem is not wholly wrong: Jonson has created a beauty quite unlike Philostratos' sensuality. The singer's adoration is fine and meant to be touching, but his diffident and selfless purity are modern inventions. For the love-glance and the kiss in the cup are reciprocal pledges (and as secret pledges were sins and crimes for Jonson). The sacramental language ("soul's thirst," "drink divine") is not insulated from Christian association: the singer's reason for not asking wine is precisely that the kiss will change water to wine as in Philostratos' Letter 33. The culminating return of the roses is a pledge too; although they are not (as in Philostratos) slept with first. Forgetting that "swear" was no light term in the seventeenth century, we tend to miss the outrageousness of the belief in a false miracle. All this is not to deny that the song aspires to very elevated sentiments—or even that it expresses an unfulfilled thirst for divinity.[33] But the heaven represented by "Caelia" is heaven only to her lover, whose love is less than that of the epode. It is in the latter love, in the "rage divine" of *Forrest* 12 and in the direct love of God in *Forrest* 15, that the thirst is to be quenched. Such an imitation as Forrest 9, then, is not just a "demanding literary game" (Braden): it seriously attempts to improve the devil's tunes to the point at which the reader is tempted by belief in their attractions.

It follows that Jonson brought the silva form much nearer to that of the modern thematic collection. *The Forrest* has come a very considerable distance from the rough spontaneous gathering pretended by Statius and disliked by Quintilian. It is highly polished and, at least in part, articulated into a structured sequence whose arrangement or "disposure" must have been planned from a fairly early stage. Nevertheless, Jonson's classicism has many mannerist features. It is characteristic that he should derive inspiration from the formal idea of the silva and find so many ways of symbolizing it self-referentially. His relation to classical tradition is also complicated by the otherwordly values that imbue *The Forrest*. The trees of his silva are burnt on a fire of zeal; its hylē is in process of transmutation to "a fire now," "true fire," flames of love such that "logs not burn, but men." (The omnipresence of these Christian values helps to explain how *The Forrest* came to be followed by the sacred groves of Herbert and Herrick).[34] But it is necessary to add that Jonson is far from suppressing spontaneous emotion where it would be appropriate. There is much confession of his inner life in *The Forrest,* for those who can hear it. It reveals the passionate upward striving of a poet who did not overvalue his own raw material but rather struggled to rise above the very feelings that many of his readers now seem to be most interested in attributing to him.

NOTES

1. *Noctes Atticae*, preface 6, in *The Attic Nights of Aulus Gellius*, tr. John C. Rolfe, (London and New York 1927), 1:xxix (translation mine). There is a Princeton Ph.D. thesis on the silva tradition by Ann Lawinger, Prin. 685.1977. 5668, which however I have not consulted.

2. Cf. Poliziano's verse lectures of 1480–90, which he called *Silvae;* Bacon's *Sylva Sylvarum* (London, 1627); and Dudley North, Baron North *A forest of varieties* (London, 1645, but written 1610–12). On the various senses of *silva* in Renaissance rhetoric, see Walter J. Ong, *Ramus: Method and the Decay of Dialogue* (Cambridge: Harvard University Press, 1958), pp. 118–19.

3. Cicero, *De Oratore* 3.26.103 "silva rerum, sententiarumque." See also Cicero, *Statius,* tr. J. H. Mozley (London: Heinemann and New York: Harvard, 1928), 1:xi.

4. David Vessey, *Statius and the Thebaid* (Cambridge: Cambridge University Press, 1973), p. 37.

5. As Vessey elsewhere appreciates: *Statius and the Thebaid*, pp. 15 n., 16. Contrast Mozley's predictable reaction to the mannerism of the *Silvae:* "to our taste, at any rate, they appear artificial and exaggerated in tone, and lacking in real sentiment, also for the most part much too long."

6. *Instit. Orat.,* 10.3.17–18.

7. J. C. Scaliger, *Poetices libri septem* (Lyons, 1561), p. 150.c.1; facs., ed. August Buck (Stuttgart-Bad Cannstatt: Frommann 1964). Jonson knew Scaliger's *Poetices* well, for he used it both in his formal criticism and in *The New Inn*. See *Ben Jonson's Literary Criticism,* ed. James D. Redwine, Jr. (Lincoln, Neb.: University of Nebraska Press, 1970), p. xxiii.

8. There were also partial models in ancient literature. Horace's *Odes* had thematic organization but not generic variety; the *Planudean Anthology* had both, but lacked moral weight.

9. See Robert H. Macdonald, *The Library of Drummond of Hawthornden* (Edinbrugh: Edinburgh University Press, 1971), pp. 228–32. Jonson admitted to Drummond that his knowledge of French had been inadequate when he wrote his tribute to Sylvester (*Epig.* 132, *Conversations with Drummond* 29–31; in Ben Jonson, *Works,* ed. C. H. Herford and Percy and Evelyn Simpson, 11 vols. [Oxford: Oxford University Press, Clarendon Press, 1925–52], 8:83 and 1:133), but claimed that it had since improved. He refers to Ronsard's *Amours* in *Underwoods* 27.22–24. For evidence of his knowledge of Italian, see Daniel Boughner, *The Devil's Disciple: Ben Jonson's Debt to Machiavelli* (New York, 1968), p. 139.

10. It burgeoned in the nineteenth century; Coleridge's *Sybilline Leaves,* Whitman's *Leaves of Grass,* and Stevenson's *Underwoods* are perhaps the most familiar instances. Herrick calls *Hesperides* "This Sacred Grove" in "To the Queene," l. 3.

11. Partly translating the Latin note before *Timber:* "Rerum, et sententiarum, quasi [Hylē] dicta a multiplici materia, et varietate, in iis contenta. Quemadmodum enim vulgo solemus infinitam arborum nascentium indiscriminatim multitudinem *Sylvam* dicere: Ita etiam libros suos in quibus variae, et diversae materiae opuscula temere congesta erant, Sylvas appellabant Antiqui: *Tymber-trees.*" This in turn came from Caspar Gavartius's commentary in his edition of Statius (1616). See Herford and Simpson, 11:213. Jonson's fondness extending the generic metaphor by plays on *leaf, shrub,* etc. shows also in the titles of *Underwoods* 20 ("A Satyricall Shrub") and 21 ("A little shrub growing by").

12. G. A. E. Parfitt, "Ethical Thought and Ben Jonson's Poetry," *SEL* 9 (1969), 123–34.

13. But see the appreciative comment by Stephen Orgel in *The Jonsonian Masque* (Cambridge: Harvard University Press, 1965), pp. 192–94.

14. On seventeenth-century poems as landscapes, see James Turner, *Politics of Landscape* (London: Blackwell, and Cambridge: Harvard University Press, 1979), ch. 1.

15. On these ironies, see Paul J. Alpers, "The Milton Controversy," in *Twentieth Century Literature in Retrospect,* ed. Reuben A. Brower, Harvard English Studies 2 (1971), p. 275.

16. *Ben Jonson and the Cavalier Poets,* ed. Hugh Maclean (New York: Norton, 1974), p. 20.

17. Wesley Trimpi, *Ben Jonson's Poems: A Study of the Plain Style* (Stanford: Stanford University Press, 1962), p. 114.

18. Cf. Judith Kegan Gardiner, *Craftsmanship in Context: The Development of Ben Jonson's Poetry*, S.E.L. 101 (The Hague and Paris: Mouton, 1975), p. 71.

19. For rejection of the muses as a convention of satire, see Trimpi, *Ben Jonson's Poems,* pp. 99–100.

20. Gardiner, *Craftsmanship in Context,* p. 65.

21. William Kerrigan, "Ben Jonson Full of Shame and Scorn," *Studies in the Literary Imagination* 6 (1973), 199–217.

22. Parfitt, "Ethical Thought," p. 129.

23. *The Poetry of Meditation,* rev. ed. (New Haven: Yale University Press, 1962), p. 101.

24. See H. Neville Davies, "The Structure of Shadwell's 'A Song for St. Cecilia's Day 1960,'" in *Silent Poetry,* ed. Alastair Fowler (London: Routledge, 1970), pp. 206–19, esp. p. 209. Davies gives a history of the tradition as far back as the sixth century.

25. *Forrest* 12.83–84. In Jonson's time, "pyramid" (derived from Pyr, "fire") usually meant a sharp, flamelike or spirelike obelisk form: see example in Leslie Hotson, *Mr. W. H.* (London: Hart-Davis, 1964), p. 86. Its symbolic value was often aspiration or ambition: see *The Poems of John Milton,* ed. John Carey and Alastair Fowler (London: Longmans, 1968), pp. 722–23, n. to *Paradise Lost* 5.758–59. Another relevant association is with stellification: see Arthur Henkel and Albrecht Schöne, eds., *Emblemata; Handbuch zur Sinnbildkunst des xvi und xvii Jahrhunderts* (Stuttgart: J. B. Metzlersche, 1967), col. 1223, on the SIC ITUR AD ASTRA emblem. The pyramid-obelisk might have any number of faces larger than two; for its identification with the tetrahedron, see *OED,* s.v. "pyramid," 2, definitions from 1570 (Billingsley). For immortalizing pyramids elsewhere in Jonson, see *Epig.* 133.194 ("The citie since hath rais'd a Pyramide") and *Underwoods* 77.25–28, in a poem with a pyramidal line-total:

> . . . though I cannot as an Architect
> In glorious Piles, or Pyramids erect
> Unto your honour: I can tune in song
> Aloud; and happ'ly) it may last as long.

26. In this connection, Ian Donaldson has drawn my attention to the fact that *The Forrest* and *Underwood* both begin, like the *Divina Commedia,* with a statement of the poet's age. On forest entanglement and individua-

tion, see C. G. Jung, *The Collected Works*, tr. R. F. C. Hull, vol. 13 *Alchemical Studies* (London: Routledge, 1968), pp. 194–97.

27. Statius' *Silvae* 2.3 is on "The Tree of Atedius Melior."

28. *De Oratore* 3.30.118.

29. Cf. Gardiner, *Craftsmanship in Context*, p. 62.

30. See Gordon Braden, *The Classics and English Renaissance Poetry*, Yale Studies in English 187 (New Haven and London, 1978), pp. 166–70.

31. And only an allusion to Matthew 22:30 can make a good pun of its otherwise awkward line "But grant us perfect, they're not known."

32. The bursting of the discoverers' bubbles of originality is recounted in Braden, *The Classics and English Renaissance Poetry*, p. 167.

33. The notorius ambiguity in "I would not change for thine" now falls into place: Jonson means the reader, if not the lover, to glimpse a higher aspiration than Celia. On the ambiguous lines, see J. G. Nichols, *The Poetry of Ben Jonson* (London: Routledge, 1969), pp. 163–64.

34. Herbert has several obvious connections between the individual epigrams of *Lucus*: the subsequence on Urban VIII and the name "Roma," and the continued development of stone imagery.

HELEN GARDNER

"A Nocturnal upon St. Lucy's Day, being the shortest day"

In commenting upon Donne's "Nocturnal" in my edition of *The Elegies and Songs and Sonnets* in 1965, I contented myself with saying that Grierson had suggested that the poem was inspired by a serious illness of Lucy, Countess of Bedford, in 1612 and that others have wished to connect it with Anne Donne: either with Donne's anxiety over her health while he was abroad with Sir Robert Drury from November 1611 to September 1612, or with her death in 1617. I now realize that I was wrong to handle the possible connection with Anne Donne so summarily and should have referred to the most cogent attempt to see the poem as inspired by Donne's desolation at the death of his beloved wife, that of Louis Martz in *The Poetry of Meditation*, recurred to in *The Poem of the Mind*.[1] I feel happy to have an opportunity to make amends in a volume published in his honor by providing some new arguments in support of his view. They are speculative, as are most discussions of the dating of Donne's lyrics, and, even if we could reach certainty, this would not increase the value of the poem as a profound expression of the sense of utter and irremediable loss.

Gosse referred only briefly to "A Nocturnal," oddly describing it as "a most curious ode" in which Donne "amid fireworks of conceit . . . calls his mistress dead, and protests that his hatred has grown calm at last."[2] Grierson thought that Gosse was right to suggest that "the death of the lady addressed is assumed, not actual," but he disputed Gosse's connection of the poem with "Donne's earlier and troubled loves." For, as he said justly, he could find "no note of bitterness, active or spent, in the song. It *might* have been written to Anne More. It is a highly metaphysical yet sombre and sincere description of the emptiness of life without love." Grierson was greatly impressed by the affinities he perceived between the "subtle, passionate, sonorous lyric," "Twickenham Garden" and "A Nocturnal," declaring that "the thought, feeling, and rhythm of the two poems are strikingly similar." Since Lady Bedford lived at Twickenham Park from 1608, he assumed that "Twickenham Garden" was "addressed" to her and, if so, " so also, one is tempted to think, must have been" "A Nocturnal," since Lucy was the Countess's name. It was his desire to see both poems connected with Lucy Bedford that made Grierson accept Gosse's suggestion that the death of "the lady addressed" was "assumed, not actual," and propose the Countess's serious illness in the winter of 1612 as the occasion that gave rise to the poem. Yet Grierson had doubts. "A Nocturnal" he saw as "a sincerer and profounder poem" than "Twickenham Garden" and owned "it is more difficult to imagine it the expression of a conventional sentiment." He made an attempt to meet this objection by referring to "the Petrarchian convention" as affording "a ready and recognized vehicle of expression" for the "mutual feeling" he presumed to exist between Donne and his wealthy patroness. Having expressed these views in his general introduction on "The Poetry of Donne," Grierson recurred to the subject at the beginning of his commentary on the *Songs and Sonnets,* again linking "Twickenham Garden" with "A Nocturnal" and both with Lucy Bedford. He quoted a letter reporting that she was critically ill on November 23, 1612 and, supposing the illness was typhoid, thought it probable that on December 13 she was still in a critical condition and "Donne may have written in anticipation of her death." "But," he added, "the suggestion is hazardous. The third verse speaks a stronger language than that of Petrarchian adoration." He then withdrew slightly: "Still it is difficult for us to estimate aright all that was allowed to a servant under the accepted convention." He added: "It is noteworthy that the poem is not included in any known MS. collection made before 1630. The Countess died in 1627."[3] It is difficult to know how seriously Grierson took the final implication: that the poem may have been written as late as 1627, the year of the Countess's actual death.

Grierson was justified in seeing some likenesses between "Twickenham Garden" and "A Nocturnal"; but he gave less than adequate weight to the differences. Although he speaks of both poems as "addressed to" a lady, both are, in fact, soliloquies, not monologues that assume the presence of another person who is being addressed. Both are seasonal poems and are given what is comparatively rare in Donne's lyrics, a natural setting.[4] We are not, as we so often are, in "one little roome" which is made "an every where." We are in a garden in spring, on the one hand, and in a completely barren landscape at midnight, at the very dead of winter, the nadir of the year, on the other.[5] In both poems the state of the speaker is contrasted with the setting. In "Twickenham Garden" the contrast is obvious and conventional: between the sweetness and fresh life of spring, the season of hope, and the melancholy and bitterness of the rejected lover. In "A Nocturnal" the contrast is original and highly metaphysical: between the deadness of the landscape, which is within the natural order of things, a temporary withdrawal of life that is even now at the moment of its turn toward renewal, and the absolute deadness of the lover, which is outside the natural order, is extra-temporal. For Love, the great Alchemist, has produced in him a quintessence, or elixir of nothingness, that unimaginable Nothing to which the natural world will return at the end of days, as it emerged from it in the beginning.[6] Lastly, in addition to having ideas in common,[7] the two poems are similar in their metrical form and versification. Each is in a stanza of nine lines, made up of decasyllabic and octosyllabic lines, employing four rhymes, except that the fifth, the medial line shrinks to six syllables in "A Nocturnal" and its rhyme looks forward, whereas the medial rhyme in "Twickenham Garden" looks back. Both poems have a slow, unvarying pace with comparatively little inversion of stress and powerful rhymes, giving much end-stopping. The whole effect is meditative, undramatic, and uncolloquial. Yet, in spite of these similarities, the dissimilarities between the two poems are even more striking. They differ profoundly in the nature of the relation between the lover and his mistress and, strikingly, in their textual history.

"Twickenham Garden" handles a stock theme of the sonneteers, the lament of a lover whose mistress denies him her love. Donne imports into this a characteristic intensity and bitterness that is alien to the tradition. Self-betrayed, his lover brings into the garden "The spider love, which transubstantiates all / And can covert Manna to gall," and the serpent, the tempter through whose guile Paradise was lost. Unlike all other daughters of Eve, his mistress will not yield to temptation; but her truth to her husband, or to another lover, springs from her cruelty rather than from her virtue. The religious ideas glanced at are devoid of any religious significance. The association of the spider, who "turns all into excrement and gall,"[8] with the Eucharistic transformation of the wafer into the Host is witty but profane: it degrades the holy, rather than sanctifying the secular. The lady is not allowed to gain any credit by resisting the temptation of the serpent. "A Nocturnal" is also a lament, but it mourns the separation by death of two lovers who had in life been wholly united to each other in a mutual love: a union such as Donne celebrated in "The Good-morrow," "The Anniversary," or "The Canonization." This perfect union has been broken by the woman's death, not by any failure of love on the part of either lover, so that there is no remorse or blame in the poem, but only grief. In other poems in which he wrote of a perfectly mutual love Donne employed religious language and religious symbolism: but he used them to exalt human love and give it almost the status of religion, not to give it a religious dimension. "A Nocturnal" is unique among the *Songs and Sonnets* in that it is "fundamentally religious," as Louis Martz asserted in 1954.[9]

Martz rightly pointed to the title of the poem and to its closing four lines as setting a tone of religious devotion, of rites to be performed. St. Lucy's Day, December 13, is the twenty-four hours from midnight to midnight. A Nocturn is one of the three divisions of the office of Mattins, the first of the canonical hours, which is said at midnight. By the old Julian Calender December 12 had by the sixteenth century become the day of the winter solstice;[10] but, since a name is more easily memorized than a date, St. Lucy's Day was popularly regarded as the shortest day following the longest night. By its title the poem is a midnight office for the "long nights festivall" that "shee enjoyes." At its conclusion the poem has become something else. For her it is a Festival in that other world which to him on earth is a darkness; for him it is the Vigil[11] or Eve of her Feast:

> Since shee enjoyes her long nights festivall,
> Let me prepare towards her, and let me call
> This houre her Vigill, and her Eve, since this
> Both the yeares, and the dayes deep midnight is.

The title and the closing lines point to religious exercises: the first office of the celebration of the Feast of a Saint and the work of penitence, prayer, and fasting of the Vigil that precedes the Feast and is the preparation for it. In the body of the poem no explicitly religious terms are used. Nothing is said about that other world into which "shee" has been withdrawn. We are only told that to speak of "her death" is to use a word that "wrongs her." In its austere acceptance of the finality of death and of the mystery that lies beyond death, the poem has a deep religious reverence and reticence. There is no "rage against the dying of the light," nor any pretense of comfort, except what might be thought the cold "Comfort to a youth that had lost his Love" which Herrick offered:

> What needs complaints
> When she a place
> Has with the race
>   Of Saints?
> In endless mirth
> She thinks not on
> What's said or done
>   On earth:
> She sees no teares,
> Or any tone
> Of thy deep grone
>   She heares:
> Nor do's she minde,

> Or think on't now,
> That ever thou
>   Wast kind.[12]

Although the word is not used, the poem is an analysis of mortification or "dying to the world." That this process has not been brought
about by deliberate, willed abnegation of the world but has been
forced upon the speaker by the loss of what gave the world all it had
of value is not important. Acceptance of a discipline imposed is as
serious as the voluntary choice of a discipline. It is in its sustained
seriousness of tone that the poem is so impressive. It is impressive
also in that it is not a palinode, or retractation, by a poet who has
discovered the insufficiency of human love. His mortification is the
fruit of Love's alchemy. It is Love that has made him a quintessence
of nothingness because he and she were "one, and anothers All."
The lovers who are called upon to study him are not to learn by their
study to leave a love which reaches but to dust, but generously
bidden to "Enjoy your summer all." They may, as Donne had in
"The Anniversary," put aside the thought of death and of ultimate
parting with the cry "Let us love nobly, and live."

Different as "Twickenham Garden" and "A Nocturnal" are in
the feelings about a woman that they embody, they are alike in the
impossibility of either of them reflecting Donne's relations with his
aristocratic, wealthy, and pious patroness. We have many letters
from him to her both in verse and prose, and there are references to
her in his letters to Goodyer, who had been instrumental in bringing Donne to her notice. The verse-letters hyperbolically exalt her
beauty and virtue; the references to her in letters to Goodyer show
anxiety to please and not offend her. It seems highly improbable
that she would have been pleased to have been represented in a poem
as either the recipient of unwelcome attentions, particularly as the
poem ends with a cynical slur on the lady's virtue, or as having been
involved in a passionate love affair with the poet. The title "Twickenham Garden" is not invariably found attached to the poem in the
manuscripts, but it is sufficiently widely distributed to be given
weight. If accepted it must date the poem after 1607, when the

Countess took up residence at Twickenham, and the gloomy and cynical tone that Donne has imported into the conventional theme of the unhappy lover in the "soote season, that bud and blome furth bringes," normally treated in a tone of gentle melancholy, may be more probably ascribed to his circumstances at a time when his fortunes were at a very low ebb than to unsuccess in a love affair. A melancholy letter to Goodyer, printed in *Poems* (1633) immediately following a letter to Lady Bedford referring to verse that "your Ladiship did me the honor to see in a Twicknam garden," echoes the mood of the poem: "Because I am in a place and season where I see every thing bud forth, I must do so too, and vent some of my meditations to you; the rather because all other buds being yet without taste or vertue, my letters may be like them. The pleasant-ness of the season displeases mee. Every thing refreshes, and I wither, and I grow older and not better. My strength diminishes, and my load growes."

Textually everything is against any connexion between "Twick-enham Garden" and "A Nocturnal." "Twickenham Garden" is one of the most widely circulated of the *Songs and Sonnets*. It is found in all the substantial collections of Donne's poems and in a great many manuscript miscellanies. "A Nocturnal" is extant in only seven closely related, very full collections and is not found in any extant manuscript miscellany. It is possible to arrive at some tentative conclusions about its date by remembering what we know of Donne's attitude toward the circulation and publication of his poems and by comparing it with other poems whose circulation was re-stricted.

As a young man Donne had no wish for a reputation as a poet outside a circle of friends. In a letter sending a friend his *Paradoxes,* he asked for an assurance "upon the religion of your friendship that no coppy shallbee taken of these or any other my compositions sent to you." He explained that this showed "not a distrustfull but a free spirit," for, he added, "I meane to acquaint you with all myne: and to my satyrs there belongs some feare & to some elegies & these perhaps shame."[13] But in 1611, perhaps emboldened by the success of *Pseudo-Martyr,* whose publication in 1610 he followed up by the

lively *Conclave Ignati* and its English translation early in 1611, he
seems to have been thinking of the publication of his poems. He
writes to Goodyer in Latin to tell him he has an opportunity to go
abroad for a considerable time, although it means leaving his wife
and children, and he wants to discuss the matter with him. He asks
Goodyer to put aside those papers of his Goodyer had accepted with
a pledge of speedy restitution. If his Latin epigrams and his satirical
Catalogus librorum are not among them, then they are not. (Presumably this means "it doesn't matter.") He goes on to say that they
(that is, his papers)

> are about to undergo the last Judgement—that is, my final revision.
> Some of them will suffer their Purgatory, so that they may come forth
> in a correcter form. Other things of mine, copies of which have crept
> out into the world without my knowledge will, however, confess—
> their originals having been destroyed by fire—that they have been
> condemned by me to Hell. The rest, which are either virgins (save
> that they have been handled by many) or else so unhappily sterile that
> no copies of them have been begotten, will sink away and dissolve
> into utter annihilation (a fate with which God does not threaten even
> the wickedest of sinners).[14]

It seems very unlikely that Donne, his mind full of the prospect
of his travels with the Drurys, would be occupying himself with
sorting and revising his works unless he was thinking of publishing
them. But if this were so, the plan was abandoned for something
much more impressive: to come before the world as the author of a
long, serious poem, *The Anatomy of the World*. The title at once
suggests a moral poem or satire. What reputation Donne had as a
poet rested on his *Satires*, which Jonson presented with the neat
phrase "Rare poemes aske rare friends" to Lucy Bedford, and the
only long poem he had so far attempted, *Metempsychosis*, dated by its
preface August 16, 1601, was subtitled *Poema Satyricon*. Wesley
Milgate has reminded us that Pope "commended Donne's epistles,
Metempsychosis, and satires as his best," and that Joseph Warton
remarked that Donne had "noble talents for moral and ethical
poesy." I have always suspected that the inspiration to write an
"Anatomy" preceded the notion of a further celebration of the vir-

tues of Elizabeth Drury beyond the "Funeral Elegy" he had composed for her, and that Louis Martz was right in holding that the two themes of her virtue and the general decay of the world are connected by ingenuity rather than by any logical propriety: that "the poem has a central inconsistency which defeats all Donne's efforts to brings its diverse materials under control."[15] No such central defect mars *The Second Anniversary,* published five months after, while Donne was in France. But if Donne had hoped to win new admirers and possible patrons by appearing before the public as a grave, moral and religious poet, he missed his mark and learned from Goodyer and George Garrard that instead he had won disapproval for what was regarded as extravagant praise of the dead girl, and in particular had offended his best patron, Lucy Bedford. In replying to Garrard, Donne wrote: "the fault that I acknowledge in myself, is to have descended to print anything in verse, which though it have excuse even in our times, by men who professe, and practise much gravitie; yet I confesse I wonder how I declined to it, and do not pardon my self."[16]

In the period of just over two years between his return from the Continent in September 1612 and his ordination in January 1615, Donne wrote a good many occasional poems. Most of them are the product of his desperate need to find patronage. Soon after his return he approached, through friends, the powerful favorite, Rochester, told him he had resolved to take orders, and asked his protection and assistance in the matter of preferment. Rochester seems to have dissuaded Donne from his purpose and urged him not to abandon hope of a secular career. He made overtures to the King on Donne's behalf, but without success, and contributed generously to Donne's support during this difficult time. At the beginning of 1613 Donne "descended to print" with his Elegy on Prince Henry, and also wrote a charming Valentine's Day Epithalamion for Princess Elizabeth's marriage to the Elector Palatine on February 13, 1613. Soon after he went to stay with Goodyer at Polesworth and, leaving him on Good Friday to visit Sir Edward Herbert at Montgomery Castle, was inspired to write one of his finest religious poems, "Good Friday 1613: Riding Westward" and the curious poem "The Primrose," whose title in the second edition of the poems was given the addition "being in Mountgomery Castle, uppon the hill, on which it is situate." In December Rochester, now made Earl of Somerset, was married with great splendor to Frances Howard. Donne's Epithalamion, with its apologetic prelude, was delayed by the illnesses of himself and his family during the winter and most of the spring of 1614. In February 1614 Lady Bedford's young brother, Lord Harington, friend of Prince Henry, died of smallpox. Donne's tribute to him was also belated. In addition to writing his Epithalamion for Somerset, he had responded to a suggestion from Garrard of another wealthy noblewoman who would be pleased to receive some verses. This was the Countess of Salisbury, for whom Donne wrote a poem he dated August 1614. It must have been later than this that he completed and sent to Lady Bedford the "Obsequies to the Lord Harington," the longest and finest of his Epicedes, for at the close he declared he would write no more verses:

> Doe not, faire soule, this sacrifice refuse,
> That in thy grave I doe interre my Muse,
> Who, by my griefe, great as thy worth, being cast
> Behind hand yet hath spoke, and spoke her last.

By the time he sent the "Obsequies" to Lady Bedford Donne had made up his mind that the only course open to him was to enter the ministry. To his obvious embarrassment, he found himself, as he wrote to Goodyer on December 21, 1614, "brought to a necessity of printing my Poems, and addressing them to my L. Chamberlain," that is, to Somerset. He intends to do this "not for much publique view, but at mine own cost, a few Copies." He realizes how incongruous this may seem, but is "under an unescapable necessity" and asks Goodyer if he may borrow "that old book of you."[17] No copy of this projected limited edition of Donne's poems has ever come to light. In my edition of the *Divine Poems* in 1952[18] I put forward the hypothesis that the five manuscripts of Group I, which all descend from a single common exemplar, preserve the selection of his poems that Donne was making at the close of 1614.

All the poems included are canonical and none of them can be dated after Donne's ordination. Although there are minor variations in the order in which the poems are copied, all the manuscripts end with the "Obsequies" and, so, with Donne's interring of his Muse. A rigorous selection has been made of the verse-letters: only two of the many addressed to the Countess of Bedford are included, along with those to Lady Carey and to the Countess of Salisbury. Almost all the short letters to Donne's men friends are omitted. The selection of the love poems has been much less rigorous. All the manuscripts include thirteen Elegies (one of them being a Funeral Elegy) and the greater number of the *Songs and Sonnets*. They all omit six short pieces: "The Computation," "The Expiration," "Witchcraft by a Picture," "A Jet Ring Sent," "The Paradox," "Negative Love." These slight pieces may well have come under the censure Donne passed on some of his poems at his first attempt to collect them, as deserving only to be left to perish. "Farewell to Love" is also missing, a poem that is very rarely found in manuscript.[19] Apart from its obvious impropriety, it is clumsily written, although it has some striking lines and phrases. Its rarity in manuscript may point to its being more a draft than a finished poem. Two more of the *Songs and Sonnets* are missing: "A Nocturnal" and "The Dissolution." I cannot suggest any reason why these two poems should have been omitted if they were in existence in 1614.

There is a third occasion when Donne referred to his copies of his poems: in a letter sent to Sir Robert Ker on the eve of his going abroad in 1619 as chaplain to the Doncaster embassy to the German Princes. He sends Ker his "Poems, of which you took a promise" and, going beyond what he had promised, sends "another Book," *Biathanatos,* which he says he had kept very close—"no hand hath passed upon it to copy it, nor many eyes to read it." He asks Ker to "Reserve it for me, if I live, and if I die, I only forbid it the Presse, and the Fire: publish it not, but yet burn it not; and between those, do what you will with it."[20] Alan MacColl has suggested, with great plausibility, that the "Poems" sent to Ker, which would seem to have been a very substantial collection, since the lengthy *Biathanatos* accompanying them is referred to as "another Book," are the source of the collection found in the four manuscripts of Group II.[21] With a few insignificant exceptions the Group II manuscripts are canonical. The collection they preserve is much fuller than that in Group I and is not so tidily sorted into kinds. It adds to the poems the prose *Paradoxes and Problems* and, significantly, includes the unfinished poem "Resurrection, imperfect," which points to a derivation from an author's loose papers. It is in this collection that we find "A Nocturnal" and "The Dissolution." Otherwise they are only found in the Dolau Cothi manuscript, closely related by its text and the poems it contains to Group II; in the Luttrell manuscript, which added poems from a Group II manuscript to a basically group III collection; and in the O'Flaherty manuscript, which is an expansion and resorting of Luttrell. The absence of these two poems from the collection preserved in Group I is a strong argument for dating them after Donne's ordination and for looking at them together and in association with the few poems we know that Donne wrote after he had declared that he had interred his Muse.

"The Dissolution" is an unsatisfactory poem. Its metrical form, a verse-paragraph with lines of varying length and irregular rhymes, which Donne used so brilliantly for dramatic effect in "Woman's Constancy" and "The Apparition," is unsuited to a poem that is a meditative soliloquy unvarying in tone. The initial conceit of the lover's absorption into his body of the first elements of fire, air, water, and earth, into which the body of his mistress had been dissolved by death, is grotesque, as is the final development of it into an explosion, through the excess of fire and fuel, which will release his soul to be catapulted after hers and overtake it. Yet it has an obvious relation to "A Nocturnal" in its subject and in its protest at the word "death"—"This (which I am amaz'd that I can speake)/This death,—although here there is not the religious suggestion of "A Nocturnal": that to speak of "her death" is to use a word that "wrongs her." Its failure points up the aesthetic beauty of "A Nocturnal." It owes this largely to its setting, which provides an initial impression of a universe of death, of "privations" and of "absence, darknesse, death; things which are not." John Hollander has drawn attention to the powerful combination of metrical stress and rhyme on the word "not," making it not a negative particle, but adjectival.[22] I would go further and say it gives the word rather the status of a substantive, an essence of negation, the equivalent of "nought." The setting is reverted to at the close of the final stanza, which opens with the summary, paradoxical "But I am None," the powerful stress on this negative substantive being reinforced by the internal rhyme with "Sunne." This last assertion of non-being passes into a strangely moving sense of affirmation, the last line of the poem echoing the first with a difference, for what at first is pure statement—"Tis the yeares midnight, and it is the dayes"—ends as the motive for a new way of life. The two uses of "since" join "her long nights festivall" with his midnight hour. The beautiful repetition of the verb "Enjoy," in "since shee enjoyes" links this world with the other, and the implication of the last stanza is that as, in the world of time, the lowest depth of winter is the moment when the terrestrial sun begins to renew his strength, so, in the spiritual world, the arrival at the sense of absolute non-being is the moment at which the soul recognizes that its "being's heart and home" is in the world of eternity where "shee" has gone before him. For as "there is a budding morrow in the midnight," so "on the shores of darkness there is light."[23]

It is characteristic of the poems that Donne wrote after his ordination that they did not circulate widely and that they are mostly occasional, arising out of circumstances. Exceptions are the poem on the "Sydnaean Psalmes" and the paraphrase of Lamentations, which may be regarded as arising out of the concerns of his profession.[24] Thus, the Latin poem to Herbert (printed in *Poems,* 1650) is written on the new seal he has adopted on taking orders. The "Hymn to Christ, at the Author's last Going into Germany" is headed in one manuscript "At the Sea-side going out with the Lord Doncaster. 1619." While this is a little too precise for credence, there can be no doubt that the poem was occasioned by Donne's imminent departure on May 12, 1619. This poem had a wider circulation than most,[25] which is paralleled by the number of manuscripts of Donne's *Sermon of Valediction,* preached at Lincoln's Inn on April 18, 1619, which the poem strikingly echoes. Donne ap-

pears to have regarded the journey with misgivings and feared that
he might not return. He wrote both the sermon and the poem with
this in mind, and it is likely that he would let friends have copies of
what he thought might be his last poem. The poem to Mr. Tilman,
who was ordained deacon in December 1618 and priest in March
1620, is a reply to Tilman's own poem. It is found in only two
collections (Dobell and O'Flaherty) and in a miscellany where it
follows the poem it answers. Of the two hymns that Donne wrote
during his serious illness in 1623, the "Hymn to God my God, in
my sickness" is extant in only one collection (Stowe 961) and on a
loose sheet among the papers of Sir Julius Caesar, who has endorsed
it with the date on which he received it, "in December 1623." It is
the poem of a man awaiting imminent death. The other, known as
"A Hymn to God the Father" from the title given to it in the
edition of 1633, is more widely distributed.[26] This can be ac-
counted for if we accept Walton's story that Donne on his recovery
had it set to music and sung at St. Paul's. It is much more general,
less tied to actual circumstances than the other hymn, and has
indeed been included in hymnals although quite unsuited to con-
gregational singing, as the other could not conceivably be. In 1625,
reluctantly, Donne yielded to a request of Sir Robert Ker for a poem
on the death of the Marquis of Hamilton. He apologized for its
feebleness, and with some justice, in a letter to Ker, adding "Had
you commanded mee to have waited on his body to Scotland and
preached there, I would have embraced the obligation with more
alacrity."

There remain the three Holy Sonnets which are found only in
the Westmoreland manuscript. They are unconnected in subject
with each other; but they are alike in that none of them springs out
of a particular occasion. Two are concerned with Donne's spiritual
state; the third with the state of the universal Church. This last can
be roughly dated from the reference to a church which "rob'd and
tore / Laments and mourns in Germany and here." This must refer
to the collapse of the Protestant cause after the disastrous defeat of
the German Protestant Princes at the Battle of the White Mountain

in October 1620, and the passionate sympathy felt in England for the plight of fellow Protestants. The sonnet that speaks of his dead wife would seem to have been written at much the same time. The tone of the poem suggests that Donne's bereavement was not recent, and the closing lines refer to a thwarting of his worldly hopes.[27] Donne had returned from his travels with Doncaster restored in health and spirits and had every right to expect he would now get preferment. He had been handsomely treated while abroad, and in Holland, where he had preached before the Elector Palatine and his wife, he had been given by the State General one of the gold medals struck to commemorate the Synod of Dort, a signal mark of honor.[28] He returned to England on January 1, 1620, and in the following March the Deanery of Salisbury became vacant. It went to a certain Dr. Bowles, and, according to Chamberlain, writing to Carleton, "poore Dr. Dun is cast behind and fallen from his hopes." A year later, in March 1621, the Bishop of London died. Chamberlain, recording the current gossip, wrote that, in what R. C. Bald calls an ecclesiastical "general post," Donne was to have the Deanery of Salisbury, but two months later the news had changed, and Donne was to have the Deanery of Gloucester. In the event he had neither and wrote an abject letter of complaint to Buckingham on August 8, reminding him "how narrow and penurious a fortune I wrestle with in thys world" and referring to himself as "a clodd of clay" awaiting whatever kind of vessel Buckingham chose to make of him. A month later the longed-for preferment came and Donne knew from the King that the Deanery of Paul's was to be his.[29] He was finally elected November 22, 1621. The third of the Westmoreland sonnets provides no clue to a possible date; but its general mood of discouragement makes it seem likely that it was written during the same period as the other two, that is, at some time between the close of 1620 and September 1621 when Donne at last had the prospect of what he had looked for in vain for some twenty years: security, in work that gave him scope for the exercise of his talents.

While I cannot claim to have offered any conclusive external arguments to support the view that "A Nocturnal" expresses Donne's desolation at the loss of his much-loved wife, I hope I may have suggested some considerations that make this view very probable. The most telling argument is the poem's restricted circulation, which is a feature of the poems Donne wrote after 1615 as a whole, and, particularly, its absence from the very full selection from poems written before that date preserved in the manuscripts of Group I. Having, in 1611, begun to revise his poems and sort them into those he thought worthy of preservation and those he thought should be left to perish, he gave up any idea of publishing them and instead wrote and published the two *Anniversaries* as if, in addition to pleasing his new patron, Sir Robert Drury, he wished to add to his reputation as a controversialist a reputation as a serious, moral poet. Disgruntled by their reception, he concentrated in the years 1612–14 on writing, for private circulation, a kind of public poetry, celebrating two splendid court weddings, writing obsequies for Prince Henry (which he allowed to be printed) and for Lord Harington, and addressing complimentary verses to the Countess of Salisbury and, possibly, also to the Countess of Huntington. Two poems dating from these years that were not written with the ulterior motive of pleasing the great and the wealthy are both occasioned by purely personal circumstances: that he was journeying toward the west on Good Friday 1613, and that a few days later he was staying with his old friend Edward Herbert at Montgomery Castle.[30]

Except for the verses on the translation of the Psalms by Sidney and his sister and the *Lamentations of Jeremy,* the poems Donne wrote after his ordination are inspired by personal circumstances, as if some strong inner compulsion made Donne break his promise in the Harington Elegy to write no more poems. The most profound of his personal experiences after that date were the loss of his wife in August 1617, his leaving England and his orphaned children behind him in May 1619 to venture abroad, where he feared he had dangerous enemies among the Jesuits, and when his own health was bad and his spirits low, and the illness that brought him to the verge of death in the winter of 1623. I would like to add, as a bad time for Donne, the failure of the Doncaster embassy to preserve peace between the Catholic and Protestant Princes of Germany and the disappointment of his own hopes of advancement after his return from the Continent. It would be strange that only the first, and personally the most grievous, of these crises in Donne's life did not drive him to express his feelings in poetry.

If we accept that "A Dissolution" and "A Nocturnal" were written about the death of Anne Donne, we can see a psychological progression from the blank opening of "The Dissolution"—"Shee' is dead"—and its treatment of grief in purely physical terms as an oppression weighing down the whole body, to the calm tone of memory in the opening of the Westmoreland sonnet, where Donne can now think of his love for his wife as having led him to the love of God. "The Dissolution" ends with the hope that, overburdened with passion (which longs for her physical presence), with sighs (which shorten life), with tears, and with despair, his body will perish, releasing his soul to overtake hers. "A Nocturnal," inspired like "Good Friday 1613: Riding Westward" by a day, explores the sense of absolute loss profoundly, with metaphysical and religious overtones, to arrive at a sense of dedication for another life: "Let me prepare towards her." The "Hymn to Christ" of 1619 regards the coming journey as a "Divorce to All" that he had loved or by whom he had been loved. He goes alone in his "winter"

Where none but thee, th'Eternall root of true love I may know.

In so going he chooses "an Everlasting Night." The Westmoreland sonnet revolves the same notion of God as a jealous lover, but takes the sorrows and disappointments of this life as God's strategy to bring men wholly to him. I regret that in revising my edition of the *Divine Poems* I did not reconsider my tentative dating of the sonnet as written before the Hymn, for I now think it is more likely to have been written after Donne's return from his travels. It is much quieter in tone, containing a beautiful tribute to his wife, and a thankful sense of what his love for her had taught him. There is no longing for death in it, but only an attempt to see his loss of her and the disappointments of his worldly hopes as tokens of God's chastening love, for "whom the Lord loveth, he chasteneth."[31]

NOTES

1. *The Poetry of Meditation* (New Haven: Yale University Press, 1954), pp. 214–16; *The Poem of the Mind* (New York: Oxford University Press, 1966), pp. 17–20.

2. *The Life and Letters of John Donne* (London: Heinemann, 1899), i. 74.

3. *Poems of John Donne* (London: Oxford University Press, 1912), ii. xxii–iii and 10.

4. "The Ecstasy," "A Lecture upon the Shadow," and "The Primrose" are also set out of doors.

5.

'Tis the yeares midnight, and it is the dayes,
Lucies, who scarce seaven houres herself unmaskes,
    The Sunne is spent, and now his flasks
    Send forth light squibs, no constant rayes;
        The worlds whole sap is sunke:
        The generall balme th'hydroptique earth hath drunk,
        Whither as to the beds-feet, life is shrunke,
        Dead and enterr'd. . . .

W. A. Murray, 'Donne and Paracelsus,' *RES* 25 (1949), 115–23, saw the poem as presenting Donne lying on his bed, which has become a tomb bearing his corpse, the "generall balme" having regressed from his body down into the earth. He took the "flasks" of the spent sun to be pieces of bottle glass in the windows of the bedchamber; but did not explain how at midnight these could emit even "light squibs." He was followed in both these misinterpretations by Richard Sleight in *Interpretations,* ed. John Wain (London: Routledge and Kegan Paul, 1955), pp. 32–58.

6. Donne discusses the doctrine of creation *ex nihilo* at some length in his Essays in Divinity, commenting on the words *In the Beginning.* He declares that the doctrine is beyond reason and is an *Article of our Belief,* and ends his discussion by saying: "Of this we will say no more; for this *Nothing* being no creature, is more incomprehensible than all the rest." (*Essays,* ed. Evelyn M. Simpson [Oxford: Oxford University Press, Clarendon Press, 1952], pp. 15–20 and 27–32).

7. In both other Lovers are called on: to come with "chrystall vyals," or to "study" the lover, and to enjoy their summer—a brief time compared with the "long nights festivall" that "shee enjoyes." In both use is made of the idea that plants and stones, although they cannot move, can "detest, and love."

8. See the fable of the bee and the spider in Swift's *The Battle of the Books*.

9. *The Poetry of Meditation*, 115 n. 4. He was countering J. B. Leishman's difficulty in believing that Donne wrote the poem "after the actual death of his wife in 1617, when he had been two years in orders."

10. H. W. Garrod in his selection of Donne's poetry and prose in the Clarendon English Series (Oxford, 1947), noting that the actual day of the winter solstice differs periodically, declared that December 13 was not the shortest day in any year in Donne's lifetime. This irrelevant piece of information set off Donaphan Louthan on a search through contemporary almanacs that resulted in the most fantastic "explication" of the poem known to me. He discovered that December 12, 1594 was both the shortest day and the day on which Lucy Harington was married to Lord Bedford. The poem thus mourns her defloration or 'erotic death' on her wedding night; see *The Poetry of John Donne* (New York: Bookman Associates, 1951).

11. In the early church Vigils were celebrated at midnight, from association of watching with the idea that the Last Trump would sound at midnight. The offices were followed by a celebration of the Eucharist, as in the ancient liturgy for Holy Saturday, which is followed by the first Mass of Easter. From the fourth century they were moved back to precede nightfall on the day before and became a time of penitence, prayer, and fasting in preparation for the Feast.

12. *Poetical Works,* ed. L. C. Martin (Oxford: Oxford University Press, Clarendon Press, 1956), p. 314.

13. Burley MS. See Evelyn M. Simpson, *Prose Works of John Donne,* 2nd. ed. (Oxford: Oxford University Press, Clarendon Press, 1948), pp. 316–17 for a transcript of the letter.

14. The letter is the first of the letters to Goodyer printed after the "Elegies on the Authors Death" in the *Poems* of 1633. I have to thank John Sparrow for a translation more elegant than I could have made of Donne's contorted Latin. The interest of the letter is that it lends support to the view that some of the variants found in the manuscripts of Donne's poems have arisen from his revision of poems in his possession which had been circulating in their original form.

15. *The Poetry of Meditation,* p. 229. Subsequent attempts by scholars

and critics to defend the unity of *The First Anniversary* have not convinced me.

16. *Letters* (1651), pp. 238–39. Donne's letter to Goodyer uses much the same words (*Letters,* pp. 74–75). He attempted to write a verse-letter of exculpation to Lady Bedford but broke off after writing twenty-five embarrassed and not very convincing lines. He had, after all, not only written in praise of the dead Elizabeth Drury. He had also. written a verse-letter to Lady Carey and Mrs. Essex Rich, extravagantly praising their beauty and virtue, from Amiens in the early months of 1612.

17. *Letters,* pp. 196–97.

18. *The Divine Poems of John Donne,* ed. Helen Gardner (Oxford: Oxford University Press, Clarendon Press, 1952), 2nd rev. ed., 1978.

19. It is found in Stowe 961, the only collection to include the "Hymn to God my God, in my sickness," in O'Flaherty, in the large late miscellany Stowe 962, and in a miscellany at Harvard, where the name "Mr. An: Saintleger" is written against the title.

20. *Letters,* pp. 21–22.

21. See "The Circulation of Donne's Poems in Manuscript," in *John Donne: Essays in Celebration,* ed. A. J. Smith (London: Methuen, 1972), p. 35. MacColl's B. Litt. thesis (1967) on this subject in the Bodleian gives a full account of the manuscripts of Donne's poems with contents lists.

22. *Vision and Resonance* (New York: Oxford University Press, 1975), p. 53.

23. Aye, on the shores of darkness there is light,
    And precipices show untrodden green:
    There is a budding morrow in the midnight;
    There is a triple sight in blindness keen. . . .

Keats, "To Homer"

24. "Upon the translation of the Psalms" (extant only in O'Flaherty) must have been written after 1621 when the Countess of Pembroke died. It expresses Donne's dissatisfaction, shared by many of his contemporaries, with the Old Version of the Psalms. It seems likely that the paraphrase of Lamentations (extant in two manuscripts of Group II, O'Flaherty, Bridgewater, and the second of the Osborn manuscripts) was undertaken with the idea of providing worthier material for use in worship. Donne's mind may have turned to Lamentations in the years 1620–22 when disaster had overtaken the Protestant Churches in Germany.

25. In addition to Group II, Luttrell, and O'Flaherty, it is found in Dobell, Stowe 961, Bridgewater, Osborn 2, and its collateral, Phillipps.

26. It is found in Group II, Luttrell, O'Flaherty, Dobell, Stowe 961, and in three miscellanies in one of which it is provided with a setting.

27.   But why should I begg more love, when as thou
      Dost wooe my soule, for hers offring all thine:
      And dost not only feare least I allow
      My love to saints and Angels, things divine,
      But in thy tender jealosy dost doubt
      Least the World, fleshe, yea Devill putt thee out.

28. See Paul R. Sellen, "John Donne: The Poet as Diplomat and
Divine," *HLQ* 39, no. 3 (1976) for an account of Donne's important
standing in the embassy, ranking after Doncaster and Sir Francis Nether-
sole, and for the significance of the leaving gift to him of the gold medal.

29. See R. C. Bald, *John Donne: A Life* (Oxford: Oxford University
Press, Clarendon Press, 1970), pp. 370–74.

30. See John Hayward, *John Donne: Complete Poetry and Selected Prose*
(London: Nonesuch Press, 1929), p. 464 for a letter to Sir Robert Harley,
dated "1613, April 7, Montgomery."

31. Hebrews 12:6.

FRANK MANLEY

Toward a Definition of Plain Style in the Poetry of George Herbert

Halfway through Herbert's "A Wreath" something peculiar happens. The poem explodes, and out of the dust and debris something else emerges: or rather something else should emerge. What happens instead is that the film reverses itself and runs backwards; the pieces come together again, but it is not the same.

The poem begins with the desire to weave a garland of praise for God. It is the primary impulse of all devotional poetry except that in this case, because of Herbert's superior technical ability, the weaving will seem to take place on the page itself. The last few words of one line are carried over and inverted at the beginning of the next, thus implicating them both:

A wreathed garland of deserved praise,
Of praise deserved, unto thee I give,
I give to thee, who knowest all my ways.

And then it happens. Herbert suddenly realizes that there is a corollary between the weaving motion of the lines he has just written and the crooked, winding ways of his spirit, "wherein I live," he says. "Wherein I die, not live." Deviousness, Herbert realizes, is a form of deceit whether in one's life or in one's art, for life is simple, straightforward, directed in all things toward God:

life is straight,
Straight as a line, and ever tends to thee,
To thee, who art more farre above deceit,
Then deceit seems above simplicitie.

What began as an act of praise, therefore, ends up as a humble
petition for simplicity:

> Give me simplicitie, that I may live,
> So live and like, that I may know, thy wayes,
> Know them and practice them: then shall I give
> For this poore wreath, give thee a crown of praise.[1]

It is difficult to say precisely what happens at the crucial moment when the poem alters direction, but it seems probable that
Herbert perceived something more than a general resemblance between what was happening on the page and what he saw occurring
in his own heart and soul. He was also aware, perhaps, of a causal
connection between the sorts of devices he was using in his poetry
and the deviousness of character that led to those devices—the
realization, in other words, that he was guilty of spiritual pride in
seeking the perfection of his poetry instead of simply using it to
worship God.

The most interesting thing about the poem, however, is not
this dramatic moment of truth but the fact that the poem rights
itself and, on a technical level at least, continues on as though
nothing had happened. The ending of one line is still carried over to
the beginning of the next, weaving the poem together on to the very
end, but the words are no longer inverted. They are simply repeated, thus giving an illusion of straightforwardness. The device is
not effective enough or perhaps not concealed enough, however, to
offset the realization that the technical complexities of the poem run
counter to the desire for simplicity it expresses. Even the overall
rhyme scheme suggests the circular pattern of a wreath. The first
few lines rhyme *abab;* the next four *cdcd;* and the last few reverse the
beginning and complete the circle, rhyming *baba.*

In a very fundamental way the poem would seem to be at odds
with itself, and one wonders why. What was it that allowed Herbert
to say one thing and do another? Is it really a piece of poetic
hypocrisy, or is it instead a mature acceptance of the nature and
limitations of art? Would it have been better for Herbert to stop
where he was and throw the poem away when he realized what was

happening; or was that part of the overall strategy from the very beginning? Or was it perhaps discovered in process and then capitalized on? To what degree, in other words, is art, artifice, deviousness, duplicity—however one would want to consider it— essential to the nature of poetry? These are crucial and extremely difficult questions for a devotional poet. The obvious danger is that the poet will become too intent on the poem itself and forget the larger purpose the poem should serve in leading the mind to God. If it fails in that, it fails altogether, even though it succeeds as a poem. But where is one to draw the line?

Herbert was aware of the danger, of course; hence his ambivalent attitude toward poetry. On the one hand it was a "Lovely enchanting language, sugar-cane / Hony of roses." On the other hand he conceived of it as a whore wearing an embroidered coat. "Beautie and beauteous words should go together" (pp. 176–77), but Herbert knew they do not. It was the same old platonic delusion: physical beauty is not a reflection of virtue in the soul. The disparate claims of what Herbert conceived of as art and what he regarded as the greater reality of truth or life or devotion (all of which he seemed to equate) formed one of the central conflicts of his thought and one of the most significant tensions in his poetry. Throughout *The Temple* Herbert evinces an intense desire to get out of the complications of self as he knew it—sophisticated, intellectual, introspective, and above all else subtle, complex, and self-divisive—into what he conceived of as the simple, straightforward life of the country parson or, more distant, the early Christians, clothed in the homespun language of the gospels. In Herbert's mind poetry seems to have been connected with the double-mindedness of the divided self, whereas life, truth, and devotion were associated with the integral self he imagined himself as capable of becoming if only he could resolve his innate contrarieties and focus his entire being on God.[2] One might quarrel with the underlying assumptions, aesthetic and otherwise,[3] but this conflict in Herbert led to some of his finest poetry, such as "The Forerunners" and "Jordan" I and II, in which he confronted the problem directly and—the choice is strange—somewhat paradoxically within the medium of poetry itself. Taken to their logical extreme these poems constitute a poetry designed to get out of poetry, or at least to move beyond any concept of poetry Herbert was previously acquainted with, into something simpler, more immediate and direct, like truth or life itself.

But what sort of poetry could that possibly be? Plain style as we ordinarily conceive of it would not do since it is an even more stylized form of art designed to conceal art and give the false impression of simplicity. The reader might be fooled, but not the poet. Herbert could strip his style, of course, but if he were to strip it too far, he would be in danger of falling into the prosaic flatness of most religious poetry. Despite Herbert's protestations to the contrary, "My God, My King" and "Thou art still my God" are not poems, not as they stand anyway, without being shored up by the context in which they appear. If he had written a simpler sort of poetry, a new sort of plain style, we might have expected Herbert to avoid some of the excesses of his pattern poems—the sort of things Summers admired as hieroglyphs—[4] but he would still have had to deal with the complexity and difficulty inherent in poetry itself, and he would still have been in danger of focusing his attention on the wrong thing. For poetry is necessarily difficult and requires the qualities of paradox, metaphor, compression, ambiguity, complexity of mind, and emotion to be truthful to itself and not reductive of experience. To write poetry at all requires a great deal of attention to matters of craftsmanship—writing, rewriting, adjusting, tinkering, arranging, all of which to a devotional poet with an excessively scrupulous conscience might very well seem like an exercise in pride. And yet that same scrupulous poet would know that poetry, like a bear cub, has to be licked into shape: the dilemma would seem to be insoluble. If the poem was scrupulously rewritten, rewriting was done in danger of focusing the attention of the poet pridefully on his own creation, and if he resisted the impulse and refused to rewrite, he would obviously fail to achieve the poem, which would remain half-articulate and only partially developed. Either way he lost. If he became caught up in the poem, he was in danger of losing God, and if he concerned himself only with God, he was in danger of losing the poem he had intended to present to God.

It would be possible, of course, to quit writing altogether, as Shakespeare's Claudius quit praying,[5] and perhaps that would be the only logical conclusion. And yet it is obvious from such poems as "The Quiddity" and "The Forerunners" that poetry was an important part of Herbert's life and devotion. St. Thomas More once said that God made vegetables for growth, animals for innocence, and man to worship him in the tangle of his mind. Poetry for Herbert was a way to worship God through the use of the intellect, a method of remaining and dwelling with God. "It is," he wrote in "The Quiddity," "that which while I use/I am with thee, and *most take all.*" (p. 70). And yet if he also felt that his intellect was a source of pride and an occasion of sin, would it not be better for him to cease writing altogether than to offend God in what should be the act of prayer?

One solution—a partial, temporary solution only—was to turn poetry against itself and cause it to self-destruct. In poems like "Jordan" I and II Herbert creates the illusion that the poem, the actual poem, consists of only the last few lines or perhaps even the last few words. Everything else in the poem is simply a prelude. The first two stanzas of "Jordan" (I), for example, are made up of a series of questions about the nature of contemporary poetry. It is only in stanza 3 that some of these questions begin to be answered as Herbert turns from negative to positive, from critic to poet himself, presenting in the very last line the ideal poem or perhaps the Platonic form of all true poetry complete in itself in all its stark simplicity. Consider the effect:

> Who sayes that fictions only and false hair
> Become a verse? Is there in truth no beautie?
> Is all good structure in a winding stair?
> May no lines passe, except they do their dutie
>   Not to a true, but painted chair?
>
> And sudden arbours shadow course-spunne lines?
> Must purling streams refresh a lovers loves?
> Must all be vail'd, while he that reads, divines,
>   Catching the sense at two removes?
>
> Shepherds are honest people; let them sing:
> Riddle who list for me, and pull for Prime:

> I envie no man's nightengale or spring;
>   Nor let them punish me with losse of rime,
>   Who plainly say, *My God, My King.*

In "Jordan" (II) the effect is the same, but the poem is much more personal. The problem is not in contemporary poetry; it is in Herbert himself. When he first began to write, he says, he was so carried away with the initial excitement that he tried to go beyond himself and like Macbeth fell "on the other." The intent was good. "Nothing could seem to[o] rich to clothe the sunne." But the result was fundamentally prideful. Herbert discovered that he wove himself into the sense with "wreaths of fame and interest," as Marvell was later to put it.[6] In the last stanza the mistakes of the past give way to the present, however, as Herbert speaks of a voice that came to him and suggested a different direction, a new way of writing or a new perspective on writing he might use to simplify his verse:

> But while I bustled, I might heare a friend
> Whisper, *How wide is all this long pretence!*
> *There is in love a sweetnesse readie penn'd:*
> *Copy out only that, and save expense.*

Just as in "Jordan" (I) the poem serves as a vehicle to lead out of itself, and it works: the effect is achieved. But it is clear that a poet can write only a certain number of poems like that and still get away with it. The problem still remains. How is one to write something other than an anti-poem that turns the devices of poetry against itself and gives the effect of leading out of itself into another form of discourse? How is it possible to write an entire poem in that new discourse, and what would it consist of?

There is probably no satisfactory answer to a question like that, certainly none that one can formulate abstractly as a critical principle. But the "Jordan" poems themselves suggest a possible solution. For they not only announce a new poetic, they suggest that they are written in terms of that new form of discourse or at least from the vantage point of its perspective. The contrast between past and present in "Jordan" (II) would seem to indicate as much:

> When first my lines of heav'nly joyes made mention,
>   Such was their lustre, they did so excell,

That I sought out quaint words, and trim invention;
My thoughts began to burnish, sprout, and swell,
Curling with metaphors a plain intention,
Decking the sense, as if it were to sell.

Thousands of notions in my brain did runne,
Off'ring their service, if I were not sped:
I often blotted what I had begunne;
This was not quick enough, and that was dead.
Nothing could seem too rich to clothe the sunne,
Much lesse those joyes which trample on his head.

As flames do work and winde, when they ascend,
So did I weave my selfe into the sense.
But while I bustled, I might heare a friend
Whisper, *How wide is all this long pretence!*
There is in love a sweetnesse readie penn'd:
Copie out onely that, and save expense.

Despite what Herbert says in the last few lines, this is obviously not
a simple poem: it seems to contradict and perhaps even violate
itself. Herbert says he learned not to curl with metaphors a plain
intention, and yet he seems to think in terms of metaphor. His lines
burnish, sprout, and swell with them—from a rank garden to a
woman at her dressing table to a merchant or perhaps a whore,
"Decking the sense, as if it were to sell." The metaphors come so
fast it is difficult to untangle them, and the same is true of "Jordan"
(I) with its flickering images of women and deceptive cosmetic
surfaces that play behind the verse. In both poems the texture of
associative images is extremely rich and complex, and what is true
of imagery is also true of the syntax of individual lines. What does
Herbert mean by this, for example? He seems to use the pun on
"sunne" almost metaphorically:

Nothing could seem too rich to clothe the sunne,
Much lesse those joyes which trample on his head.

Or what does this mean?

Shepherds are honest people; let them sing:
Riddle who list, for me, and pull for Prime.

And what does that have to do with the line that immediately
follows—"I envie no mans nightengale or spring"—? One knows,

of course, but it requires a great deal of imagination on the part of the reader to follow it. The lines are open, not closed as in the pattern poems.

But how is this new style, and what, if anything, is plain about it? For the reader, I suspect, not a thing. The language may be straightforward, or at least colloquial, but the thought is muscular and difficult to follow. For the poet, though, it is a different matter: the language mirrors the way his mind works. These poems and others like them in *The Temple* proceed not according to a fixed, predetermined form like a pair of wings, an altar, a circle, or any of the other "hieroglyphs" Herbert wrestled into language, but according to the mind's own patterning, and the result is a kind of poem that is not neat—not in essentials, anyway—not orderly or highly polished, but jagged, with great logical gaps the reader must bridge himself if he is to follow the surge and rapidity of the thought. It is the kind of poetry where thought is metaphoric, and metaphors are not developed as in a conceit, but piled on one another associatively. Herbert is not so concerned with the effect the poem will have on the reader or the reader's ability to follow the various turns and involutions of the overall movement as he is in the direct, authentic expression of his own thoughts and emotions. It is a form of plain style that mirrors the mind's own complexity.

This is not to say that Herbert satisfied himself with the first thing struck out in the fervor of composition and no longer revised his poetry. He probably revised just as extensively as before, but with a new objective in mind: the desire to be truthful to something inside himself, not something outside. Revision, therefore, would tend to retain difficulties of thought and expression since its primary purpose was not to smooth or polish, but to clarify. If the poems that resulted from this process turned out to be difficult, it was only because the mind itself is complex, though in its workings simple and direct.

Take for example "The Crosse," where Herbert speaks of his inward anger and frustration—the crossing—experienced presumably at having humbled himself and accepted a position at Bemerton only to discover that because of sickness he was unable to function even there. Because of the interior nature of the language a number of individual lines are extremely difficult, as here in the abrupt and surprising beginning:

> What is this strange and uncouth thing?
> To make me sigh, and seek, and faint, and die,
> Until I had some place. . . .

Or here, where again we perceive behind the lines, complicating them, a flickering image of Christ's crucifixion:

> to take away
> My power to serve thee; to unbend
> All my abilities, my designs confound,
> And lay my threatnings bleeding on the ground.

Or here, where the workings of the mind are simple and direct, but the statement almost impossible to unravel:

> I am in all a weak disabled thing,
> Save in the sight thereof, where strength doth sting.

The sight referred to is presumably the sight of the literal crucifix Herbert seems to be meditating on from the very beginning, but the poem never makes this clear. It simply moves on to an ironic awareness of the tone of whining and complaint: "Besides, things sort not to my will" (pp. 164–65).

This paradoxical plain style is found in almost all of Herbert's finest, most widely anthologized poetry, such as "The Collar," which like "The Crosse" is also intensely personal and suffused with a sense of frustration, anger, and wry self-irony. Consider, for example, the image of the rope of sands:

> Forsake thy cage,
> Thy rope of sands,
> Which pettie thoughts have made, and made to thee
> Good cable, to enforce and draw,
> And be thy law,
> While thou didst wink and wouldst not see.

An hourglass? Perhaps. But it need not be limited to that any more than the transition from cage to rope to cable to law needs be an explicit and logical. Or consider the abrupt shifts from secular to ecclesiastical reference and back again in the same image and often in the same word, as the reference to "board" (meaning both table and altar) at the very beginning: "I struck the board, and cry'd, No more." The same duality of reference is picked up a little later on in the images of harvest, corn and wine, with their simultaneous application to the eucharist. Throughout the poem there is an obscure afterimage of the priest at the altar, which at times comes forward, at times recedes. But more than in the images or any individual lines and expressions, the inwardness of the poem manifests itself primarily in the overall structure with its abrupt shifts of speaker as Herbert turns from one aspect of the self to another without identifying them, without even indicating where one leaves off and the other begins. This is what almost all readers of the poem have the most difficulty with. The effect is one of interior confusion and turmoil, but it is also a graphic representation of the way the mind actually works, the various internal voices seeming discrete and at the same time blending obscurely together since they are, after all, simply aspects—various elements and impulses of the same personality.

This same style or mode of discourse is found almost always in Herbert's most extreme, far-fetched instances of metaphysical imagery, which seem to be not the result of calculation, but a direct psychological flaring-out. In "The Bag," for example, it is present in the image of the wound in Christ's side as a mail box (as well as in the rest of the poem, particularly in the duality of structure and the strange, mythical retelling of the story of Christ's incarnation and death); in "The Forerunners," in the perhaps more effective but equally surprising image of the coming of age and the grey hair that accompanies it as chalk marks on the side of the head made by the harbingers of the king, who go before him on progress and indicate what rooms he will need to occupy when he comes;[8] or in the surprise reversal of imagery at the conclusion of "Decay," where the fire that will consume the world at the second coming is regarded not as an act of justice, but an act of mercy and love when God's real presence and warmth will return and fill once again a world grown cold and pinched by sin:

> I see the world grows old, when as the heat
> Of thy great love, once spread, as in an urn
> Doth closet up it self, and still retreat,
> Cold sin still forcing it, till it return,
>   And calling *Justice,* all things burn.

Or consider the images of fire and water in "Church Lock and Key," their relation to one another and to the title:[9]

> I know it is my sinne, which locks thine eares,
>   And bindes thy hands,
> Out-crying my requests, drowning my tears;
> Or else the chilnesse of my faint demands.
>
> But as cold hands are angrie with the fire,
>   And mend it still;
> So do I lay the want of my desire,
> Not on my sinnes, or coldnesse, but thy will.
>
> Yet heare, O God, onely for his blouds sake
>   Which pleads for me:
> For though sinnes plead too, yet like stones they make
> His blouds sweet current much more loud to be.

Or in this instance, observe how Herbert blends the image of a skeleton with that of a young man about town complimented for having put on some weight and both with Christ's passion and death. Notice the ease and lack of strain with which it all happens:

> Death, thou wast once an uncouth hideous thing,
>   Nothing but bones,
>   The sad effect of sadder grones:
> Thy mouth was open, but thou couldst not sing.
>
> But since our Saviours death did put some blood
>   Into thy face;
>   Thou art grown fair and full of grace,
> Much in request, much sought for as a good.

The same style is also present where one would least expect it—in Herbert's most abstract allegories. "Love III," for instance, moves from the humorous fiction of a priest invited to a party, to a simultaneous awareness of the eucharistic feast, to the entry of the soul into heaven, and finally to the realization that all of these are subsumed into the abstract nature of love itself. The poem swings effortlessly from one level of awareness to another except when the stage-sets collapse and we plunge abruptly, with the shock and surprise of a metaphysical image, through the surface to the sense of wonder and awe that underlies it, as when the host asks the guest, who is too shy to look at him, "Who made the eyes but I?" And when the guest protests that he has misused them ("Truth Lord, but I have marr'd them: let my shame / Go where it doth deserve"), the reply once again flings us out of the fiction of the poem into an entirely different dimension of meaning: "And know you not, sayes Love, who bore the blame?" The same effect is felt in the last shocking realization that the imagery of cannibalism that underlies the Christian sacrament of communion is true to the basic nature of love itself, which desires to give itself completely and be absorbed body and soul into the very substance and being of the loved one:

> You must sit down, sayes Love, and taste my meat:
> So did I sit and eat.

As Donne wrote in one of his sermons:

> Love is a Posessory Affection, it delivers over him that loves into the possession of that that he loves; it is a transmutatory Affection, it changes him that loves, into the very nature of that that he loves, and he is nothing else.[10]

The style I describe in this paper is scattered throughout *The Temple,* at times appearing primarily in terms of language and syntax, at other times in image, structure, or simply the associative process itself. Since we do not know the order in which the poems were written, it is impossible to speak of chronology. The poems in *The Temple* do not come together to form a neat, orderly sequence. By the time he put the collection together, Herbert had come to realize perhaps that order was not what he had once thought it was and that there was a deeper current to his life and art than he had previously realized. Reading the collection as a whole one catches a glimpse of this deeper organic unity:

> The poems of *The Temple* . . . constitute an important human argument: a man's attempt to discover himself, to define and refine away

what is selfish and vacillating and cowardly in his nature, to fix a goal for his life's course, and to submit himself to the demands imposed by that goal. It happens by a series of historical and personal accidents that this *agon* is stated in terms of a specific religious system, the middle Anglicanism of Herbert's day; but it is none the less general for that, and a useful way to regard it, if we are unable to accept it on its own terms, is as a metaphor of the dilemma that in one guise or another confronts all thoughtful men in every time and place.[11]

The style described in this paper is part of that organic process. As Herbert learned to accept the demands of the goal he had chosen and became more and more fully himself, the realization that he could write in such a way as to remain truthful to himself and still be simple, direct, plain-spoken, and authentic could not have been the least of his discoveries. The poetry he came to write is not the simple, pietistic verse one would expect to be written by the country parson Herbert sometimes wished to become but expresses the man as he actually was. It is the poetry of a country parson who is also a complex, sophisticated individual. Compared to the pattern poems, the artistry seems flawed at times and gives the impression of being downplayed, if not actually thrown away, but it is in fact the most artful of all because the most subtly informed and realized, not with the surface of the mind only, but with the full powers of the total man surface and subsurface, conscious and unconscious, rational and irrational.

NOTES

1. *The Works of George Herbert*, ed. F. E. Hutchinson (Oxford: Oxford University Press, 1941), p. 185. This edition is used for all subsequent references.

2. See also "Variety" (I), "Content," "The Windows," and "Praise" (I).

3. See, for example, Helen Vendler, *The Poetry of George Herbert* (Cambridge: Harvard University Press, 1975), p. 203, who argues quite correctly that the success or failure of a poem has nothing to do with whether the structure is open or closed. It is important to remember, however, that Vendler is speaking of poetic success and failure, not the success or

failure of the poem as an act of devotion. To that only Herbert can testify. The real problem is that of intentionality, but Herbert does not seem to have thought of it that way.

4. Joseph H Summers, *George Herbert: His Religion and Art* (Cambridge: Harvard University Press, 1954), pp. 73–146. Summers' concept of hieroglyphic form caused an entire generation of readers to admire Herbert for all the wrong reasons. The notion of a hieroglyph is not only alien to the nature of seventeenth-century poetry, it is based on a faulty sense of aesthetics that sees Herbert's pattern poems at the center of his poetic accomplishment. Following Summers, Helen Vendler makes a good case for the pattern poems, particularly "Paradise" and "Heaven" (Vendler, *The Poetry of George Herbert,* pp. 202–30), but it is the perfectly obvious, perfectly valid experience of most readers that Herbert's pattern poems are primarily literary curiosities, like the poems of Robonus Maurus in the *Patralogia Latina,* in which a picture of a knight will have a web of words thrown over it, with poems running down the spear, over the helmet, across the shoulders, a poem for each foot and under each foot, with each individual poem a part of the larger sequence of the web itself. Such things are complex, but they are not necessarily good poetry. Herbert's pattern poems are more important for what they reveal about Herbert himself, and his attitudes toward external forms, structure, and institutions than they are either as poetry or as acts of devotion. Despite its opaque style, Arnold Stein's *George Herbert's Lyrics* (Baltimore: The Johns Hopkins University Press, 1968) is probably the best book on Herbert. Stein recognizes the desire for simplicity as central to Herbert's life and art, but his account of Herbert's "art of plainness" is too vague to be of much use. He also tends to think of plain style as a form of art that conceals art, which will not do for Herbert at all.

5. With the words, it will be remembered:

> Pray can I not,
> Though inclination be as sharp as will.
> My stronger guilt defeats my strong intent,
> And like a man to double business bound,
> I stand in pause where I shall first begin
> And both neglect.

6. In "The Coronet," a poem very similar to Herbert's "A Wreath" in its realization of prideful intent while still in process.

7. Summers, *George Herbert,* pp. 90–92.

8. "The Forerunners" exhibits the same duality of structure as "The Bag," as though they are two poems yoked by violence together.

9. In the Williams manuscript the title is "Prayer." See Hutchinson's textual footnotes, p. 66.

10. John Donne, *Sermons,* ed. George R. Potter and Evelyn M. Simpson (Berkeley and Los Angeles: University of California Press, 1953–62), 1: 184–85.

11. Dudley Fitts, "Introduction" to his selection of Herbert's poetry reprinted in *The Laurel Poetry Series,* ed. Richard Wilbur (New York: Dell Publishing Co., 1962), p. 13. Stanley Fish's notion of a disappearing Herbert (*Self-Consuming Artifacts* [Los Angeles: University of California Press, 1972], pp. 156–223) seems based on an imperfect understanding of Christian theology. To lose one's life is to find it. One becomes more fully himself.

CLEANTH BROOKS

Andrew Marvell: Puritan Austerity
with Classical Grace

Andrew Marvell's "The Garden" and "To His Coy Mistress" are, by common consent, two of the finest lyric poems in English. Yet the clash between the world views they involve, though calculated to bring up the ever-thorny question of the poet's sincerity, has been little discussed. "To His Coy Mistress" carries so much conviction that it is difficult to dismiss it as simply an exercise. On the other hand, Marvell's known Puritan leanings suggest to many readers that such poems as "The Garden" must surely represent his real convictions. What I shall be concerned with here, therefore, is what gives both poems that sense of conviction and their seeming inevitability as dramatic "statement."

For all their apparent oppositions and contradictions, the two poems have much in common. They share several themes, one of which, I believe, has received in the past less attention than it deserves: the theme of time in relation to eternity.

I suggest that we try to imagine the lover of "To His Coy Mistress" to be the same man who steps into "The Garden" and savors its cool delights. Let's imagine that he has been unable to persuade his coy mistress to yield. Now, after having run through his "Passion's heat," he has indeed found in this delightful place "Love['s] . . . best retreat." Nature, no coy mistress, offers her innocent pleasures wholeheartedly. Would he, in this situation and this state of mind, find the "lovely green" of nature more "am'rous" than the "white" and "red" of his mistress? An hour before, let us suppose, he has used the phrase "vegetable Love" to dismiss rather contemptuously a love affair that had little to recommend it except

the longevity and slow growth characteristic of plant life. But if the
"Fair Trees" of the garden are indeed more amorously attractive
than any woman, would not their love be also a despised "vegetable
Love?" These questions help us see, I think, how much each poem
depends on a given dramatic situation, on the mood of the character
speaking the poem, and on the tone in which he makes his various
utterances.

Let me begin with time and mortality. The lover of the coy
mistress never relaxes his concern with the swift rush of time. His
account is studded with references to events in the far-off past, such
as Noah's flood, or to events that are to occur only in some very
remote future, such as the conversion of the Jews.

All this witty hyperbole is meant, of course, to render prepos-
terous so slow-paced a courtship and to prepare for the sudden
speed-up of time found in the middle third of the poem—a rush
that will soon take the lovers out of life altogether and strand their
bodies in "Desarts of vast Eternity." The strategy, of course, is to
present with laconic irony a bleak reality that exposes the earlier
fantasy of timelessness for the posturing that it is. Having done so,
the lover is ready to urge his conclusion: the only course is to beat
time at his own game, to live with such breathless speed as to make
the sun lag behind them.

Though a reference to speed—that of the lovers' outracing the
sun—occupies the final couplet, the dominant image of the closing
lines of the poem is one of eating. The lovers are to devour their
pleasures greedily. Far from being the love birds of tradition, they
are "am'rous birds of prey"—snatching and tearing at the flesh of
their kill. Like them, time also is a devourer, but with jaws ponder-
ous and slow as he gradually masticates all that is mortal.

It is not a pretty picture, this scene of ravenous gluttony: the
lovers tear their pleasure with "rough strife through The Iron Gates
of Life." Nobody seems to know what this refers to. (Someone has
even taken the gates to be the lips of the vagina, in which case
"iron" seems an oddity.) For me, the image that comes to mind is
simply that of feeding time for a pair of hawks mewed up in an iron
cage. They will not wait for their keeper to finish poking through
the bars the meat he brings. They snatch at it and pull it through

themselves. What seems obvious, at any rate, is a sense of creatures savage and violent; and the violence suits the poem, for the poem is realistic and even desperate.

Such images indicate one way in which "To His Coy Mistress" differs from most of the carpe diem poems of this period. Another instance of grim insistence on the physical and realistic is the allusion to the rotting corpse and the grave-worm. True, the worm here is not the never-dying worm of the Scriptures, cited by generations of hell-fire preachers. This worm is a quite matter-of-fact worm, doing what he may be expected to do to every all-too-mortal carcass. Yet, if one is to look for Marvell's Puritanism, I think a trace of it may be found here. The note of horror sets up a reverberation that is deeper and more powerful than is to be heard in any other carpe diem poem that I can think of. Compare it with the Anglican Herrick's masterpiece, "Corinna's Going a-Maying." Marvell's poem is not necessarily "better," but it is of another order.

For most readers, the voice heard in this poem cannot be that of a Puritan but has to be that of a libertine—someone, say, like the Earl of Rochester. Yet Puritan and libertine were more closely allied than we are in the habit of supposing. The libertine of Marvell's day was not a pagan suckled in a creed outworn. He had almost certainly been brought up on the Ten Commandments and the Apostle's Creed. In short, he was typically a lapsed Christian, whether now cynical, indifferent to, or defiant of, his heritage. Yet it would be difficult for him to expunge completely what he had been brought up to believe and that to which his society still gave more than lip-service.

As I have already suggested, the general tone of Marvell's poem is not precisely classical. When Catullus reminds his Lesbia that both will eventually have to descend into everlasting night, the note sounded is different. *Nox est perpetua una dormienda* is sufficiently somber to give urgency to his plea that Lesbia give him her love while she may. But Catullus' description of that perpetual night as one in which one must sleep forever mitigates much of its horror. He does not mention the grave-worm nor the lady's "virginity" being "tried" by it.

In sum, the lover in "To His Coy Mistress," in spite of his

brilliant rhetoric, highflown compliment, urbanity and grace, impresses me, I repeat, as a desperate man, though his desperation is held under firm control.

II

Time pervades "The Garden" as well as "To His Coy Mistress." The man whose thoughts constitute the poem is very much conscious of time, even though in this poem he is stepping out of its hurrying blast.

The poem begins on a note of surprise, happy surprise at what the speaker has just discovered when he enters the garden precincts: quiet and innocence. Clearly he has heretofore failed to find them in the "busie Companies of Men" or, as stanzas 3 and 4 indicate, in the society of women and the attendant disappointments in love. His discovery of quiet and innocence is as surprising to him as it is welcome. How else account for the tone of "Fair quiet, have I found thee here, / And innocence thy sister dear!" The note is one of almost shocked relief.

To assess correctly the dramatic situation out of which the garden meditation arises—whether or not we indulge the fancy that the man speaking is the lover of "To His Coy Mistress"—allows us to take in the proper spirit the teasing of the ladies that occupies stanzas 3 and 4. A literal reading would make the speaker a misogynist or at least a very sour Puritan. Though he is here sardonic about romantic love, this disillusioned lover is not a man with a settled dislike for women.

Praise of the beauty of trees and plants to the disparagement of woman's beauty brings up once more the subject of "vegetable Love." Some commentators on "To His Coy Mistress" have been apprehensive that "vegetable Love" might make the modern reader envisage a cabbage—Gilbert and Sullivan's Bunthorne, one remembers, pretends to a "passion of a vegetable fashion" and meditates on a dalliance with a "not too French French bean." They therefore take pains to point out that Marvell refers only to the "vegetative soul," the vital principle of the plant world. The next highest was the "animal soul," the animating principle of animal life. Man alone possessed the highest in the hierarchy, a "rational soul."

This is all true enough, but the concession hardly diminishes the disparagement contained in "vegetable Love." Things animated by no more than a vegetative soul constitute the very lowest rung of animate nature. The lover speaking to his coy mistress is properly contemptuous of a love that, like a plant, even a centuries-old yew or redwood, can do little more than keep growing and propagating itself. He asks for a love that has fire and passion.

What, then, does one make of the love for trees, fruit, and flowers professed in "The Garden"? How seriously—even setting aside the mocking reference in "To His Coy Mistress"—can we accept the assertion?

If we indulge a little further the supposition that the person speaking to his coy mistress is the person now admiring the garden, we may say that after having failed to convince his mistress, he is now venting his pique. In any case, his ironic assessment of the conventional tributes to female beauty plainly does not come from indifference or inexperience. This complainer against women has been very likely one of the "Fond Lovers" at whose folly he now smiles.

Still, there is more to his mood in the garden than mere revulsion from an unrequited love. It springs from genuine joy. To this man Nature is not only delightful in itself but points to delights beyond itself. It hints of a peace and innocence that transcends the mortal world. The lusts of the animal soul, of the "am'rous birds of prey," are here replaced by the contemplations of the rational soul, the bird with "silver wings" that in "The Garden" prepares itself "for longer flight."

In "The Garden" the speaker's attitude thus shifts from amused reflections on the folly and self-deception of men to happy surprise and glad relief at discovering—almost accidentally?—the true abode of quiet and innocence. Then his delight moves him toward a witty and high-spirited praise of plants and trees and to mockery of the conventional claims for female beauty. With a learned mock-seriousness, he brazens out his case with proofs fabricated by a reinterpretation of two classical myths.

With stanza 5, he gives himself up to the fruits and flowers of the garden's little paradise. He compares his "wondrous Life" to that led by an as yet sinless and solitary Adam during the first hours of his existence in an Eveless Eden. A brave new world, indeed, then made its impact on the first man's unjaded senses. It was a world to be raptly explored, devoid of distraction from anything—even the distraction provided by an Eve. Nature is regarded here as a completely yielding mistress. Her fruits and flowers offer themselves to him without hesitation or reservation. The vines press their grape clusters into his mouth. The melons before his feet seem to wish to make him stumble, and the very flowers ensnare him and pull him down upon the earth.

"Stumble," "ensnare," and "fall" are loaded terms in the Christian vocabulary. The words suggest seduction to sensual pleasures and a fall from grace; and indeed, the speaker soon becomes, like Adam, a fallen man. But Nature's embrace is innocent. There are no broken vows, jealousies, or aftermaths of remorse. (In stanza 8 the poet will develop this hint of the Eden story into an explicit reference.

Yet, though Marvell has deliberately invoked sexual overtones in describing the reception that Nature affords this grateful recipient of its peace, he never relaxes his grasp upon common sense and reality. The man in the garden has given himself up wholly to the garden's cool shade because it offers a blessed respite from the burden and heat of a day within a too-busy life. But we may be sure that he will not try to overstay his hour or so of bliss. The poem is no manifesto for primitivism. The man whose experience it describes has not resolved to live for the rest of his life in solitude as a hermit in some wilderness. He does not even suggest an anticipation of Wordsworth.

The conception of nature implied in "The Garden" seems to me thoroughly orthodox. Nature is innocent. In this poem it is not Plato's lower and grosser element on which the divine forms can only imperfectly make their imprint. It is certainly not the Manichaean's actively evil force at war with good. The natural world has been created good by a good Creator. It has not brought about man's fall. Man has only himself to blame for that. Having in mind the possible influence of his Puritanism on his poetry, we can say that on this particular issue Marvell is as orthodox as that other great Puritan, his friend, the John Milton of *Paradise Lost*. Neither holds nature in contempt.

Marvell does indeed regard the felicities that nature offers as lower than those available to the soul. A number of his poems confirm this, among them "A Dialogue Between the Resolved Soul, and Created Pleasure," "On a Drop of Dew," "Clorinda and Damon," "Thyrsis and Dorinda," and "A Dialogue Between the Soul and Body." Yet one notices that in this last-named poem the poet allows the body to make a good case for itself, even allows the body the final word—and what a telling word it is. The body argues that it is not the body that corrupts the soul, but the soul the body:

What but a Soul could have the wit
To build me up for Sin so fit.
So Architects do square and hew
Green Trees that in the Forest grew.

The body, like the trees praised in "The Garden" for their "lovely green," would, if left to itself, fulfill its own possibilities instinctively and innocently. It is the "Tyrannic Soul" that frustrates and tortures it.

One learns to respect the solid intellectual and theological base that undergirds such poems. That the poems are so based has much to do with their structural coherence and furnishes the grounding for the pointed applications of Marvell's serious wit. One might observe that even "To His Coy Mistress" can be fitted to this same theological base. For if one puts the highest valuation on the pleasures of the body, then one had indeed better seize the day and enjoy those pleasures now. They perish with the perishing of the body. One would be foolish to expect them in an afterlife, for the Scriptures are very specific on this point: in the Christian heaven there is no more marriage or giving in marriage. If one does not believe in an afterlife or, even if he does, sets highest value on the fulfillment of bodily desires, then the argument made to the coy mistress is sound.

The best evidence that the speaker of "The Garden" regards the pleasures of nature as in themselves innocent is to be found in stanza 6, where the body's delight in nature does not distract the rational soul from its higher pleasure. Indeed, it is when the body is appeased and innocently happy that the mind can "[Withdraw] into its happiness" (stanza 6). This pleasure peculiar to the rational soul points toward a transcendence that is fully developed in the final stanzas of the poem. The garden's quiet joys allow the contemplative man to become for a moment a disembodied soul and to gain some sense of what the joyful freedom of pure spirit is.

Yet how carefully Marvell manages the tone. Instead of the high spirits and hyperbole of some of the earlier stanzas or the ironic teasing in others, in stanza 7 he is precise, restrained, careful not to overstate. The Soul, like an uncaged bird, flies only a little way from the body—goes no further than a nearby bough, where "it sits, and sings, / Then Whets, and combs its silver Wings." The image is beautifully apt: it catches the soul's timidity at being outside its familiar habitation, the joy that makes it sing, and its almost childlike pleasure in the discovery that it has silver wings, wings now preened in a sort of innocent vanity.

Stanza 7 provides a nice example of Marvell's classic restraint. Even at this high point of the experience, the metaphor used makes very moderate claims. The soul is allowed no more than a glimpse of its future bliss. It dares not presume on its spiritual powers. The poet is even very practical in justifying its actions in spreading its wings. Now is the time to prepare for the "longer flight" that some day, permanently separated from the body, it must take. When Marvell is thoroughly serious, his assertions are invariably moderate and credible.

The next stanza (8) resumes the banter we have heard earlier. In stanza 6 the speaker has perversely inverted the classic myths of Apollo's pursuit of Daphne and Pan's pursuit of Syrinx; now in stanza 8 he turns upside down the Biblical account of Eve's creation. God gave Eve to Adam not because he needed a suitable helpmeet, but because God thought his delicious solitude entirely too good for a mere mortal to enjoy (as if Marvell were unaware that Adam became mortal only *after* the creation of Eve and the breaking of God's express command, the act that brought death into the world and all our woe). But Marvell is quite cheerful in his irreverence. He can hardly be trying to delude his readers, saturated as they were in the Scriptures. His case for the delights of solitude is transparently specious.

In the next and final stanza of the poem, however, classic moderation again asserts itself. If he is playful in proposing that " 'twas beyond a Mortal's share" to live alone in the earthly paradise, he is very properly serious in implying, as the poem closes, that it is indeed beyond any mortal's share to live continually in the full light of eternity. If one could do that, he would have ceased to be mortal.

Our meditator on the garden's delights has by now clearly reentered the world of time. How do we know this? From, among other things, the reference to the sundial in the final stanza. The numerals of this dial consist of artfully shaped beds of flowers. Such a chronometer is, of course, thoroughly appropriate to the garden. Nevertheless, it is a timepiece, and it reminds us that time has never stopped its motion even during an experience which has seemed a blessed respite from it.

The "industrious" bee, it is claimed, consults the clock for the time of day, and the sun duly moves through his twelve signs ("fragrant Zodiak") of the dial just as he moves through the heavenly zodiac in the course that makes up the year. Thus, the fact of time—winged chariot or no—is acknowledged. Mortal man escapes time only in brief blessed intervals, and even those escapes are finally illusory except as they possibly point to some future state. But to the contemplative man depicted in "The Garden," time is not terrifying, for *his* time does not eventually lose itself in vast deserts of eternity. For him there waits beyond time an eternity in a realm of joy that no earthly garden can do more than suggest.

III

"To His Coy Mistress" and "The Garden" are remarkable poems, but it is not remarkable that one and the same poet could write them. They reflect, to be sure, differing views of time and eternity, but they have much in common in the ideas they touch upon. In any case, they are not declarations of faith but presentations of two differing world-views, dramatizations made by a poet who, though suffused with the Christian sense of mortality and the ethic it implies, also knew his classics well and had evidently read them with sympathy.

Like a great many men of his age, Marvell was concerned to incorporate into the Christian scheme as much as possible of classical wisdom. When he chose, he could also treat with understanding and dramatic sympathy the great classical literary forms, not only as frames of reference, but as representing time-honored classical attitudes toward life and death. He makes such a presentation in "To His Coy Mistress." But as I have suggested earlier, even this pagan-classical poem bears more than a trace of Christian and even Puritan feeling, particularly in the references to death. Marvell had never lived in that happy pagan time when, as Théophile Gautier conceived it, the skeleton was unseen. Like John Webster, even in a love poem Marvell "saw the skull beneath the skin." The Christian alloy hardens the classical metal with a touch of medieval horror. It adds force to the poem's argument and gives it a sharper edge.

On the evidence of the two poems we have been comparing, Marvell was not a man who was unable to make up his mind or a waverer between commitments or a trimmer. The poems tell quite another story: they reveal a fair-mindedness, an awareness of alternatives, a sensitivity to the complexity of issues. Marvell's mind is a mind of the late Renaissance at its best. He is learned, thoroughly at home with the earlier literature of the West. He is familiar with classical philosophy as well as Christian theology. He regards both as constituting a valuable inheritance. His aim is to assimilate their lore and to develop, as far as is possible, a synthesis that will take the whole of human experience—animal and rational, active and contemplative, playful and sober, hawk and singing bird—into account.

GEORGE deFOREST LORD

Folklore and Myth in *Paradise Regain'd*[1]

Despite the austere manner in which it seems to eschew the traditional mythic allusions of epic, *Paradise Regain'd* may be seen as a deeply symbolic version of Joseph Campbell's "monomyth," an archetypal pattern in which the hero "ventures forth from the world of common day into a region of supernatural wonder"; then encounters and wins, with divine help, a victory over "fabulous forms"; and "comes back from this mysterious adventure with the power to bestow boons on his fellow man."[2]

Following another of Campbell's suggestions, we can see *Paradise Regain'd* as combining elements of the fairy-tale hero with its primary emphasis on Jesus as the ultimate hero of myth:

> Typically, the hero of the fairy tale achieves a domestic, microcosmic triumph, and the hero of myth a world-historical macrocosmic triumph: whereas the former—the youngest or despised child who becomes the master of extraordinary powers—prevails over his personal oppressors, the latter brings back from his adventures the means for the regeneration of his society as a whole.[3]

The "domestic microcosmic" aspect of *Paradise Regain'd* is evident, inter alia, in the innocence and ignorance and youth of the hero. Although Jesus asserts, in his first meditations, his early aversion to "childish play" and dedication to "public good," he sets out without any idea of how he is to fulfill the ultimate role of which he is, nevertheless, assured:

> To rescue *Israel* from the *Roman* yoke,
> Then to subdue and quell o'er all the earth,
> Brute violence and proud Tyrannic pow'r,
> Till truth were freed and equity restor'd.
> [1.217–20]

His ignorance and lack of power and submissiveness imply something like the initial weakness of the young would-be redeemer of folk tale, as does his dependence on his mother, a virtual matriarch, in the absence of his father, for what little information he has about his mission:

> These growing thoughts my mother soon perceiving
> By words at times cast forth, inly rejoic'd,
> And said to me apart: high are thy thoughts
> O Son, but nourish them and let them soar
> To what height sacred virtue and true worth
> Can raise them, though above example high;
> By matchless deeds express they matchless Sire.
>
> [1.227–33]

In his unannounced departure from home to undertake the inward adventure of self-discovery in the wilderness and in going back to his mother in the end—"he unobserv'd / Home to his mother's house private returned—Jesus is tracing the monomyth in the essentially private and domestic mode of the fairy tale. To be sure, both the "growing thoughts" she fosters and the single, approving theophany of the Father, who announces impersonally and laconically (according to Satan's report), "This is my son Belov'd, in him am pleas'd"[4] sustain Jesus as he tries to fathom the perplexed question of his identity as "Son of God" (an identity Satan will also claim for himself), and he never questions the public end to which his career is dedicated, only the means.

The uncertainty about Jesus' specific mission and the means to its accomplishment is compounded by Milton's resolute confinement of the action of *Paradise Regain'd* to his inward psychomachia. From the public point of view, represented mainly by his mother and his discomfited disciples, he achieves nothing. They are kept ignorant of the whole adventure. The negative way of his quest, through denial and privation, qualifies Jesus as more quintessentially "private" than any of his predecessors in privation, such as Odysseus or Guyon.

Thus the "adventures" of Milton's hero are microcosmic as far as the public is concerned, and we readers alone are privileged to share with Milton a knowledge of the Son's secret quest. His actions, in the context of the epic tradition, are inactions; his return home at the end of the poem something less than an anticlimax—a return, apparently, to the status quo ante that appears to deflate the great expectations he had shared with his mother and to abrogate the implications of his Father's annunciation at the Jordan. It is interesting to try to imagine the homecoming scene:

> Mother: Where did you go?
> Son: Out.
> Mother: What did you do?
> Son: Nothing.

Perhaps one of the implied conditions of the Son's inward quest is that its successful achievement must remain a secret, shared only by God and Satan, until the proper time for the beginning of his active ministry comes round. Possibly Milton felt that for the Son to divulge his inner triumph *to anyone* would somehow have tainted it. Jesus, in the necessarily private mode of his experience, is deprived of the privilege of sharing his self-revelation. The austere manner in which it is presented to us is counter to the rich celebratory style with which epic normally records heroic deeds. In any case, Milton achieves in *Paradise Regain'd* the ultimate instance of the heroism of inaction that had engaged him throughout his career: in *Comus*, "Upon his Blindness," *Lycidas, Paradise Lost, Samson Agonistes,* and other works.

Paradise Regain'd is a fairy-tale version of the monomyth in other respects. At the risk of sounding like a perverse Stephen Dedalus, I would observe that Jesus in this story is, like many folklore heroes, the youngest son. He is, moreover, the youngest of three and thus enjoys that special position of apparent inferiority and real inner strength that third sons in fairy tales often occupy. As Son incarnate he is a figure distinctly different from and, for the time being, separate from the Son of *Paradise Lost,* the "Second Omnipotence" (6.684). Of this omnipotent, omniscient figure the Son incarnate of *Paradise Regain'd* knows little, since, like other mortals he is in most respects confined to seeing the divine through a glass, darkly. Satan is not alone in regarding him as distinct and separate from that Son who with "his fierce thunder drove us to the deep" (1.90) and shares his perplexity with his fellow devils:

> Who this is we must learn, for man he seems
> In all his lineaments, though in his face
> The glimpses of his Father's glory shine.
>
> [1.91]

The Son of *Paradise Regain'd* is likewise confined to knowledge of the Old Testament and, like Satan, to uncertain predictions about the future. In knowledge, then, the contestants are evenly matched, and Satan's uncertainty about the Son's identity is a demonic version of the Son's own uncertainty. The critical difference between them, I hasten to add, lies in Satan's compulsive and vain pursuit of knowledge about his opponent as distinct from the Son's imperturbable faith in the adequacy of whatever knowledge God vouchsafes him. On the eve of his ordeal he declares:

> And now by some strong motion I am led
> Into this wilderness, to what intent
> I learn not yet; perhaps I need not know;
> For what concerns my knowledge God reveals.
>
> [1.291–94]

This serene resignation, unhesitatingly supported by faith, is reflected in Jesus' quiet, unemphatic, laconic responses to Satan:

> Who brought me hither
> Will bring me hence, no other Guide I seek.
>
> [1.335–36]

> Why dost thou then suggest to me distrust,
> Knowing who I am, as I know who thou art?
>
> [1.355–56]

> Thy coming hither, though I know thy scope,
> I bid not or forbid; do as thou find'st
> Permission from above, thou canst not more.
>
> [1.494–96]

They all had need, I as thou seest have none.
                    [2.318]

Thy pompous Delicacies I contemn,
And count thy specious gifts no gifts but guiles.
                    [2.390–91]

Shall I seek glory, then, as vain men seek,
Oft not deserv'd? I seek not mine, but his
Who sent me, and thereby witness whence I am.
                    [3.105–07]

But what concerns it thee when I begin
My everlasting Kingdom? Why art thou
Solicitous? What moves thy inquisition?
Know'st thou not that my rising is thy fall,
And my promotion will be thy destruction?
                    [3.198–201]

In all these instances Jesus counters Satan's relentless attempts to
goad him into action or to declare his messianic intentions with an
intelligent brevity of speech that instantly exposes the fraudulent
motive behind the temptation. The encounters have their comic
aspect, as the obsessed Satan, in Bergsonian fashion, repeats and
repeats his vain gambits and suffers one pratfall after another. The
encounters dramatize the foredoomed failure of a lying and imprisoned intelligence to enthrall a free one. The effect is to keep Satan in
a state of frantic uncertainty that reaches its highest pitch when
Christ rejects the benefits of Greek philosophy with this devastating
response,

Think not but that I know these things: or think
I know them not; not therefore am I short
Of knowing what I ought: he who receives
Light from above, from the fountain of light,
No other doctrine needs, though granted true.
                    [4.286–90]

The Son's gnomic utterances express essential truth unadorned, and
his longer speeches, almost devoid of imagery and rhetorical com-

plexity, also imply an innocence that can express itself artlessly. Against this artlessness Satan's more figurative and involuted style is powerless.

Satan's desire for knowledge of the Son is, as I have said, in the service of his compulsion to convert him from trust in God to a premature exercise of his destined messianic role. The "wiser" older brother, we might say, tries to subvert the secret strength of the younger, which is essentially beyond his comprehension. Such jealousy is a persistent element in folklore, as one sees in Cinderella and her older half-sisters, in Cordelia and her two evil older sisters, in Joseph and his brothers, and in many other cases. Satan's machinations are bound to fail, if only because he cannot dissociate knowledge from the corrupting, self-serving exercise of power, and he is therefore incapable of recognizing the Word incarnate. As in *Comus* and *Samson Agonistes* this hero is never seriously tempted, and the interest of his career lies elsewhere than in the drama of temptation. The suspenseless, virtually actionless character of his encounters is characteristically Miltonic, implying that the human spirit is the arena where any real action occurs. If there is a dramatic element in *Paradise Regain'd,* it may be found in the Son's gradual self-definition, culminating in a sudden, blinding self-revelation. It may also be found, in Jung's terms, in the dramatized encounter between the Son, considered as self, and Satan, considered as ego. A similar relationship can be seen in Cordelia in conflict with Regan and Goneril. Although Satan and Regan and Goneril are older, they have never developed beyond the infantile ego, which can relate to others only in terms of its own drives, and therefore cannot comprehend that infinitely larger entity, the achieved self. Thus too, as in countless fairy tales, *As You Like It* among them, the despised and often dispossessed youngest child defeats his evil older brother, even though the older brother seems to have the power to arrange things pretty much as he likes. For Milton and Shakespeare worldly power is anatomized as weakness and other-worldly weakness as the only real strength.

An even more important fairy-tale aspect of the relation of Jesus and Satan is seen in the main model for *Paradise Regain'd,* the Book of Job. Whereas Satan proposes the testing of Job and has divine permission to afflict him in any way he wishes, the Father in *Paradise Regain'd* takes the initiative in offspring Jesus to Satan as a subject for temptation. In both texts the Father withdraws during the trial of his favorite son, and Satan becomes his surrogate. In folklore terms this apparently harsh paternal behavior would correspond to that stage in the young hero's development at which the father is seen as an ogre. Job's wife and friends seem bent on persuading him to take such a view, but they fail. The idea, of course, never occurs to Jesus, because his faith is founded upon an unshakable trust in the divine goodness. Job's God finally speaks to him, though incomprehensibly, out of the whirlwind, but the only direct communication Jesus has with the Father is the brief theophany at the River Jordan. In view of Jesus' divine nature, that is sufficient. Unlike Job, the Son is given no rewards at the end of the poem, the point being, I suppose, that there is nothing the Father could give him that he lacks. The Son's final utterance on the pinnacle of the temple, "It is written, thou shalt not tempt the Lord thy God," is an impersonal declaration in his Father's words of the underlying truth which Satan has labored to destroy. As Jesus utters them, the words apply equally to himself and to Satan, but the accompanying miracle, which he does not anticipate, gives them a further and astounding application to himself. In refusing to tempt God, Jesus manifests the truth that he *is* God. Poised dizzily on the spire of the temple with, one would imagine, his arms outstretched to maintain his balance, the concluding ordeal of the Son is to symbolize the New Testament figure of the crucified Jesus triumphantly raised upon the apex of the Old Testament.

II

We may now look back to trace other elements of the monomyth in its microcosmic, fairy-tale form in *Paradise Regain'd* in a way that may shed light on the vexed question of its genre.

The opening lines that imitate through Spenser the discarded proem of the *Aeneid* imply, in the "Virgilian progression," Milton's adherence to a threefold poetic career from pastoral, through georgic, to epic:

> I who erewhile the happy Garden sung
> By one man's disobedience lost, now sing
> Recover'd Paradise to all mankind,
> By one man's firm obedience fully tried
> Through all temptation and the Tempter foil'd
> In all his wiles, defeated and repuls't,
> And Eden rais'd in the waste Wilderness.

"The happy Garden" emphasizes the pastoral aspects of *Paradise Lost,* but the prelapsarian labors of Adam and Eve in "lopping and propping" their garden and their arduous labors after the Fall, whether in Adam's sweaty toil to win his bread or in Eve's birth-labors, imply the georgic tradition, going back to Hesiod's *Works and Days* and summed up in the Virgilian phrase, *labor improbus.* "The happy Garden," lost "by one man's disobedience," gives place, in *Paradise Regain'd,* to "the waste Wilderness," an inversion of Eden's "wilderness of sweets." Now, Milton seems to say, we come to the true epic, the recovery of Paradise "to all mankind" through the unmatched heroic achievement of "one man's firm obedience fully tried / Through all temptation" and the "raising" of Eden in compensation for its earlier "razing."

Paradise Regain'd thus completes the central myth of loss and redemption projected in *Paradise Lost* from its very beginning and affirmed emphatically at its close in Michael's final promise to Adam of "a paradise within thee happier far." Once the enclosed garden of Eden is seen as an irrecoverable and *local* paradise, the way is open for Adam and Eve to take the first steps in the human saga that will lead to the mission of Jesus in the wilderness. Like them he *wanders,* the verb suggesting resignation.

If *Paradise Regain'd* is to be construed in some ways as the culminating epic in Milton's career, we must try to understand why its style is so austere that it succeeds in excluding many of the features of epic: heroic *action,* divine interventions, allusiveness, sublimity of style, and figurative richness. The repression of these grand aspects of the traditional epic is clearly appropriate to the

themes of privacy and deprivation that provide the thematic keynote
to Jesus' ordeal. The negative way is reflected in the privations of
this chastened style. The style also suggests the essential humility of
Jesus and corresponds to the fairy-tale aspect of the solitary adventures of a little-known youth. Finally, by directing our attention
toward the inward journey, a meditation in process, the austerity
annuls the outer copiousness and richness of setting that are appropriate to traditional epic. The polychromatic garden gives place to a
monochromatic desert. The fecundity of Eden yields to the sterility
of the Transjordanian wilderness. The total effect is to contract the
infite variety of *Paradise Lost* into a desolate and largely featureless
milieu in which topographical features are almost entirely irrelevant.

The Son's forty-day journey differs from the voyages of Odysseus
or Gilgamesh or Aeneas or Dante or Beowulf or Satan (in *Paradise
Lost*) in having no geographical goal. His point of departure is the
Jordan where he was baptized, but the time is not specified:

> So they in heav'n their Odes and Vigils tun'd.
> Meanwhile the Son of God, who yet some days
> Lodg'd in *Bethabara,* where *John* baptiz'd,
> Musing and much revolving in his breast,
> How best the mighty work he might begin
> Of Savior to mankind, and which way first
> Publish his Godlike office now mature,
> One day forth walk'd alone, the Spirit leading,
> And his deep thoughts, the better to converse
> With solitude, till far from track of men,
> Thought following thought, and step by step led on,
> He enter'd now the bordering Desert wild,
> And with dark shades and rocks environ'd round,
> His holy meditations thus pursu'd.
>   [1.183–95]

The many present participles contribute to the rapt, musing mood
of this passage and suggest the passivity of the traveler. "One day"
he walked forth alone: the temporal vagueness is augmented by the
line "He enter'd now the bordering Desert wild." When is now? It's
when he entered the desert. Temporal vagueness here suggests the

"once upon a time" with which all fairy tales begin, and it discounts the importance of chronology. In the forty days that follow, chronology is all but forgotten, and place, to the extent that it is described at all, does not mark progression in a journey; its notations are purely symbolic or for atmosphere, the Son's "holy meditations" being interrupted only by nightfall or by Satan's visitations. Such *places,* in most instances, are not *placed,* being unconnected by time or movement or geographical relation to any other "places." It is inner time and place that matter, as Jesus meditates on the time and place and manner in which he may "first / Publish his Godlike office now mature," a public event that does not occur in the poem and which constitutes a prelude to his destined career. His inward journey, then, has nothing to do with the times or places where events occur, except for the culminating pinnacle of the temple. The passage, in its simplicity, may seem to anticipate the style of Wordsworth on one of his reflective excursions into the natural scene except that it is quite devoid of Wordsworth's unceasing interest in the natural scene. Jesus' detachment from his milieu is another major manifestation of the intense inward focus of his experience.

Outwardly the emptiness and topographical bleakness of the wilderness reflect both the privacy and the privation of the hero's quest. Inwardly, it may serve in this case, as it often does in both fairy tale and myth, as, in Campbell's words, "a free field for the projection of unconscious content."[5] In emptying himself of will and submitting to a blank and undifferentiated environment, in exposing himself to Satanic suggestion, Jesus also submits to the repertory of visions and ideas projected on that blankness by the Satanic imagination. In his sharing of these visions, despite his resolute rejection of the implications Satan finds in them, must there not be, in Jesus' own imagination, a degree of participation? For him as well as for the Tempter, they have meaning and interest. Were he utterly indifferent to them, the whole experience would be meaningless, and he would not be moved, as he sometimes is, to make extended analytical rejections of the motives for action Satan fallaciously claims for them. In response to Satan's argument that it is the Son's urgent duty to seize "Occasion's forelock" and assert himself as Messiah, Jesus defines his role with compelling cogency and force:

> All things are best fulfill'd in their due time,
> And time there is for all things. Truth hath said:
> If of my reign Prophetic Writ hath told
> That it shall never end, so when begin
> The Father in his purpose hath decreed,
> He in whose hand all times and seasons roll.
> What if he hath decreed that I shall first
> Be tried in humble state, and things adverse,
> By tribulations, injuries, insults,
> Contempts, and scorns, and snares, and violence,
> Suffering, abstaining, quietly expecting
> Without distrust or doubt, that he may know
> What I can suffer, how obey? who best
> Can suffer, best can do, best reign, who first
> Well hath obey'd; just trial e'er I merit
> My exaltation without change or end.
>
> [3.182–97]

Repeatedly, Satan projects a polychromatic and animated image of one culture or another, crammed with exotic names and compelling details. He is a geographer and historian, the custodian, as it were, of time and place. Invariably, however, Jesus nonsuits his gambit by rejecting the temptation to seize the time and place for the beginning of his career, and his language is as insistently abstract as Satan's is specific. Despite its austerity, however, the Son's style has a sinuous, interconnected clarity and an intellectual tightness whose sublime simplicity cancels Satan's virtuosity. Since Satan has intimations of his doom, and since the Son's reign will be eternal, Satan's point of view is limited to specific historical opportunities which the Son can serenely refuse. Offers of power, of fancied strange delights, and threats of violence cannot shake his twofold piety as Son of God and Son of Man.

At key moments in the poem the wilderness through which the Son wanders is presented as a maze or labyrinth. And so it must seem to one fixated on time, space, and goal, like Satan:

> The way he came not having mark'd, return
> Was difficult, by human steps untrod;
> And he still on was led, but with such thoughts
> Accompani'd of things past and to come
> Lodg'd in his Breast, as well might recommend
> Such solitude before choicest Society.
>   [1.297–302]

Dwelling amongst untrodden ways, this second Adam tests his progenitor's admission to the independent-minded Eve that "solitude is sometimes best society" (*Paradise Lost* 9.249); unlike Eve, who is "amazed" by the physical and rhetorical involutions of the Serpent, the Son, with Providence his guide, never questions the validity of the route he follows. Though isolated and physically disoriented in the wasteland, Jesus nonetheless proves Satan's vain boast in *Paradise Lost* that "the mind is its own place" in the calm confidence he evinces: "Who brought me hither / Will bring me home, no other guide I seek" (1.335), and he reminds Satan of his ghastly discovery that he is "never more in Hell than when in Heaven" (*Paradise Lost* 1.420). "Oracles are ceast," he declares and continues:

> And thou no more with Pomp and Sacrifice
> Shall be inquir'd at Delphos or elsewhere,
> At least in vain, for they shall find thee mute.
> God hath now sent his living oracle
> Into the World to teach his final will,
> And sends his spirit of Truth henceforth to dwell
> In pious hearts, an inward Oracle
> To all truth requisite for men to know.
>   [1.457–64]

In dismissing oracles like "Delphos," Jesus is differentiating himself from a long line of epic heroes whose rites of passage require a guided visit in pursuit of visionary or oracular knowledge in the underworld, as Odysseus visits Tiresias, Aeneas, the Sybil and the spirit of Anchises, as Dante traverses Hell with Virgil, or as Guyon descends to the care of Mammon. In the wilderness Jesus thus enacts the double role of the heroic seeker of truth and as the source of "all truth requisite for men to know." "Place," again, is displaced, and the ancient identification of Delphi as the navel of the world is replaced with the Christian revelation of the oracle within. Thus Jesus' rite of passage is distinguished from all others in being a descent into the truth within himself, the individuation there achieved being independent, virtually, of the time or place where it occurs. His enunciation of this truth exposes Satan's essential unreality:

> To whom our Saviour with unalter'd brow.
> Thy coming hither, though I know thy scope,
> I bid not or Forbid; do as thou find'st
> Permission from above; thou canst not more.
> He added not; and Satan bowing low
> His grey dissimulation, disappear'd
> Into thin air diffus'd; for now began
> Night with her sullen wing to double-shade
> The Desert; Fowls in thir clay nests were couch't;
> And now wild Beasts came forth the wood to roam.
> [1.493–502]

These lines, which end book 1, typify a pervasive characteristic of Milton's wilderness setting. It is low and earth-bound and largely two-dimensional. There is one scene in Heaven, two devilish consistories held somewhere in the air, and a brief apotheosis when Jesus is borne up by flights of angels from the pinnacle of the temple, but the earth-bound milieu, eschewing the upward and downward sublimities of action in *Paradise Lost,* reflects the persistently humble vision of Jesus' *via negativa,* as well as the peripatetic meditative mode of his quest. In addition to this incidental observation, one might note the negative quality of the scene. Into this monochromatic landscape doubly-shaded at nightfall the Prince of Hell, now, in Milton's brilliant phrase "a gray dissimulation . . . disappears into thin air diffus'd," assuming, or being absorbed into, the insubstantiality of his new status as Prince of the Air. Even birds nest on the ground. What little energy is left in the waning light is transferred rather perfunctorily to unspecified wild beasts who now "come forth the woods to roam." We are witnessing them through the serenely indifferent eye of the Son. All the conventional elements of romantic horror are here, as in countless scenes in Spenser's fairy land, or in *Macbeth's* spine-chilling "Light thickens, and the crow makes wing / To the rooky wood," but Milton somehow contrives to divest them of horror. The tone, like the scene, does not reflect but, rather, absorbs the horror, leaving the Savior "unalter'd."

That Jesus does not "alter" in response to any of the temptations again suggests that, unlike other heroes undergoing rites of passage, his individuation has already been achieved before the story begins. The self into which he descends at the outset of his meditations is perfect and fully formed. His ordeal is then a matter of self-discovery rather than self-fulfillment.

The Tempter, in the first encounter, according to Campbell's monomyth, may be seen as a "threshold guardian" on the borders of a zone of magnified power. Beyond him "is darkness, the unknown, and danger; just as beyond the parental watch is danger to the infant and beyond the protection of his society danger to the member of the tribe."[6] Jesus is capable of converting this zone of danger to beneficial uses, whereas a more conventional hero would jeopardize not only himself but his "tribe," as does Eve in her solitary excursion. As threshold guardian and Prince of the Air, Satan has power over space and time, moving the Son of God up and down and around at will and simultaneously exchanging his gray dissimulation (reminiscent of Archimago) for a repertory of ephemeral identities that counterpoint the Son's unchanging self. Satan, as the quintessential ego, is fundamentally unchanged through all his metamorphoses, a threshold guardian through whom Jesus passes as easily as Alice going through the looking glass.

If Jesus has already achieved the fundamental goal of true selfhood before the events of *Paradise Regain'd* begin, the poem may seem to lack action, to amount to little more than a series of demonstrations of his spiritual perfection, with all the activity left to that energetic virtuoso, Satan. On the other hand, the main action of the poem may, paradoxically, be a kind of inaction, Jesus' persistent determination to refrain from untimely or inappropriate deeds. If, as we have seen, according to Campbell, the fairy-tale hero "achieves a domestic, microcosmic triumph," this occurs in Jesus' private interior victory. If the hero of myth achieves "a world-wide macrocosmic triumph," this is the inevitable and undoubted consequence of Jesus' secret victory. The fact that Milton utterly ignores Jesus' active career indicates his conviction that it is the destined sequel to his ordeal in the desert.

The series of temptations must then be regarded as moments in a process of self-discovery. "Wand'ring the woody maze" for forty days of total deprivation, he undergoes the temptation to turn stones into food (and thus enact the social gospel of charity), the manifold temptations of the banquet (2.302–405), the offer of wealth and political power to redeem Israel (2.406–86), of glory (3.1–144), of "zeal and duty" in assuming the throne of David (3.145–250), of world empire (3.251–443), of Roman "wealth and power, / Civility of Manners, Arts, and Arms, / And long Renown" (4.44–194), and the rich delights of Greek culture (4.195–366). Milton is thus recapitulating major episodes in the epic tradition that he is radically revising, and Satan's attitude toward such achievements is quite orthodox, according to tradition. After Greece fails, "quite at a loss, for all his darts were spent" (4.366), Satan now turns to other strategies to shake his steadfast victim. Returning him to the wilderness ("What dost thou in this world?") he employs all the special effects in his repertory to harrass and disturb the Son with darkness, cold, ugly dreams, thunder, "fierce rain with lightning mixt, water with fire / In ruin reconcil'd," hurricane winds, "infernal ghosts and hellish furies," who howl, yell, and shriek and brandish fiery darts. But these Dantean apparitions are, like the dismal night of their occurrence and the impresario conducting them, "unsubstantial" (399). On the fair morning that ensues, the Son answers Satan's solicitous inquiries with a stroke of deflating *sprezzatura,* "Mee worse than wet thou find'st not" (4.486). Clearly, there is dramatic interest in the interplay between Satan's versatile arts and the artlessness of the Son's rejoinders. Perhaps, on the other hand, the Son's artlessness is the art that conceals art in the spontaneous simplicity of truth.

This last encounter with specious terrors and double darkness is a hyperbolic reprise of the first, and the two episodes bracket the seven temptations enumerated above—analogues, perhaps, for the seven deadly sins—isolating the visionary mode of Christ's ordeal in the wasteland from events in the "real" world that precede and follow them: the Son's baptism and his triumphant stand on the pinnacle of the temple.

Incarnation has cut the Son off from all direct access to the Father (except for the epiphany at Jordan), and the action of the poem consists, finally, of the gradual discovery, through essentially *human* resources, of the nature of his career as Son of God and savior of mankind. The climax on the temple spire is a culminating revelation of his divine identity, one in which the Logos moves beyond the realm of discursive language and debate to an almost wordless epiphanic mode. His rescue and succor by the angels is outside the framework of the action proper, and a nine-word coda brings him back to the point of his departure: "hee unobserv'd / Home to his Mother's house private return'd." Unlike other heroes of the monomyth, the hero of *Paradise Regain'd* undertakes a dark voyage in which space, time, direction, and destination are sublimely indifferent matters. In fact, that they should be sublimely indifferent is essential to the successful completion of his quest. From a public standpoint, he has achieved nothing. From Milton's point of view of the *via negativa* as the essential way he has fulfilled his quest so perfectly that not a trace of it can be discerned at the poem's end except by those who have the privilege of sharing Milton's vision.

III

From this brief survey of questions about the genre, hero, action, and style—all interrelated—the main conclusion I would draw is that *Paradise Regain'd* is an epic poem that modifies radically traditional aspects of epic. The career of the meditative hero, outwardly inactive, must be rendered in a style shorn to a large extent of those qualities that contribute to the grandeur of traditional epic: rich and elaborate imagery (there are almost no similes in the poem);

classical allusions; rhetorical, metrical and syntactical inversions, suspensions, and variations; and sensuous sound patterns that have so much to do with the incantatory and sonorous effects of the *Aeneid* or *Paradise Lost*. Vocabulary is abbreviated. The diction is chastened.

All such tendencies toward a lower and more austere style appear most conspicuously in the passages of narration and in the speeches of the Son. Since Satan's speeches are repeated invitations to regress into an inappropriate and outmoded course of heroic deeds, his language tends to be more conventionally epic. The temptations he offers recreate experiences and deeds that are central to earlier epic: prowess in battle, self-glorification, elaborate banquets, the advancement of an ethnic or national destiny, even the great philosophical and literary achievements of ancient Greece, which undergird so much of *Paradise Lost*. An outstanding example is Satan's animated account of Rome:

> Many a fair Edifice besides, more like
> Houses of Gods (so well I have dispos'd
> My Airy Microscope) thou mayst behold
> Outside and inside both, pillars and roofs
> Carv'd work, the hand of fam'd Artificers
> In Cedar, Marble, Ivory or Gold.
> Thence to the gates cast round thine eye, and see
> What conflux issuing forth or ent'ring in,
> Praetors, Proconsuls to thir Provinces
> Hasting or on return, in robes of State:
> Lictors and rods, the ensigns of thir power,
> Legions and Cohorts, turms of horse and wings:
> Or Embassies from Regions far remote
> In various habits on the *Appian* road,
> Or on th'*Aemilian*, some from farthest South,
> *Syene*, and where the shadow both way falls,
> *Meroe, Nilotic* Isle, and more to West,
> The Realm of *Bocchus* to the Blackmoor Sea.
>
> [4.55-72]

These seventeen lines are part of a sentence that extends to twenty-four lines and forms but a small portion of Satan's sinuous, variegated representation of Rome, geographical, political, architectural. The epic emphasis on power, wealth, and culture, to which we can supply analogues in *Paradise Lost,* lacks, nevertheless, a point of view or a vision that can discern any real meaning behind all this busy detail. The accounts of Hell and Eden in *Paradise Lost* are unified by coherent values, but this vivid heterogeneity is devoid of insight. Satan can supply an engaging tableau of imperial Rome with a lot of going and coming, and he can indicate its greatness by a catalogue of exotic places it governs, but there is no inkling of any authentic purpose or principle underlying this inventory. "Fam'd Artificers" reminds us of Daedalus, but neither the most famous of ancient mythopoeic artists nor any artist or work of art is here. Rome is an ornamental and inchoate anthill rendered in a relentlessly materialistic mode. This fact is obviously related to the fact that everything Satan has to offer is specious, but it also suggests that, in the course of his degeneration, the heroic rebel has lost whatever appreciation of the heroic he once had. Jesus unerringly exposes the hollowness of the proffered vision:

> Embassies thou show'st
> From Nations far and nigh; what honor that,
> But tedious waste of time to sit and hear
> So many hollow compliments and lies,
> Outlandish flatteries?
> [4.120–26]

Satan's speech has some of the momentum and cumulative power that is so evident in *Paradise Lost,* with "the sense variously drawn out from one verse into another," but the offer ends in anticlimax as he feebly concludes, "to me the power / Is given, and by that right I give it thee" (4.103–104). Since he cannot identify any recognizable value in the gift, he is easily put down by the laconic simplicity of Jesus' rejoinder.

Jesus' apparent inaction, "deeds above heroic / Though in secret done," is heroic conduct of a unique order, since on it depends not only the restoration or preservation of a nation but the opportunity for the salvation of all mankind. Only an achievement of this illimitable magnitude can cancel the consequences of the Fall. Unlike Adam and Eve, the hero of such an ordeal must achieve his triumph by resolutely denying himself any form of self-assertion, any impulse of the will that might lead him to exercise his power prematurely and to some limited end, like Achilles or Aeneas. The acts of Jesus, then, are a disciplined and total obedience to the promptings of the Spirit. With the rejection of traditional modes of heroic behavior, Milton must find a form and a style that adequately express the *via humilis* Jesus pursues. By blending the usual epic preoccupation with the sublime with the humbler mode of the fairy tale, the dualistic style of *Paradise Regain'd* is responsive both to the secret character of Jesus' ordeal and to its enormous implications for the human race. Jesus' experiences in the wilderness are folklore and romance, much influenced by Spenser, while their public consequences are celebrated in the sublime epic quality of the climactic epiphany and apotheosis.

The interaction of Satan's and Jesus' styles may be understood as a conflict between two modes of epic value, patterned, it may be, on the aggressive and self-assertive Achilles as contrasted with the much-enduring Odysseus. Whatever power he still has, no one has ever thought of Satan as the hero of this poem. Irrevocably lost, his vain hope is to subvert the power of the new hero through secondhand versions of old epic temptations. Ultimately the difference in their utterances goes beyond modes of action, values, and styles. Satan's speeches are self-defeating because they are solely governed by the egoistic compulsion towards personal power, and they mask a hollowness. Jesus' speeches are always in the service of belief in the transpersonal divine, and he speaks with the sublime simplicity of truth.

Since the hero of *Paradise Regain'd* is both man and God incarnate, his self-defining ordeal, though limited to a sense of divine destiny that is inscrutable and to a purely human wisdom supported by that sense of destiny, puts him in a different class of heroes from the others under consideration. Nonetheless, the privation of knowledge about his divine career places Jesus firmly among the other heroic figures whose rites of passage yield revelations that lead to the founding of a new society or the restoration of an old one. Thus *Paradise Regain'd,* in following the self-denying and self-fulfilling career of Odysseus and in rejecting systematically the collective, secular vision of the Roman empire, exemplifies strong affinities with the mythical *via negativa* of the *Odyssey* and the *Inferno* while rejecting implicitly both the philosophical individualism of later Greek culture and the collectivistic power-centered social principles of the *Aeneid*. In his final epic Milton succeeded brilliantly in producing a hero apparently stripped of heroic power, in the mode of the unestablished No Man of Homer's *Odyssey*, who exemplifies, through his total rejection of appeals to the ego and his profound, godlike, aversion to the exercise of godlike power toward inadequate ends, the essential reality of the achieved self.

Paradise Regain'd then appears to be a palinode of the *Aeneid* and a liberal, enfranchised version of the *Inferno*. For a variety of reasons Milton does not need the elaborate Augustinian and Thomistic categories of sin that are deployed so elaborately in the *Inferno*. While Milton's hero encounters more tempting versions of damnation than Dante can depict in his hideously stratified Hell, the Son of God, in his divine intuitions, his wise passiveness, his established self, is indifferent to the manifold modes of sin, except to the degree that Satan offers opportunities for him to violate his mission. Milton's Jesus, as God incarnate, exemplifies the *coincidentia oppositorum*, the union of opposites, that establish him as the ultimately heroic antihero.

NOTES

1. Barbara Lewalski's article on *Paradise Regain'd* provides a brilliant historical and critical account of the poem and a judicious and full survey of the best secondary sources. It is to be found in *A Milton Encyclopedia*, edited by William B. Hunter, Jr., John T. Shawcross, and John M. Steadman, 8 vols. (Lewisburg and London: Bucknell University Press, 1978–80), 6: 80–105. The associate editors of the *Encyclopedia* are Purvis E. Boyette and Leonard Nathanson.

2. *The Hero with a Thousand Faces* (Princeton: Princeton University Press, 1968), p. 38. This is the edition cited throughout.

3. The text of *Paradise Regained* used throughout is John Milton, *Paradise Regained, the Minor Poems, and Samson Agonistes,* ed. Merritt Y. Hughes (New York: Odyssey, 1957).

4. The omission of the "I" suggests that either God or Satan is repressing the full identity of the great I AM, complicating Jesus' problems of self-discovery.

5. Campbell, *The Hero with a Thousand Faces,* p. 79.

6. Ibid., pp. 77–78.

BALACHANDRA RAJAN

Milton, Humanism, and the Concept of Piety

It may seem odd to begin a paper on humanism by suggesting that the term may be outgrowing its usefulness. "Outgrown" is a word deliberately used. A term is made useful by its discriminatory force, its significant separation of what it admits from what it excludes. Humanism today, detached from the constraints of a specific location in history, can appear as a habit of mind, as a response to life, as a commitment to man the measure, and in other forms of inchoate expansiveness. I prefer to write of Christian humanism and will begin by observing that while humanism is undermined by what it will not leave out, Christian humanism is threatened by what it is obliged to contain. This effort at containment is, ironically, among the principal characteristics by which Christian humanism is to be identified. To say that a Christian humanist is a Christian who is also a humanist is not necessarily a sign of mental exhaustion. It is rather to draw attention to an array of latent antipathies to which the term directs us through its own composition. The nature of Christian humanism is most strikingly affirmed by the manner in which it resists its own dissolution.

The forces of dissolution are familiar and it is no contribution to scholarship to list them; but their cumulative importance can be underestimated when they are considered as they frequently are in isolation. Since humanism began as a renegotiation of relationships with the classical past, the initial confrontation is between the classical and the Christian. While the former can be typologically accommodated to the latter it does not follow that the Christian humanist is totally at ease with the accommodation. The structures of supersession must be opened not simply to demonstrate a theory, but to reconcile one's own divided loyalties. Moreover the conversation with antiquity that humanism institutes acknowledges the uses of the past and must eventually acknowledge the capacity of that past to provide enlightenment in its own right and not simply to furnish examples of providentially planned obsolescence. We cannot wholly avoid the historical view of knowledge as the sum of the best that has been known and taught. However, the view of truth as historically acquired is in potential collision with a view of the truth as synchronic, final and revealed, as given to rather than found by the understanding. This conflict between the historical and the visionary is deepened by the Reformation insistence on the inward, overwhelming, and self-authenticating nature of the experience of relationship with the divine.

A humanist is committed to a strong sense of the capacity of reason to know the nature of things. A Christian humanist is committed to an equally strong sense of the limits of reason. He is a humanist haunted by the dangers of humanism. The knowable must be approached with confidence and the unknowable with piety. The line between must be drawn by a capability that overreached itself in the primal event that initiated history and which is continually seeking to reenact its own hybris.

Adam, when first seen in the garden, is described as formed for contemplation and valor. His hyacinthine locks (Professor Frye advises us to attend to the hair style, not the coloring)[1] have Apollonian evocations, though we must remember that in *Lycidas* the sanguine flower is inscribed with woe. Milton is concerned throughout his literary life with the relationship between contemplation and action, between what Sidney calls "well-knowing" and "well-doing."[2] He is concerned with the latent divergence that Arnold develops into the opposition between Hebrew and Hellene. It is not too much to say that Milton renegotiates the balance between withdrawal and involvement at every stage of his work, redefining the terms themselves as he reconsiders the interplay betwen them. The reconsideration does not take place in the abstract and is not carried forward simply as an aesthetic exercise. Rather it pits the answering force of the mind against the assault of circumstance, gaining the mind's "new acquist" of "true experience" (*Samson Agonistes*, 1755–56)[3] from the events of history, whether tragic or fortunate.

Contemplation may be that "contemplation of created things" by which we ascend the scale of nature to God (*Paradise Lost*, 5.507–12). The scale, as we know, is the articulating structure in Milton's program of education.[4] Contemplation thus directed enables the soul to possess itself of true virtue, but since well-knowing is the basis of well-doing, it also fits us to perform "justly, skilfully and magnanimously, all the offices both private and publike of peace and war."[5] The civic paradigm is joined to the platonic love of the good and that conjunction might be said to be humanist; but both are joined in their turn to Christian dependence on "the heavenly grace of faith."[6] Contemplation can also be more inward looking. In the Ignatian meditative tradition as defined by Louis Martz,[7] the self learns to know and make itself by finding its location within the divine drama and seeking its salvation through that drama. In the Protestant tradition, as defined by Barbara Lewalski,[8] the self makes itself by seeking and recognizing the image of God from which it has turned away as its quintessential nature. Both are forms of piety which can consort with humanism, but one tends to lead to an individual understanding. The other is more capable of being collectivized because it acknowledges a universal psychic history, which, if it is creatively directed, will complete the circle of exile and return.

The image of God offers us one more area in which the Christian awareness of the limits of reason encircles the classical confidence in man's rational capability. In classical thought man's erect stature is the sign of that gift of reason which distinguishes him from the lesser creation. Pico in his oration on the dignity of man, suggests that the power of choice rather than the gift of reason may be the distinctive manifestation of our uniqueness.[9] When God tells us in *Paradise Lost* that "reason also is choice" (3.108) and Milton tells us in *Areopagitica* that "reason is but choosing" (2:527), these two possibilities are being synthesized in a manner crucial to Milton's scheme of understanding. In Christian thought, however (including Milton's thought), man's erect stature is taken as the sign of the presence of the divine image in himself. The image includes reason but is more than reason. It is to be found according to Ussher "in the perfection of his [Adam's] Nature, indued with Reason and Will, rightly disposed in Holiness and Righteousness, Wisdom and Truth; and accordingly framing all Notions and Actions, both inward and outward."[10] Milton describes the image in his prose as consisting of "Wisdom, Purity, Justice, and rule over all creatures" (2:587). He describes it in his poetry as composed by "Truth Wisdom Sanctitude severe and pure" placed in "true filial freedom" and thus bestowing "true authority" (*Paradise Lost,* 4.293–95). At first glance it may seem that these descriptions differ from their classical precedents only by being more inclusive, by involving the whole man rather than a single faculty. But an image is inexorably sustained by that which it images: it can have no existence apart from its source. The very word declares a concept of creative dependence, which for Milton finds its ideal form in a sonship of which "true filial freedom" is the manifestation. Such a dependence is not necessarily consonant with humanist confidence in the sufficiency of reason.

In indicating some of the contentions that lie in the nature of Christian humanism it is not intended to mobilize these elements in battle array under the respective banners of humanism and Christianity. The aim is rather to suggest that a Christian humanist mind, because of its mixed persuasions, cannot avoid being involved in these contentions. It also cannot choose like Browne's "great amphibium" to live in "divided and distinguished worlds."[11] Nevertheless the one world in which it has to live is constituted rather than sundered by the forces to which it is subject. The integrity achieved is all the more characteristic and possibly all the more enduring because it is built out of a complex of resistances. Uneasy alliances, or, in Yeats's phrase, "a brief forgiveness between opposites,"[12] remain the stuff out of which literature is made. Professor Patrides, for example, has advised us of the precarious copresence in Spenser of hedonism and a "predominantly" Christian

outlook.[13] As he goes on to suggest, similar potential disjunctions
are kept in relationship, largely by virtuosity, in the writings of
Bembo, Michelangelo, and Tasso. Indeed one of the strongest
statements of the poetics of contrariety is made by Tasso when he
argues that "the art of composing a poem resembles the nature of
the universe, which is composed of contraries." One can almost see
Blake waiting in the wings of this remark. Tasso then maintains
that "such a variety will be so much the more marvellous as it brings
with it a measure of difficulty, almost impossibility."[14] "Imperious
impulse held all together" is Yeats's characteristic finding about the
period.[15]

Piety in a Christian humanist thus takes its place amid a
complex of forces by which its own content may be modified. One
might think at the outset that piety, because of its meditative
connotations, is among the forces that are inward-pulling, that it is
concerned less with structures of meaning in the external world and
in the disclosures of history than with understanding achieved
within the self and carried into a narrow range of personal relationships. But piety can also be outward-looking, and when Tasso
commends the piety of Aeneas as a heroic virtue, he is thinking of
the behavior of a man among men in the performance of a historic
obligation, as well as of the behavior of a man before the gods.[16]
Earlier, in the *Discourses on the Heroic Poem,* he has explicitly told us
that "epic illustriousness is based on lofty military valour and the
magnanimous resolve to die, on piety, religion and deeds alight
with these virtues."[17] Milton's reference in *The Reason of Church
Government* to "the deeds and triumphs of just and pious Nations
doing valiantly in faith against the enemies of Christ" (1:817) is not
without its remembrances of Tasso's statement.

Milton's own placing of piety is difficult to establish to the
satisfaction of the scholar because his uses of the term are not very
frequent. It occurs only twice in the *De Doctrina,* where one would
expect it to occur most often. Elsewhere in the prose and in the
poetry it can be found considerably more frequently but relatively
seldom in significant usages.[18] Obviously the concept is not to be
pursued with a concordance. It must be apprehended via its reflec-

tions in such terms as, for example, "purity" and "justice" and "uprightness" and more particularly as the coming together of that cluster of qualities in which the image of God in man is made manifest.

To be pious is presumably to be dedicated to virtue and so *Comus* takes its place among the adumbrations of piety, providing us with yet another reading of the lady's much-discussed chastity. The downward metamorphosis in *Comus,* as befits a play built on the hinge of a classical myth, is the undoing of "reason's mintage / Character'd in the face" (529–30). Since the "human countenance" in *Comus* is "the express resemblance of the Gods" (68–69), we are anticipating later and fuller statements; but given the decorum of the masque, the anticipations have to be restrained. If we look at the downward transformation in the light of a subsequent understanding we can note that Milton, appropriately enough in celebrating wedded love, finds that love is "Founded in reason, loyal, just and pure" (*Paradise Lost,* 4.755). The attributes of the image are clearly present here, and loyalty is fidelity to the creative dependence made real in that image. In *Comus* chastity likewise means the soul's loyalty to what the Elder Brother describes as "the divine property of her first being" (469). As for purity, it was Plotinus who established the idea of the virtues as purifications,[19] and the Elder Brother possibly has that in mind when he describes the upward metamorphosis as a purifying process (453–63). Loyalty to the divine principle can mean the sloughing away of what does not adhere to that principle, but Milton's view is that all created things offer themselves naturally to the ground of their own being if they are reproportioned and realigned. Purification implies not rejection but reorientation, though it follows from this that one must identify and reject incitements to disorientation, however plausible. The lady is perhaps not entirely successful in expounding this proposition, but she does embody that other Miltonic proposition declaring that we are purified by trial and that trial is by what is contrary. The mind is directed away from error and confirmed in its proper structure only by having that structure challenged. Christ in *Paradise Regain'd* must be exercised in the wilderness, as unexercised virtue is dismissed in *Areopagitica* as "unbreath'd" and in *Samson Agonistes* even patience is the "exercise of saints" and the "trial of their fortitude."[20] The idea that the mind makes itself and does not merely announce itself in action is not unique to Milton. "Knowledge," Ben Jonson tells us, "is the action of the soul."[21] Hence the "unpolluted temple of the mind" and the temple of "th'upright heart and pure" (*Comus*, 461; *Paradise Lost*, 1.18)—the places of piety where the image knows its source—become significant only in so far as they are kept in being by a living commitment, maintained within and, if necessary, against, the world.

Seen thus, piety is a public as well as a personal quality. A nation emerges and indeed can only emerge from what Ann Radzinowicz terms a purified consensus.[22] Social and even theological engineering cannot achieve a truly just society though Milton does write, in his early elation, as if the reforming of ecclesiastical institutions could liberate by itself the natural creativity that is gathered in the elect nation, England. When Milton tells us that the happiness of a nation "consists in true Religion, Piety, Justice, Prudence, Temperance, Fortitude and the Contempt of Avarice and Ambition" (11:340) he is arguing that collective self-management is an extension of individual self-discipline. The regenerate and pious individual, the gathered church, and the organic society and—according to Professor Walzer—even the new model army[23] reflect each other and call upon each other for their being. All of them, to endure, must be related images of the same source.

In *The Reason of Church Government* Milton contemplates celebrating "the victorious agonies of Martyrs and Saints" as well as "the deeds and triumphs of just and pious Nations doing valiantly in faith against the enemies of Christ." Resistance is commemorated in the language of high achievement, but Milton shows his awareness of the norms of history when he also speaks of deploring "the general relapses of Kingdoms and States from justice and God's true worship" (11:817). It should be noted that to stand fast, to refrain from seizing the day, to maintain the pious integrity of the self resolutely against the assault of evil, to patiently await the divine deliverance, are responses that declare themselves in Milton's

work as early as *How soon hath Time* and *Comus*. The later work does
not renounce the earlier; it merely accepts the underlining of events.
Nevertheless the pious nation of which Milton speaks, the just
individuals joined in a creative society, are an important ideal in
Milton's middle prose and an ideal which does seem within the
grasp of history.

Milton's mind is too inclusive for him not to sound the note of
warning even in the elation of his early prose. "The doore of grace,"
he writes, anticipating the doors of heaven in *Paradise Lost*," "turnes
upon smooth hinges wide opening to send out, but soon shutting to
recall the precious offers of mercy to a nation." God was "at the
door," however, in 1642, not knocking upon it but called by the
voice of his bride. It was the time of the just and pious nation
or—to use language only slightly different—of the "great and War-
like Nation, instructed and inur'd to the fervent and continuall
practice of *Truth* and *Righteousness*." *Areopagitica* moderates the
mood of elation for the view of truth as a fully formed entity,
self-evident to the eye of the understanding, it substitutes a view of
truth as gathered, sifted, and discriminated from error in ac-
cumulating and evolving acts of choice. Nevertheless the nationali-
zation of piety is very much part of the tone of *Areopagitica*. The
seeking enterprise is a collective enterprise. The torn body of Osiris
is put together by a society of believers for whom the act of remaking in the external world is almost the universalized statement of
the equivalent reconstitution of the divine image in themselves.[24]

Areopagitica is a crucial humanist statement not only because it
reaches outward to a creative society built upon a religious and
moral consensus but also because it reaches back through its firm
understanding of the making of truth as an evolutionary movement.
We come to what we know not by virtue of what we know. We
close up truth to truth, and each act of closing up is a further
discovery of structure. But the "homogeneal and proportionall"
body will only be fully known at the end of time, and the making of
truth is therefore coextensive with history. Reflection will indicate
that such a view is deeply humanist, not only in its social orientation and not simply because it admits the uses of the past but

because it goes further, making the past indispensable in the creative constitution of the present.

Areopagitica is Milton's maximum statement of involvement, of men making themselves and finding each other in acts of relationship that also remake society. Many have documented what follows, the solidifying frustration of the interregnum years, the invincible reluctance of England to become the second Israel. The nation "inured to the fervent and continual practice of truth and righteousness" becomes the nation "in good or bad Success, alike unteachable" (5:450). Not to retreat under the tauntings of history was impossible, but we have to ask ourselves how far the retreat was really carried. Christian humanism finds itself by balancing itself between the promptings of involvement and withdrawal. Involvement beyond a certain point is a surrender to the pragmatic and the politic. It can minimize to the point of near-obliteration the religious sense of creative dependence on a reality other than the secular. On the other hand, withdrawal beyond a certain point can result in virtual abandonment of the secular, taking its stand on the incompatibility of the two cities and on our inviolable membership of the true one. In either event, Christian humanism ceases to exist. One term of the paradox is devoured by the other.

As the historical imminence of the just nation dissipates itself, the inward persuasions of piety can be expected to strengthen. *Paradise Lost* is after all about its title. Yet it is also a reminder that the doors of grace, though not as wide open as they once were, are not and never will be closed. Milton's thought, moreover, is rich in adumbrations of patience and of waiting, of the apparent dominance of evil and of the right commitment resolutely pursued in the face of the world's mockery. It is tempting to argue that he does not change his mind but simply readjusts its balances. Yet, as has already been suggested, to readjust the mind beyond a certain point is to change it.

The failure of a revolution to which Milton committed so much of himself raised what remains a threatening question. Are not all revolutions born to be betrayed? The answer is that the only revolution that will not be betrayed is that resulting from the reconstitution of the individual upon the ground of his all-but-lost creativeness. By profoundly acknowledging his dependence upon the divine, by rebuilding his self around the acknowledgment, he can create a structure that is able to consolidate itself and that is not consumed in "eternal, restless change" (*Comus,* 595). Individuals who, by reaching out to divine grace, are embarked on a restoration of the divine image in themselves can find each other, learn from each other, and come together in a society based on a common commitment. But the number in that society is not to be predicted and the meaning of the enterprise can bear no relationship to the extent of its enrollment or the degree of its worldly success. This view can be described as defensive; but it is not as defensive as the post-Augustinian view that requires us to be in the world but not of it and to maintain our citizenship of another country in an environment inherently hostile to our loyalties.

The place of piety in this view is prescribed by *Paradise Lost* itself when, in its opening book, it sets up the temple of the "upright heart and pure" to contrast it with the mind as its own place, almost as if the hybris of humanism were being set against the humility of Christian understanding. Christ's first victory, as the poem depicts it, is partially imaged in "the deeds and triumphs of just and pious nations." His victory on the cross is imaged in "the victorious agonies of martyrs and saints." In returning yet once more to *The Reason of Church Government,* we note not only the continuities of Milton's thought, but the manner in which history may be discerned as the recurrent mirroring of two events, which are figures of eternity. The distinct nature of these events in time contrasts with their unity beyond time.[25] All that happens manifests the divine design, but the extremities of manifestation make it apparent that the world sets the conditions for our contention with the world. We may transform it at best or, at worst, refuse to be transformed by it. The outcome—whether it is creative change or creative resistance—must be built on the reconstitution of the individual mind as a place of piety, sanctity, and justice. Milton did not as Helen Gardner alleges "invent" the destruction of paradise;[26] but he uses that destruction like other signposts in his poem to point to the primacy of the interior kingdom and the initiating reality of the paradise within. "Tyranny must be" as Michael points out implacably, until the interior tyranny is ended (*Paradise Lost*, 12.90–96). A revolution can be no more than an insurrection if no revolution has taken place in the self.

The paradise within is not the mind's place but the place of the sanctified mind, freely dependent on the creative will of God. The question to be answered is whether the paradise within is any more than a pietistic retreat anchored to the divine but disconnected from or, at best, indifferent to the secular. It is hard to conclude that Milton is proposing the disintegration of the elect nation into a miscellany of hermits. Yet in that last exchange between teacher and student, Adam's recital and Michael's confirmation are strongly directed to specifying the terms of the renewed self rather than to indicating, however tentatively, the social and cultural extensions of that renewal. It is true that Michael exhorts Adam to add "deeds" to his "knowledge answerable" (12.581–82) and that the critic's heart bounds with relief at that liberating word. But the deeds seem to consist of adding faith, virtue, patience, temperance, and love to one's pietistic equipment or of performing certain wholly unspecified actions for which faith, virtue, temperance, and love are prerequisites. In any case the aim of the "deeds" seems to be to complete the structure of the paradise within rather than to apply that structure to the remaking of society and the nation. One is reminded of Eliot's formula of "prayer, observance, discipline, thought and action."[27] It is difficult to determine whether "action" comes rousingly at the end of the sequence or dangles limply at the end of the chain.

My own estimate is that Milton follows the inward pull of piety nearly as far as he can without dissolving the entity that is Christian humanism. The entity remains in being because Michael has followed the lesson that "Tyranny must be" with an eloquent outline of the direction that history can take if men remain loyal to the creative promise. Raphael had spoken of earth as possibly the shadow of heaven (5.574–76), and Michael forecasts the movement from "Shadowy types to truth" (12.303). Raphael had thought of body working up to spirit on the ontological scale, and Michael now sees the fleshly world giving way to the spiritual in the historical unfolding. Strict impositions can yield to free acceptances. Servile fear can give way to filial, to a sonship and a dependence spontaneously rising from a deep sense of the holy (5.478–79, 497; 12.300–306). It is a visionary statement but is not outside the limits of history if those who stand within history direct that history to its redemptive promise. The facts, however, are sadly different. Realism does not allow us to evade these facts, but to be overwhelmed by them is to show inadequate "patience." Michael, we must remember, undertakes to teach Adam true patience and the tempering of "joy with fear / And pious sorrow." The joy attaches itself to the visionary possibilities, the sorrow to the desecration of the ideal by the actual. But it is "pious sorrow." The basis of integrity remains. All is not lost to mourning.

Nevertheless it is a time to mourn. The earth which was created as the nucleus of perfection and which once hung "self-ballanct" and as it were, weightless on its center, now rolls through time "under her own waight groaning" (7.242; 12.539). The world goes on "to good malignant, to bad men benigne." Truth which was once strong next to the Almighty, is now in retreat "bestruck with slanderous darts." (12.535–38; 2:562–63). The nation, for whom a work doctrinal and exemplary was to be written, has dwindled to "fit audience through few." (1:815; 7:31). In such circumstances the poet-prophet is reduced to a citizen on the margins of society, the exiled conscience of that people whom he rebukes. It is not surprising that Milton elucidates the term "prophet" in *De Doctrina Christiana* as applying "not only to man able to foretell the future but also to anyone endowed with exceptional piety and wisdom for the purposes of teaching" (6:572). Christ as the "living oracle" who teaches God's "final will" is imaged in that "living oracle" which the "spirit of truth" becomes in "pious hearts." As a prophet, the poet must lament the "evil dayes" in which he has been chosen to live. As a teacher he must show the way of creativeness to those whom his judgment calls to account. It is not sufficient to endure the time. The man of piety must also work within it.

In the standard view of Milton's work, *Paradise Regain'd* is seen as the poem of furthest withdrawal, the apex of retreating refusals. Suggestions put forward by Arnold Stein, Barbara Lewalski, and Irene Samuel that the poem is rather a quest for identity, an advance into heroic knowledge, a definition of right action by disengagement from its parodies,[28] have more to be said for them individually and collectively. In establishing a model of Christian self-knowledge through these searchings and definitions, Christ is, as might be expected, resolutely consistent. Yet the very purity of the demonstration must question humanist assumptions of the possibility of a secular knowledge that does more than corroborate Christian understanding. One way of moderating the latent confrontation is to point out that Christ in *Paradise Regain'd* is concerned with salvation, not with culture. In addition, one may note that Christ is himself and not John Milton and that Christ's function in the poem is to establish what is quintessential in his nature through a properly worked-out structure of refusals. Christ's destiny outside the poem, on the other hand, is to transform the history from which he seems to have abstained, to complete the learning he seems to have rejected, and to act both creatively and decisively, notwithstanding his apparent denial of action. It is not the text but the reader who must bring into relationship the historical Christ and the Christ within the poem. Because of the confinements which the biblical account imposes the poem itself can only delineate the positive by its way of dismissal of the negative and therefore cannot be rich in opportunities for humanist statements. Nevertheless, when at a moment of deep frustration Satan asks Christ, "What does thou in this world?" (4.372), the reader should not complain that he does not know the answer.

In a poem designed in this way the logic of refusal is crucial and that logic must evolve in response to Satan's specific strategies of incitement. Since the Bible is helpfully brief about these strategies and since the elaborations, both literary and nonliterary, of Luke and Matthew provide no compelling organization of precedent, Milton has some room for maneuver. As Barbara Lewalski shows, he makes use of his opportunities to define by, Christ's resistances,

Christ's true roles as prophet, priest, and king.[29] He also moves us in the second temptation from the senses (the banquet), through the passions (Parthia and Rome), to the intellect (Athens). The progression characteristically invites us to look not just at what the whole man refuses, but also at what the whole man by virtue of his refusals accepts. The "retreating refusals" school does have something to be said for it. Christ is driven back by Satan's strategies. The purpose, from Satan's point of view, is to "corner" him or—to put it in current terms of merchandising—to make Christ the offer he cannot refuse. From Christ's "corner" the purpose is to ascertain the extent of the inessential, to discover what he can discard without threatening himself. Thus the banquet is refused in favor of a higher hunger. The higher hunger, as understood by Satan, is responded to by the offers of Parthia and Rome. The exterior kingdoms are then refused in favor of the kingdom of the mind, taking the hunger to a yet higher level. Satan, in a move of some dexterity, then offers Christ the kingdom of the mind. If the world is relinquished in favor of the mind and the mind is then offered it would seem that there is no other place to retreat to and that checkmate can confidently be called. Christ's response is profoundly consistent rather than dexterous. In rejecting Athens he simply points out that the mind is not its own place. "God attributes to place / No sanctity, if none be thither brought" is Michael's teaching to Adam (11.836–37). Christ affirms that sanctity and affirms it as final, quintessential, and not to be discarded. The kingdom of the mind can only be constituted by creative dependence on the will of God. In his nature, Satan cannot offer that dependence. He has therefore no alternative but to challenge it. In the third temptation he is broken on that challenge.

Paradise Regain'd is thus a tautly discovered definition of the true basis of piety. While it may not be finally antihumanist, it profoundly questions the hybris of humanism by calling for the ordering of learning by a standard that cannot be derived from learning, however extensive. While it does not renounce all action, its definition of those actions which it is fitting to undertake excludes most of the actions that are undertaken in this world. It is

not quietist since Christ was not a quietist. But it is a poem stead-
fastly severe in its exclusions.

In one of his many references to the Samson story, Milton tells
us that Samson "thought it not impious but pious to kill those
masters who were tyrants over his country, even though most of her
citizens did not balk at slavery." The quotation comes from the
First Defence (4:402). It is part of a justification for regicide which I
find intellectually frightening. I would prefer patience rather than
the sword to be the exercise of saints, and there are obvious dangers
when the sword is wielded by a minority with no mandate except its
own invincible sense of its election. Even in a more fictive world I
would not seek to put Samson forward as a model of piety, still less
as an example of Christian humanism. Nevertheless Samson does
carry into human perseverance the lesson which Adam learns from
Michael on the hill. Adam realizes that

> to obey is best
> And love with fear, the only God, to walk
> As in his presence, ever to observe
> His providence and on him sole depend.
>   [12.561–64]

Samson finally walks as if in God's presence, observes God's providence even though the apparent cost seems to be the humiliation of
his newly found strength and depends solely upon God, offering his
life to that dependence. God calls from the highest of hills in
Paradise Lost for "prayer, repentance and obedience due" (3.190–
91). Samson repents to the extent of profoundly acknowledging his
transgression and renders obedience as God requires it of his "faithful champion." According to Milton's play he stood "as one who
prayed" (*Samson Agonistes,* 1637). According to the *First Defence* "he
first made prayer to God for his aid" (4:407). I must emphasize that
Samson's act in the temple is not a triumph of purified selflessness, a
declaration of the soul lost in God. The mixed motives of service
and self-vindication remain equally present in his final words.
Nevertheless and almost because of his impurities, Samson is Miltonic man, embodying in human fallibility the paradigms that
Adam learns and Christ ideally substantiates. The play is a powerful

reminder that right knowing and right doing do not depend on being educated in Athens; it uses an Athenian form for this purpose.

Humanism is outward-looking, a rehabilitation of secular knowledge, which necessarily expands into the renewal of commerce between the mind and the world. Christian humanism restrains that expansion by insisting that the mind is what it is by virtue of its derivation from a higher principle. The new philosophy submits hypothesis to the test of evidence and so, in Bacon's phrase, "buckles and bowes the mind to the showes of things." The new religion responds to the new science by calling not on external facts but on an interior evidence to which both the shapes of institutions and the potential arrogance of the mind are buckled and bowed. Meditative practices, whether Ignatian or Protestant, commit the making of the self to an internal dialogue between man and his Creator. The events of sacred history, the educative testimony of the biblical record, locate the soul and guide it in its experiential seeking of itself. These cumulative inward persuasions, so prominent in seventeenth-century shapes of understanding, do not rule out the possibility of action; but action if it is not to be self-destructive must be shaped by certain standards, which must be maintained even if no action results from them. As far as Milton is concerned, the failure of the English revolution lends force to these inward propulsions. The primacy of the interior kingdom, always acknowledged as a structural fact, now becomes the main objective of individual and collective effort. The creative consequences for society and history of the achieving of that kingdom are not denied, but they are kept at an appropriate distance. First things must come first, and the events of the day underline the nature of those first things. If the just and pious nation is to be brought into being, it can only be brought into being on the just and pious ground of the individual mind—the image of God incarnate in the whole man and sustained by creative dependence on the divine will.

We have outlined an interplay of forces and it is necessary to note that Milton's mind moves within that interplay, abandoning none of its constituents, but accommodating itself to the force of external events and the momentum of its own evolving understanding. Within the field of relationships there will be statements that are quietist and others that rejoice in involvement. I do not wish to propose one settlement as superior to the others or to argue that the last settlement is the best. We are dealing not with absolute understandings but with ways of engagement with the world that the world urges upon us and within which we must stand and find the truth. Nevertheless *Areopagitica* is a text which seems to me to be distinctively located in the overall interplay. Its insistence that virtue must be exercised, its view of the exercise as collective rather than solitary, its understanding of the truth as gathered in the world rather than retrieved within the self bring together the historical and the visionary, the sacred and the secular, the interior seeking and the exterior making to an extent not possible with other patterns of settlement. But *Areopagitica* is the response to a certain historical moment, and its tempered confidence has to be surrounded by other dispositions of thought that address themselves more fully to the disillusionment of high expectations betrayed. The whole array of dispositions then becomes a response not only to a range of historical moments but to the rhythm of relationship between those moments. We are taught something by the totality which we could not be taught by any single work.

NOTES

1. Roland Frye, *Milton's Imagery and the Visual Arts* (Princeton: Princeton University Press, 1968), p. 268.

2. Philip Sidney, *A Defence of Poetry*, ed. J. A. Van Dorstein (London: Oxford University Press, 1966), p. 29.

3. All references to Milton's poetry are from *John Milton: Complete Poems and Major Prose*, ed. Merritt Y. Hughes (New York: Odyssey Press, 1957).

4. See Balachandra Rajan, "Simple, Sensuous and Passionate," *RES* 12 (1945), 289–301.

5. *Complete Prose Works*, ed. Don M. Wolfe et al. (New Haven: Yale University Press, 1953–), 11:380–81. All references to Milton's prose are from this edition.

6. Ibid.

7. Louis Martz, *The Poetry of Meditation* (New Haven: Yale University Press, 1954).

8. Barbara Lewalski, *Donne's Anniversaries and the Poetry of Praise* (Princeton: Princeton University Press, 1973), pp. 108–31; Barbara Lewalski, *Protestant Poetics and the Seventeenth-Century Religious Lyric* (Princeton: Princeton University Press, 1979); U. Milo Kaufmann, *"The Pilgrim's Progress" and Traditions in Puritan Meditation* (New Haven: Yale University Press, 1966). Given the distinctions made between image and likeness it is interesting to note Milton's reference to "that which is our beginning, regeneration, and happiest end, likeness to *God,* which in one word we call *godlines*" (*Complete Prose,* 11:571). "Of Education" defines the end of education as "regaining to know God aright, and out of that knowledge to love him, to imitate him and to be like him" (*Complete Prose,* 2:367).

9. Pico dell Mirandola, "Oration on the Dignity of Man," in *The Renaissance Philosophy of Man,* ed. Ernst Cassirer, Paul Oskar Kristeller, and John Herman Randall Jr. (Chicago: University of Chicago Press, 1948), p. 219.

10. Ussher, *A Body of Divinitie,* 8th ed. (London, 1702), p. 92.

11. Thomas Browne, *Religio Medici,* 1:34.

12. William B. Yeats, "On Baile's Strand," in *Collected Plays* (New York: Macmillan, 1952), p. 170.

13. Paper read at the North Central Renaissance Conference, Ann Arbor, November 1979.

14. Tasso, *Discourses on the Heroic Poem,* trans. Mariella Cavalchini and Irene Samuel (Oxford: Oxford University Press, Clarendon Press, 1973), p. 78. The corollary of the creation as the ideal poem is the godlike status of the poet. See Tasso, *Discourses,* p. 31, Sidney, *A Defence of Poetry,* ed. J. A. Van Dorstein, pp. 24–25.

15. *Autobiographies* (London: Macmillan, 1956), p. 291.

16. Tasso, *Discourses,* p. 44.

17. Ibid., p. 43.

18. The index to the Columbia University Press edition of Milton's works lists a total of sixty-four occurrences—five in the poetry and fifty-nine in the prose.

19. Plotinus, *Enneads* 1.6.6.

20. *Paradise Regain'd* 1.156; *Complete Prose,* 11:515; *Samson Agonistes* 1287–88.

21. "Timber or Discoveries," in *Ben Jonson. The Complete Poems*, ed. George Parfitt (Harmondsworth, England: Penguin, 1975), p. 399.

22. Ann Radzinowicz, *Toward "Samson Agonistes"* (Princeton: Princeton University Press, 1978), pp. 75–76.

23. Michael Walzer, *The Revolution of the Saints* (Cambridge: Cambridge University Press, 1965), pp. 270–97.

24. *Complete Prose* 1:797, 1:707, 1:616, 2:549–51. Balachandra Rajan, "Osiris and Urania," *Milton Studies* 13 (1979), 223–24.

25. The relationship between Christ's victories can be treated as a progress from shadowy types to truth, as stages in the education of the reader, as stages in the poem's formation as a self-revising artifact, or as limited declarations of a totality to which they provide cumulative access. Combinations of these views are possible. While my preference for the fourth view is implied in the language of the main text, I do not regard the question as settled.

26. Helen Gardner, *A Reading of "Paradise Lost"* (Oxford: Oxford University Press, Clarendon Press, 1965), pp. 80–81. Don Cameron Allen, *The Legend of Noah* (Urbana: University of Illinois Press, 1949).

27. T. S. Eliot, "The Dry Salvages," in *Four Quartets* (London: Faber and Faber, 1944), p. 33.

28. Arnold Stein, *Heroic Knowledge* (Minneapolis: University of Minnesota Press, 1957); Barbara Lewalski, *Milton's Brief Epic* (London: Methuen, 1966); Irene Samuel, "The Regaining of Paradise," in *The Prison and the Pinnacle,* ed. B. Rajan (Toronto: University of Toronto Press, 1973).

WILLIAM FROST

Translating Virgil, Douglas to Dryden: Some General Considerations

"In no country, I suppose," wrote George Gordon in 1930, "in the last four centuries has Virgil been so steadily translated as in England." During the first two of these four centuries—from Henry VIII to William III—England was the kind of evolving country (I shall argue) in which Virgilian influence, in translation as well as imitation, was apparently intrinsically appropriate. This was the period of England's emergence, with its unique self-consciousness, as a nation distinct from (though allied to) Europe; and it was also the crucible period in which England's national cultural institutions—religious, literary, and political—gradually took their modern shapes. To make my central point about Virgil's appropriateness during these two hundred years I shall draw on what I take to be the previously unrealized fact—at least, it has certainly been unrealized until recently by *me*—that from Gavin Douglas in 1513 to John Dryden in 1667 between fifty and sixty British translators completed versions of all or part of Virgil.[1] I shall begin by introducing representatives of this group as briefly as possible, then proceed to my argument about Virgil, England, and the last of the fifty-odd translators, Dryden, in relation to his so numerous predecessors.

The group includes three anonymous and still unidentified translators; six whose identity, concealed at the time, has come to light; five better known for other translations—Sandys's Ovid, May's Lucan, Fanshawe's Camoens, Stapylton's Juvenal, and Creech's Lucretius[2]—than for what they made of Virgil; twelve better known for original works than for *any* translation: Surrey,

Jonson, Crashaw, Vaughan, Waller, Howard, Cowley, Denham, Oldham, Temple, Dryden, and Addison; and at least three who markedly influenced translators of Virgil who came after them: Douglas, May, and Dryden.[3] In repect to form, not more than two used prose;[4] at least two—Surrey (blank verse) and Stanyhurst (classical hexameters)—were inventors or experimentalists; at least four—Jonson, Sandys, Waller, and Denham—contributed to the development of the heroic couplet; and a contrasting pair, Lisle in 1628 and Fanshawe twenty years later, looked back to Spenser for their inspiration. In respect to translating scope, three complete Virgils (*Eclogues, Georgics,* and *Aeneid*) existed by 1697: Ogilby's, Lauderdale's, and Dryden's (though Lauderdale's was not published in full till the eighteenth century). Separately from these, there had appeared three complete *Aeneid*s; three complete sets of the georgics; and four of the eclogues. In addition, some thirty-five translators had published a Virgilian fragment, an eclogue or georgic or two, or some part of the *Aeneid;* translation of this sort included Surrey's *Aeneid* 4 (1557) and 2 (1554); Stanyhurst's *Aeneid* 1–4 (1582); Jonson's fragment of 4 in *Poetaster* (1601); the Waller-Godolphin *Aeneid* 4 (1658); Harrington's Eclogues 1 and 9, plus *Aeneid* 1–6 (1658, 1659); and Denham's *Aeneid* 2 (1656) and 4 (1668).[5]

II

What drew these particular poets or versifiers to Virgil, of all authors? Was it that, as T. S. Eliot and more recently Frank Kermode have reminded us, Virgil was long considered the supreme classic, the *poeta,* master of the true poetic language by comparison to which all others are vernaculars?[6] I suggest that while this consideration may have played a part in drawing translators to Virgil's work, another was perhaps more significant: of all ancient poets much studied in the Renaissance and post-Renaissance, it is Virgil whose works are most easy and obvious to connect with the fortunes or misfortunes, the past and the future, of the nation to which he belonged—and this at the most critical turning point, the transition from republic to empire, in that nation's significant history. Rome in those days could be a paradigm for any developing commonwealth or kingdom, or even for any cult or system of beliefs; and Virgil—in his *Eclogues, Georgics,* and *Aeneid*—was nothing if not the poet of Rome. It is thus probably no accident that Virgil drew to himself, as political life revived in Europe after sixteen centuries, so many writers who were themselves personally committed to public involvements of a political, religious, or generally ideological kind.

These members included four privy councillors (Fanshawe, Howard, Lauderdale, and Mulgrave); at least six MPs (Wrothe, Digges, Waller, Lewkenor, Temple, and Addison) and one Irish MP's son (Stanyhurst); one bishop (Douglas); one monk (temporarily)—Stapylton; five priests, clergymen, or preachers (Stanyhurst, Brinsley, Biddle, Milbourne, and Sacheverell); at least one schoolmaster (Vicars); and upwards of a dozen individuals—including some of the foregoing—who took stands on matters of public controversy. It has been thought that one of these latter may have been Phaer, because he dedicated his *Aeneid* to Queen Mary Tudor; among the others Biddle, Brinsley, Stanyhurst, and Vicars wrote controversial religious works, Wrothe moved to impeach Charles I, Harrington argued during the Interregnum for a republic, Boys petitioned in 1660 for a free parliament, Duke concocted a lampoon on a popish plot informer named Bedloe and (probably) another on Titus Oates, Tate wrote most of *Absalom and Achitophel, Part II,* and Sacheverell preached the inflammatory sermon attacked in Defoe's "Shortest Way with the Dissenters." It is consequently not surprising that at least a dozen Virgilians found themselves, at one time or another, either in hot water or in close proximity to it. Douglas was ousted from his bishopric while visiting the English court, Brinsley was "persecuted by the bishop's officers" (a much later bishop),[7] Jonson was jailed for an anti-Scottish passage in *Eastward Hoe,* Biddle was often imprisoned, was once exiled to the Isles of Scilly, and had his books condemned to be burned. Waller was imprisoned, fined, and exiled for his part in "Waller's Plot" to deliver London to the royalists; Cowley prepared his poems for publication while in jail as a suspected spy; Crashaw died self-exiled in Italy; Boys, after submitting his petition for a free parliament, had to hide out to escape imprisonment; Harrington was committed to the Tower of London in 1661; Fanshawe was removed from his ambassadorship to Portugal for taking too much initiative in treaty-making without consulting London; Caryll was briefly imprisoned during the popish plot hysteria; Lauderdale, outlawed in 1694, died in unhappy circumstances in Paris; Sacheverell was impeached, convicted, and forbidden to preach for three years; and Tate, having lost his laureateship on George I's accession, later died impoverished in the Mint. It might be added that Surrey was beheaded, that Godolphin was shot dead while on active service for the royalists at the Battle of Shagford, and that Stafford was the son of Viscount Stafford, the most prominent victim of the popish plot.[8] Two, finally—perhaps the worst fate of all—were pilloried, by much better poets, for bad verse-writing: Ogilby in *Mac Flecknoe*—

> Let Father *Fleckno* fire thy mind with praise,
> And Uncle *Ogleby* thy envy raise

and Vicars in *Hudibras*—

> We should, as learned Poets use,
> Invoke th'assistance of some *Muse;* ...
> Thou that with Ale, or viler Liquors,
> Didst inspire *Withers, Pryn,* and *Vickars,*
> And force them, though it were in spight
> Of nature and their stars, to write; ...
> Canst make a Poet, spight of fate,
> And teach all people to translate;
> Though out of Languages in which
> They understand no part of speech—

a passage in which Butler also brings in, in a footnote, Harrington: "[Vicars] Translated *Virgils Aeneides* into as horrible a Travesty in earnest, as the French *Scaroon* did in Burlesque, and was out-done in his way by the Politique Author of *Oceana.*"

Here, however, Dryden's doubly alliterative use of Ogilby as a symbol of poetic ineptitude represents an aesthetic judgment by comparison to which Butler's should not be seriously taken as more than an ideological one. Ogilby is not in fact a notably more interesting poet than Dryden makes him sound, whereas both Vicars, "a minor master in the Jacobean manner," and Harrington, some of whose "terse forcible lines" have been found to be "his best merchandise,"[9] are by no means the total disasters the partisan Butler, in his hatred of any Presbyterian or republican tendencies, succeeds in implying.

So much for the sad fates, or narrow escapes, of several of the Virgilians. I have not meant to suggest that Virgil was to blame, or that these translators would have been better off had they never turned his pages; only that the kind of temperament that drew some of them to study him so closely seems also to have drawn them to involve themselves with their contemporary worlds in definite and even potentially dangerous ways.

A word more about three of these "involved" or "activist" translators. May, whose *Georgics* exerted a continuing influence on later Virgil-translators and whose Lucan made him generally famous (he even produced an admired Latin continuation of the *Pharsalia*), was alleged by his enemies to have been motivated to associate himself with the roundheads out of pique at not being chosen by the court to succeed Ben Jonson as poet laureate. However that may be, his association with them resulted in his becoming an important public figure as one of the two secretaries of the Long Parliament and also as its historian, an historian some have found more impartial even than Clarendon. As an activist, he can be contrasted with the theorist Harrington, author of the Utopian *Oceana* (1656), of whom one of his modern editors writes as follows:

> It is ironic that this Introduction should be necessary. Two hundred years ago one would hardly have presumed to "introduce" the political theory of James Harrington to an educated American audience. At the time of the American Revolution, just a century after their author's death, Harrington's writings, which had already exerted a profound influence on the governments of the proprietary colonies of Carolina, New Jersey, and Pennsylvania during the seventeenth century, reached the peak of their popularity in this country, and Harrington himself enjoyed among American political theorists and practitioners a reputation second only to that of John Locke... if one wishes to discover the original *rationale* of many of the characteristic features of the government of the United States—such, for instance, as the writ-

ten constitution, the secret ballot, the rotation of membership in the Senate—one must look not to *The Federalist* or to the other writings of our Founding Fathers, but rather to Harrington's *Commonwealth of Oceana.*[10]

As for John Denham, his closeness to politically significant happenings, his devotion to Virgil, and his determination that his own original poetry be seen, like Virgil's before him, as specifically rooted in the public concerns of his time—all these matters have been thoroughly documented. In 1638 John Hutchinson, future parliamentary general, governor of Nottingham, and regicide, married Lucy Apsley, sister of a contemporary of Denham's both at Trinity College, Oxford and later at Lincoln's Inn; she preserved in her commonplace book the manuscript of what is apparently an early draft of Denham's 1636 translation of *Aeneid* 2–6, from which he published, in revised form, *The Destruction of Troy* (most of *Aeneid* 2) in 1656. From this manuscript it can be determined that one of the revisions Denham made before publishing in 1656 changed a line in the translation so as to echo a line in his 1642 version of *Cooper's Hill;* and this was a line (2.307) translating a line (2.306) of the *Aeneid* in which Virgil himself had echoed a line in his own first georgic (1.325); thus Denham was deliberately categorizing *Cooper's Hill* as a modern georgic. But *Cooper's Hill* itself was adjusted over the course of time by its author to allude to changing national circumstances, just as Virgil's poetry was felt to have done: the 1642 *Cooper's Hill* implicitly advised subjects not to provoke their ruler to crush them without mercy, while the 1653 version (four years after Charles's execution) was rewritten so as to imply just such a picture of disharmony in the state as Virgil (whom Denham called "my old Master") had seen as following the assassination of Julius Caesar. Thus Denham, associating *Cooper's Hill* with Georgic 1 and *Aeneid* 2, suggested a connection between the circumstances of Charles's death and "the subsequent constitutional disorder."[11]

A final point: as with some other translators of Virgil, Denham's interest in the *res publica* had aspects both contemplative and more empirical. Elevated to public office after the restoration, he was responsible for launching, in the last years of his life, the career of a notable contributor to British civilization, Christopher Wren. In Denham's eyes the supreme power of the state was to be, ideally, the supreme detector and rewarder of creative power in the citizen: in his ode on Cowley's death he parallels the relation between Virgil and Augustus Caesar to that between Cowley and Charles I—"Both by two generous Princes lov'd."[12]

III

By comparison with his fifty or so predecessors, Dryden as a Virgilian stands out in at least three ways. He is the only one who produced both a very large body of Virgilian translation and a very large body of original works—verse, prose, and drama. He is the only one who all his life combined a career as the first poet of his age with a keen and steady involvement in the events and controversies of his time. Finally, he is the only one who, making translation itself a special kind of literary calling, associated himself with others in this work, encouraged or solicited their efforts, and became himself, in the last fifteen years of his life, as much a dynamic center of energy for the recapture of the classical past as Jonson had been for the production of the Jonsonian kind of original verse in his own last years. It is significant that one of Dryden's earliest poems congratulates a Virgil translator, Howard, on his version of *Aeneid* 4, and that one of the prefaces of his last decade, that to *Cleomenes* in 1692, acknowledges the dedication to him of Creech's translation of Horace eight years earlier.

Considering the translators of Virgil as a group, one might therefore predict that Dryden would be the sort to find several years of devotion to translating Virgil a congenial prospect; and if one looked—as many *have* looked—at his original poetry, plays, and essays for evidence in them of the influence of classical authors, it would be no surprise to find what is in fact the case: that Virgil was in his mind and often at the tip of his pen from his earliest days of authorship to the last years of his extended and vigorous life.

Relevant evidence is amply spread over the period of Dryden's productivity, from 1660 to 1697. It peaks in such Virgilian years as 1667 and 1693; but to simplify consideration of it I will present some facts only about the decade most readers might consider central to Dryden's own accomplishment as an original writer: namely, 1678–87. To begin with *Religio Laici* (1682): though Horace is perhaps the presiding *genius loci* for this poem, Virgilian associations in *Aeneid* 6.268–72, have been found for Dryden's splendid opening passage about travelers wandering by moonlight; and similar points can be made about other works of the decade. In a span of ten years, according to available studies by Dryden's editors, critics, and commentators, Virgil presents himself to the reader of Dryden at least eighty-one times, and not simply Virgil in general, who is mentioned at least twice in Dryden's prose of this period, but also all his major works, the *Eclogues* eleven times, the *Georgics* five, and the *Aeneid* with notable frequency: sixty-three times—an average suggesting that Dryden rarely went more than two months without being reminded of the *Aeneid*. His recurrences to that epic are scattered widely over most of its parts: he used book 6--much his favorite—sixteen times, book 2 ten, book 12 six, books 3, 7, and 10 five each, books 1, 4, and 5 four each, book 8 twice, and books 9 and 11 once each. Among his works of this decade, Virgilian touches occur twenty times in *The Hind and the Panther*, ten in *Mac Flecknoe*, eight in *Albion and Albanius*, seven each in *Absalom and Achitophel* and *Threnodia Augustalis*, three each in his *Preface to Sylvae*, "To Oldham," "Anne Killigrew," *All for Love*, and two other works (a play and an essay), twice in his *Troilus and Cressida*, and one each in *The Medall*, *Absalom and Achitophel Part II*, *The Duke of Guise*, and the *Letter to Etherege*. As for the kinds of appearances Virgil's works make in Dryden's, nine Virgilian passages are used as Latin mottoes, or parts of mottoes, for a work of Dryden's; nine others are quoted, also in Latin, in passages of his prose, like the *Preface to Sylvae*, or (once) in a scroll on a piece of stage scenery (in *Albion and Albanius*); and sixty-three occur at spots in his prose or verse which have been found to allude to, run parallel with, recall, echo, refer to, or be based on some specific *locus* in Virgil's poetry.[13]

Study of these allusions makes it clear that they are more than merely decorative displays of classical resourcefulness and that they often relate, at least obliquely, to Dryden's activity as a Virgil translator—an activity which had already begun during this decade with his contributions to the 1684 *Miscellany* and to *Sylvae* the next year. A significant passage in both these respects occurs in *The Hind and the Panther,* part 3, where in lines 766–85 the Panther, arguing against James II's presumed intention to reintroduce Catholicism more fully into England, draws an elaborate analogy, based on *Aeneid* 7, to Aeneas' attempt to marry Lavinia and thereby establish Trojan Lares and Penates—"Those household Poppits"—in Latinus' Italy. Here language alluding to 7.210–20, 229, and 239 may suggest that Dryden was already beginning to formulate translations of at least part of this book.

Elsewhere in *The Hind and the Panther* there is unmistakable evidence of Dryden's easy familiarity with earlier Virgil translation. At 3.1174, he makes the Buzzard (Gilbert Burnet) quote the famous catch phrase from *Aeneid* 2.50, *timeo Danaos et dona ferentes,* in almost exactly the same words as Harrington had used twenty-nine years earlier in his freewheeling version: "A *Greek* and bountiful forewarns me twice" (Dryden has merely changed "me" to "us"). In the 1650s, as Dryden may have been aware, there seems to have been a competition in ingenuity centering on the *timeo Danaos* aphorism. Publishing in 1656, Denham revised his earlier literal rendering, "The Grecians most when bringing guifts I feare" to the wittier "Their swords less danger carry than their gifts,"[14] and two years later Harrington was stimulated to create the line Dryden inserts into the Buzzard's mouth in *The Hind and the Panther.* That Dryden regarded it as actually *over*ingenious (and therefore all the more appropriate to the Buzzard's devious character) is shown by his own rendering in his complete Virgil a few years later. Preserving concision and force, he paraphrases radically:

Somewhat is sure design'd; by Fraud or Force;
Trust not their Presents, nor admit the Horse.
[II.62–63]

IV

A concluding illustration involves problems presented by the original, solutions of other translators, and the relevance of Dryden's own experience both as a student of translators and as an original (and often Virgilian) poet.

About to enter his last battle on Italian soil, Aeneas bids farewell to Ascanius, his son and successor, in terms only partly Homeric, terms deriving, in fact, more directly from the tragic dramatist Sophocles, whose unhappy protagonist Ajax Aeneas here echoes. To quote a modern critic of Virgil, Viktor Poeschl,

> In Aeneas' last words to Ascanius the poet restates, as it were, the hero's testament by foretelling the dark doom which will threaten him after Turnus' death:
>
>> From me, my son, he said, you may learn what is valor
>> and what is strenuous toil; as for what good fortune is,
>> others must teach you that.
>>
>>   [12.435]
>
> Disce, puer, virtutem ex me verumque laborem,
> Fortunam ex aliis.[15]

As Poeschl read the lines, Aeneas' tragic and heroic utterance amounts to saying, "Son, from me you can find out how the game is played; to find out how to win it, you'll have to look elsewhere." I say "as Poeschl reads the lines" not in order to question his understanding of them, which seems thoroughly consistent with Aeneas' character in the epic and with the situation at this point in book 12; but it is a fact that, as often with Virgil, the Latin, though pregnant with meaning, is so compressed that a rendering of more than simply the words, word by word, is required to transmit the force of the passage. Taken word by word, all the language yields is likely to be more or less what Mandelbaum gives us at this point:

> From me, my son, learn valor and true labor;
> From others learn of fortune—

a flat and flaccid version, even a little weaker (I think) than that of the predecessor whose work Dryden proclaimed he knew best,

Lauderdale:

> From me learn Vertue and the Art of War,
> From others Fortune take.

At least "Art of War" sharpens the impact of the first line beyond a lamely literal "true labor."

But what is an uninstructed reader to make of the cryptic "From others Fortune take" or "From others learn of fortune"? Or—to give some examples from translators Dryden may well have looked at— from Vicars' line "And fortunes power by others understand," or from the three lines (reversing Virgil's order) of Dryden's French predecessor, whose work was among those he studied carefully, Regnauld de Segrais:

> Par l'exemple d'autry crains la fortune instable,
> Et de ton pere apprends la gloire veritable,
> Mon fils, ainsi l'on marche au temple de l'honneur [!]—

which seems to be *really* saying "Whatever happens to *others*, learn how to *win* from *me!*" If one contemplates the creative freedom, license, or sheer muddle exercised here by the energetic Segrais, it will seem less surprising that, confronted by the same compressed Latin, Dryden's earliest predecessor Gavin Douglas should have expanded Virgil's ten words to thirty-seven in an effort to explore Virgilian implications:

> O thou my child, do lernyng, I the pray,
> Vertu and verray laubour till assay
> At me, quilk am thy fader, as thou wait;
> Desyre to be chancy and fortunate
> As othir pryncis, quilkis mair happy beyn.

All this is relevant, I think, to what Dryden makes of the passage. Glancing, very likely, at Lauderdale's rhyme word "War," at Segrais' noun "exemple," and also (perhaps) at Douglas's adjectives "chancy" and "happy," Dryden produces a triplet that, without the fatal garrulousness of Douglas, still clarifies Virgil's contrasting alternatives and embodies the speaker's emotion in such a way that it cannot fail to be understood:

My Son, from my Example learn the War,
In Camps to suffer, and in Fields to dare:
But happier Chance than mine attend thy Care.
                    [11.644–46]

A further reason, it seems to me, for Dryden's sureness of touch at this delicate and difficult point in book 12 is the fact that seventeen years earlier, in the course of writing one of his three greatest satires, he had already rendered the same Latin, if rendered is the proper word—translated it and wrung its neck might be more accurate. In a scene in which Aeneas-Flecknoe is bequeathing all to Ascanius-Shadwell, Dryden has him suddenly echo Virgil's *Fortunam ex aliis* and echo it in a way that shows how fully Dryden entered into the spirit of what Virgil meant. He begins the line as follows: "Success let others teach." Then he completes it with a carry-over of Virgil's sharp contrast between the "others" and the speaker: "Success let others teach; learn thou from me." And what is it that son Shadwell is to learn from father Flecknoe? Virgil's *verumque laborem* inspires Dryden to rise to an obstetrical metaphor:

Success let others teach; learn thou from me
Pangs without birth, and fruitless industry.
                    [11.147–48]

Writing heroic satire had prepared Dryden to attempt heroic poetry, and was certainly part of his preparation for the true labor of translating Virgil.

APPENDIX A: A MARTZIAN EPILOGUE

I have suggested that a reason why Virgil appealed to so many translators who, in their nonliterary lives, became MPs, went to jail, suffered for their beliefs, or defended systems of thought or government was that his poetry was seen as linked with the changing fortunes of a great and well-known nation in the first century B.C. Another reason may well have been that Virgil wrote an epic, and took an epic view of real events. To men like May, Harrington, and Denham during the civil wars in England

I think such a view easily struck home. It no doubt also did to Milton, a great Virgilian original poet whose initial decision to present his epic in ten books (rather than twelve) may have been influenced, it has been suggested, by the example of the ten-book epic of another great Virgilian poet—Camoens, recently Englished by the Virgil translator Fanshawe. In the sixteenth century both Camoens the original poet and Gavin Douglas the *Aeneid* translator can readily have seen their own nations' fortunes in terms appropriate to Virgilian epic. Six years after the appearance of *The Lusiad,* we read in W. C. Atkinson's introduction to his 1952 translation, the young king of Portugal, Sebastião, led an expedition to subdue the Moors in north Africa; it

> totalled some 15,000 foot and 1,500 horse, with 9,000 camp-
> followers of every description. Five hundred vessels were needed to
> transport it. . . . In a four-hour engagement with the Moors, under an
> African sun, it melted to nothing. Eight thousand were killed,
> 15,000 more taken and sold as slaves; possibly 100 in all succeeded in
> reaching the coast and safety. Sebastião was among the slain, having
> laid the might and prestige of Portugal in the dust. . . . [Camoens]
> died on 10 June 1580, spared at least the ignominy of seeing Philip II
> of Spain cross the frontier as king of a united Peninsula. (*The Lusiads*
> [Harmondsworth, Middlesex: Penguin, 1952], p. 20)

As for Douglas, to quote Bruce Dearing's lively article on his *Eneados* in *PMLA* 67 (1952), 859,

> Never in Douglas' Vergil does Aeneas fall short of the magnanimity
> proper to a "crysten knycht and kyng." Turnus, however, brave and
> noble as he is, exhibits the extremes of foolhardiness, stubbornness,
> and impetuosity that lead inevitably to his ruin. It is ironic that James
> IV, who was unquestionably intended to profit by the example, was
> too nearly of the temperament of Turnus. Barely three months after
> the completion of the *Eneados,* Douglas' luckless king, whom the
> poet's father had tried in vain to dissuade from an assault upon the
> forces of that English Aeneas, Henry Tudor, fell at Flodden Field and
> became himself a melancholy example for the instruction of princes
> and magistrates.

In the sixteenth and seventeenth centuries, it must not have been hard to view through the lenses of Virgilian epic the greatness and disasters of national life and one's own countrymen.

Appendix B: Virgil Translations, Douglas to Dryden

1513: Gavin Douglas, *Aeneid* (published 1553). 1554, 1557: Earl of Surrey, *Aeneid* 4, 2. 1558: Thomas Phaer, *Aeneid* 1–7, 1562: Phaer, *Aeneid* 1–9 and part of 10. 1575: Abraham Fleming, *Eclogues;* 1582: Richard Stanyhurst, *Aeneid* 1–6; 1584: Phaer's *Aeneid* completed by Thomas Twyne; 1586: William Webbe, Eclogues 1 and 2; 1588: Abraham Fraunce, Eclogue 2; 1589: Fleming, *Eclogues* and *Georgics;* 1601: Ben Jonson, part of *Aeneid* 4; 1610: Giles Fletcher the Younger, part of *Aeneid* 4; 1620: Sir Thomas Wrothe, *Aeneid* 2; John Brinsley, *Eclogues* and *Georgics* 4; 1622: Sir Dudley Diggs (anonymously), *Aeneid* 4 ("Dido's Death"); 1628: William Lisle, *Eclogues;* Thomas May, *Georgics;* by 1628: Sir John Beaumont, Eclogue 4 (published 1629); 1632: John Vicars, *Aeneid;* George Sandys, *Aeneid* 1; 1634: John Biddle, *Eclogues;* Sir Robert Stapylton, *Aeneid* 4; by 1642: Sidney Godolphin, most of *Aeneid* 4 (published 1658); 1646: Richard Crashaw, part of Georgic 2; 1647–48: Richard Fanshawe: *Aeneid* 4; 1649: John Ogilby, Virgil's works (rev. 1654); 1652: Fanshawe, part of Georgic 3; Henry Vaughan, part of Georgic 4; 1656, Sir John Denham, *Aeneid* 2; 1658: Edmund Waller, completion of Godolphin's *Aeneid* 4; James Harrington, *Aeneid* 1 and 2, Eclogues 1 and 9; 1659: Harrington, *Aeneid* 3–6; by 1660?: Sir William Temple, part of Georgic 2; 1660: Sir Robert Howard, *Aeneid* 4; 1661: John Boys, *Aeneid* 3, 6; 1665: Charles Hoole, *Georgics;* 1666: Temple, Eclogue 10 (published anonymously 1684); by 1667: Abraham Cowley, part of Georgic 2 and part of *Aeneid* 8 (published 1668); 1668: Denham, *Aeneid* 4; by 1670?: Temple, part of Georgic 4; by 1683: John Oldham, Eclogue 8 (published 1684); 1684: John Caryll, Eclogue 1, Nahum Tate, 2, Thomas Creech, 2 and 3, Dryden, 4 and (anonymously) 9, Richard Duke, 5, Earl of Roscommon, 6, Thomas Adams, 7, John Stafford [Howard], 8 and 10, Knightly Chetwood, 8 and part of Georgic 2, Earl of Mulgrave, Georgic 4; 1685: Stafford, part of *Aeneid* 11; Earl of Lauderdale (anonymously), part of Georgic 4; Dryden, parts of *Aeneid* 5, 8, 9, and 10; anon., Eclogue 3 (in Aphra Behn's *Miscellany*); 1688: Luke Milbourne (anonymously), *Aeneid* 1; anon., Eclogue 2 (in *Poetical Recreations*); 1692: Thomas Fletcher, *Aeneid* 1, with bits of 2, 3, and 4; Sir Charles Sedley (anonymously), Georgic 4; 1693: Robert Wolseley, part of *Aeneid* 6; John Lewkenor (anonymously), *Aeneid* 4; Henry Sacheverell, part of Georgic 1; anon., part of Georgic 3; 1694: Joseph Addison, most of Georgic 4; Lauderdale, Georgic 1; Dryden, *Georgic* 3; by 1695: Lauderdale, Virgil's works (published 1708 or 1709); 1697: Dryden, Virgil's works.

NOTES

1. I exclude from consideration here Spenser's renderings of two poems from the Virgilian Appendix, the *Culex* and (part of) the *Ciris,* as well as the snatches of Virgil translation scattered throughout Marlowe's *Tragedy of Dido,* Florio's Montaigne, Sandys' *Relation of a Journey,* and Cotton's Montaigne. Warm thanks are due to Professor Margaret Boddy for having drawn several Virgilians to my attention.

2. Not to mention Creech's Horace, Theocritus, and Manilius. Jonson and Roscommon each did versions of the *Ars Poetica* well known in their day; and Harrington's translating ambitions may have owed something to the fame of his great-uncle Sir John's Elizabethan version of Ariosto.

3. These influences have been studied by Florence Ridley in "Surrey's Debt to Gawin Douglas," *PMLA* 76 (1961), 25–33; Helene Maxwell Hooker, in "Dryden's Georgics and English Predecessors," *HLQ* 9 (1946), 273–310; and Adams Betty Smith in her Michigan State University Ph.D. dissertation (1970), "Dryden's Translation of Vergil and its Eighteenth-Century Successors."

4. I have been unable to locate a copy of *The Four Books of Virgil's Georgicks, in English and Latin* (1665) by Charles Hoole, formerly owned by the Lincoln's Inn Library; from Hoole's other work, I would judge that it might have been literal prose, like Brinsley's *Eclogues* and Georgic 4 earlier.

5. See Appendix B for a chronological list.

6. Cf. L. Proudfoot, *Dryden's Aeneid and Its Seventeenth Century Predecessors* (Manchester: Manchester University Press, 1960), p. 116: "Virgil . . . offers an approximation to a universal norm."

7. *Dictionary of National Biography,* s.v. "Brinsley" (1967–68 reprint).

8. Aphra Behn's 1685 *Miscellany* included her "Pastoral to Mr. Stafford . . . On his Translation of the Death of Camilla," which makes it clear that "Stafford" (actually John Howard) was the viscount's son; no doubt he and his sister Anastasia, for whose marriage, probably in 1687, Dryden wrote a pindaric celebratory ode, took their father's title as a last name in order to commemorate him. The Virgil-translating Stafford is surely also "The Honourable John Stafford, Esq." who wrote the epilogue to Southerne's *The Disappointment* (1684).

9. Proudfoot, *Dryden's Aeneid,* pp. 110, 153.

10. Charles Blitzer, *Political Writings of James Harrington* (New York: Liberal Arts Press, 1955), pp. xi, xii.

11. Brendan O Hehir, "Vergil's First *Georgic* and Denham's *Cooper's*

Hill," *PQ* 42 (1963), 547; cf. the entire article, and also O Hehir's *Expans'd Hieroglyphicks, A Critical Edition of Cooper's Hill* (Berkeley: University of California Press, 1969), pp. 149–50n.

12. Lest it be thought that the same sort of collective profile could be drawn for *any* sizable group of classics-translating Englishmen of the Renaissance and Restoration, I will mention that among the more than fifty translators of Ovid from Caxton to Dryden, public life and commitment to causes evidently held far less attraction. Setting aside the eight (Brinsley, Caryll, Duke, Milbourne, Mulgrave, Sandys, Stapylton, and Tate) who were also Virgil translators and have already been treated, Ovid translators, as far as I know, include no privy councillors; no MPs; no bishops or monks; no more than one or two (Oldham, Thomas Hall) schoolteachers, preachers, or clergymen; very few (Hall, Butler, Oldham, Settle, possibly Golding) who took stands on matters of public controversy; and not many (Hall, Christopher Marlowe, perhaps George Turberville) who seem to have been at any time in much trouble with the authorities or with their contemporaries for reasons of ideology or activism. It is true that at least five (Caxton, Turberville, Marlowe, Aphra Behn, and Thomas Rymer) saw some government service (all, except Rymer, abroad); and also true that the Ovidian group included, besides those already mentioned, a few people as well known as the dramatists Heywood and Otway, the poet Churchyard, and the murder victim Overbury; but for the sort of involvement, commitment, or peril represented by figures like Wrothe, Harrington, Boys, Sacheverell, Waller, Fanshawe, May, or Denham we seek among non-Virgil-translating Ovid-translators in vain.

13. The sources of my compilation are the notes in the volumes so far published of the California Dryden; in G. R. Noyes's edition (Boston: Houghton Mifflin, 1909, 1950) of Dryden's *Poetical Works* and in his *Selected Dramas of Dryden* (Chicago: Scott Foresman, 1910); in Montague Summers's edition of "Oedipus" in *Dryden: The Dramatic Works* (London: Nonesuch Press, 1932); in the editions of Dryden's essays by W. P. Ker (Oxford: Oxford University Press, Clarendon Press, 1926) and George Watson (London: J. M. Dent, 1962); and in R. A. Brower's articles "Dryden's Poetic Diction and Virgil," *PQ* 18 (1939), 211–17 and "Dryden's Epic Manner and Virgil," *PMLA* 55 (1940), 119–38; also in Jeanne K. Welcher's "The Opening of *Religio Laici* and its Virgilian Associations," *SEL* 8 (1968), 391–96.

14. T. H. Banks, *Poetical Works of Denham* (New Haven: Yale University Press, 1928), pp. 43–44.

15. *The Art of Vergil,* tr. Gerda Seligson (Ann Arbor: University of Michigan Press, 1962), p. 58.

JUDITH FARR

Elinor Wylie, Edna St. Vincent Millay, and the Elizabethan Sonnet Tradition

In 1931 Edna St. Vincent Millay published a volume of fifty-two sonnets entitled *Fatal Interview* which she dedicated to her friend Elinor Wylie, who had died in 1928. When she wrote *Fatal Interview* Millay was the best-known woman poet in the United States, while the poet she honored had been her equally famous rival. *Fatal Interview* took its title from the sixteenth elegy of John Donne, whose imagination had nourished Wylie in her last days, inspiring the title of her final volume of poems, *Angels and Earthly Creatures* (1929). Millay's dedication expressed not only her grief for a dead friend but implied a significant bond between two poets: the need to explore a profound emotional experience in a sequence of "Elizabethan" sonnets.

Wylie had written "One Person," the group of nineteen poems, mostly sonnets, that introduced *Angels and Earthly Creatures,* after a troubled romance which, some thought, hastened her early death. Millay's volume also recorded the progress of a disturbing attachment whose brief happiness ended in disappointment. Since both women were distinguished, celebrated, and married when they wrote of the passion that temporarily affected their lives and literary styles, their books excited biographical speculation. Who were the men so churlish as to defeat the self-esteem of women noted for beauty as for talent? Millay's joyful hedonism had been daunted before in print but never tellingly; Wylie's chilly self-possession was, despite her three marriages, well known. These sonnets revealed an ardor and despair uncommon in their work. They depicted heroes as desired and hard to win as any Stella or Delia; and though as men their charms were somewhat differently compounded—they were hand-some, remote, and imperious but could be friendly and protective—their ultimate behavior was conventional, they refused to match the speakers' devotion.

The identity of Millay's lover is conjectured; the name of Wylie's platonic beloved is known, as are his efforts to remain faithful to his wife yet considerate to Elinor. Both Millay and Wylie realized that their husbands would suffer from the fact of their love as from its vivid avowal in the sonnets. (Indeed, Eugen Boissevain found him-self quietly admitting to reporters that he and Millay were merely married friends while William Rose Benét sadly professed himself sorry that Wylie had failed to win her "one person.") Despite guilt, neither poet—like Sidney's Astrophel—was "asham'd to publish [her] disease," and each did so in sonnets imbued with the meta-phoric invention of the Renaissance.

Though Millay and Wylie were accomplished sonneteers when they began these sequences, they had never written deliberately in an Elizabethan mode. Millay's books, like *Second April* or *A Few Figs from Thistles,* contained many sonnets, many influenced by Tenny-son, Rossetti, or Keats. A few had a vague Elizabethan flavor: "I know I am but summer to your heart. / And not the full four seasons of the year." Many combined a lushness of tone with a wry modern nuance suited to her feminism and Bohemianism: "Only until this cigarette is ended ... I will permit my memory to recall / The vision of you, by all my dreams attended." Wylie's early volumes, *Nets to Catch the Wind* or *Black Armour,* contained sonnets diverse in theme, often ironic in tone. Her style was crisp, cerebral. Her frequent subject was the problem of art or, as in the famous Petrarchan series "Wild Peaches," the beauty of landscape. Many described her anguish of a woman, quite different from Mil-lay's usual speaker, who found no pleasure in human affection. Her debt where apparent was to the early Yeats or Lionel Johnson. But like Millay she had developed her own style.

Now, in *Fatal Interview* and "One Person," both poets chose to write in a consciously inherited manner in sequences that like Sid-ney's or Shakespeare's described the progress of a lover's oscillating fear and hope; in language that summoned all the old images of starry eyes, storms and fires, passing bells, bows and arrows, love-philtres, savaged hearts and pitiless gods; and with revered themes: Time's sway, seasons favorable and hostile, the need to embrace before dark and death. One opens the pages of *Fatal Interview* and is struck by how many lines could "pass" for Elizabethan: "Love like a burning city in the breast," "our arrogant laughter and sweet lust," "My needle to your north abruptly swerved." And in "One Person" Elinor Wylie employs a sensuous, evocative cadence: "O love, how utterly am I bereaved / By time, who sucks the honey of our days."[1] These sonnets, one realizes, were inspired not merely by Wylie's love for an English squire, Henry de Clifford Woodhouse, or by Millay's possible lover, the scholar George Dillon. They were celebrations of the idea of love itself and of the Elizabethan sonnet tradition that had so richly expressed it.

II

The words "Angels" and "earthly Creatures" appear in Donne's "Sermon Preached to the Earl of Exeter, and his company, in his Chappell at Saint Johns; 13. Jun. 1624." The sermon's text was Apocalypse 7: 9 and included the following passage:

> But because *Angels* could not propagate, nor make more *Angels,* [God] enlarged his love, in making man, that so he might enjoy all natures at once, and have the nature of *Angels,* and the nature of *earthly Creatures,* in one person.

In choosing these words as a title, Elinor Wylie paid an extravagant compliment to Woodhouse, who admired Donne and was for a time the "one Person" who, to her, combined two natures, divine and human. Wylie's craving to see holiness in an erotic context was characteristic of her, while her vision of the beloved as morally superior was typical of the courtly tradition. And her appeal to Donne's sermon, which contrasts the sexual nullity of angels to the (implicit) appetite of man, was appropriate to her last romance— fervent and unconsummated. Donne's influence figures prominently in three "epistles" in *Angels and Earthly Creatures;* yet, despite Donnean phrases like "beyond metempsychosis" or "the festivals and pentecosts / Of metaphysics," it is not significant in the sonnet sequence to "One Person." Though unique as narrative and for its intense emphasis on disembodied love, "One Person" evokes the sonnets of Sidney and Shakespeare. (Wylie implied her debt to Shakespeare obliquely—and cruelly—by writing on the fly-leaf of her husband's privately printed copy of "One Person," "To the onlie begetter of these insuing sonnets, all happinesse." Another copy went to Woodhouse's wife Rebecca as a Christmas gift. Both she and Benét knew who the real begetter was.)

"One Person" is the story of an attraction between a married middle-aged English aristocrat with a taste for books and nature and a somewhat younger American woman who, despite her fame as a poet, idealizes and feels subservient to him. It is told in nineteen poems, all of which are Petrarchan sonnets with the exception of the seventh (thirteen lines) and the eighteenth (sixteen lines): a miscount attributed by Carl Van Doren to Wylie's dazzled emotion. The setting of the sequence is slenderly defined. It is English, for Sonnet 1 reports that the speaker has ended her "long homesickness" for a romantic past (spent in England) by joining the beloved on his own soil. It is the country, for he reveals his love under an oak, a beech, and a willow and keeps sheepfolds. The "house" that the speaker, in an elaborate conceit, "swear[s]" "to uphold" is her lord's dynasty: the children his marriage engendered, threatened now by her adulterous love (16). But its arches, hearths, and cornices also describe those of a manorhouse like Woodhouse's Rockylane Farm in Oxfordshire; and though she sees herself as essentially foreign to his heart and home, the speaker resolves at last, in echoes of *King John,* to live "upon the fringes of [the beloved's] continent,"

> This map of Paradise, this scrap of earth
> Whereon you burn like flame upon a hearth.
>   [17]

The lovers' romance is governed by seasons, for, besides renunciation, the chief theme of "One Person" is the Shakespearean

"Time's fell hand." They are, quite conventionally, happy in spring (11) before "Time" "sets sickle to [their] Aprils" (8). In a "vernal landscape," the beloved makes an unwilling declaration of love which violates the speaker's "innocence"—or frigidity: now she is both released and caught (11). Yet autumn comes (12), and separation, prudence, and denial teach her that she can never be the beloved's "bride" (14) on earth or bear his child (12). In a last poem, she discards all hope of earthly happiness yet imagines a heaven in which both lovers like "hunted exile[s]" "sleep oblivious of any doom" "upon a bed of juniper and fern" (18).

Thomas Nashe in his preface to the first edition of *Astrophel and Stella* called its "argument cruel chastity, the prologue hope, the epilogue dispair," an analysis suited also to "One Person." Its speaker, too, must sublimate her passion in "supernatural" "ecstasy" (1) and hints only once that she has "mingled breath" with the beloved (8), a restrained equivalent of Astrophel's opulently stolen kiss. Like Sidney's or Shakespeare's, Wylie's sonnet sequence records stages in a contest between honor and desire. But Wylie's speaker, unlike her masculine counterparts, declares herself inexperienced in passion. She has "lived indifferent to the blood's desire" (5). Now, no longer "obdurate and blind / To those sharp ecstasies the pulses give" (6), she still does not express herself with Shakespeare's violence towards the lover, who makes in him a "civil warre" of "love and hate"; nor with Astrophel's frank if elegant lust for Stella, "lodestone of desire"; nor, for that matter, with the coarse ardor of Millay's persona, who upsets the usual male-female sonnet roles to describe a shy man upbraided for "the rude sea / Of [unslaked] passion pounding all day long in me!" The speaker of "One Person" yearns but never abjures her old habit of decorum. She is attracted to "the shape of danger" in her lover's face but is more at ease speaking of the "pattern of [his] soul" (2). Her posture is the conventionally suppliant one of the Petrarchan sonnet, especially of the *Astrophel* sequence. She is her lover's "child" or "hound" with the "courage of a wolf new-taught to cower" (3). Her beloved with his "sable . . . hair / Silvered" (10), recalling Shakespeare's description of his own "Sable curls all silvered o're with white," has been fretted with care because of her. Like Sidney, she is

aware of the "iron lawes of duty." Like Shakespeare, she is concerned with the idea of increase: the beloved's actual children are
more estimable to her than her fantasy of mothering his son (12).
And Shakespeare's cry "Let me confess that we two must be twaine"
could serve as epigraph to "One Person" in which Wylie is the
American "crow" enamored of a "falcon," "the brier" in love with the
"noble vine," the "vassal" bent in homage to a chivalric lord (4).

"One Person" records division: national, sexual, civil, yet not
instinctual. One of its best sonnets expresses these divisions in an
Elizabethan way, by extended mythological conceit:

> O mine is Psyche's heavy doom reversed
> Who meet at noon, part by diminished light,
> But never feel the subtle balm of night
> Fall merciful upon a body pierced
> By extreme love; and I considered first
> That you, a god more prodigally bright
> Than the lesser Eros, had enriched by sight,
> Made your own morning, and the stars immersed.
> But secondly I saw my soul arise
> And, in the hushed obscure, presume to creep
> Tiptoe upon your spirit laid asleep,
> And slant the impious beam across your eyes;
> And I believe I have my just deserts
> Lacking the shadow of peace upon our hearts.
>
> {13}

In this orderly sonnet, whose octave and sestet describe different
states of feeling, the speaker is a Psyche or soul more deprived than
her classical counterpart. Even as Wylie usually met Woodhouse in
a glen at midday, she meets her Eros at noon. The time and the
caresses sacred to lovers are forbidden her. But Eros, Hesiod says,
was the generative force which together with Erebus (Night) produced Day; thus the speaker first claims that her greater Eros has
"enriched" her vision of love by extending its ritual hours to include
"morning." Nevertheless, she cannot forbear acting out the
Cupid-Psyche myth in reverie. Her "soul"—for their bodies are not
in question—asks of his "spirit" commitment; in view of their
circumstances, an "impious" request. The final couplet, whose slant

rime implies separation and despair, recalls the penitential mode of
the Petrarchans and voices the need for "peace" which Wylie herself
fulfilled in death.

III

Donne's lines, "By our first strange and fatall interview, / By
all desires that thereof did ensue," serve as epigraph to the sonnet
sequence of Edna St. Vincent Millay, who originally planned to call
her volume *Twice Required*—a phrase from her Sonnet 14: "Since of
no creature living the last breath / Is twice required." Her earlier
choice was more apt, for in her narrative no "interview" precedes
obsessive love, and its ultimate subject is the need "to outlive
[the] anguish of parting": a "very death" of which real death is the
mere copy (47, 14). The title was changed to commemorate
Donne's tercentenary, and a few lines like "Heart, have no pity on this
house of bone: / Shake it with dancing, break it down with joy"
(29) are mildly metaphysical. But *Fatal Interview* owes as much to
the "songs and sonets" of *Englands Helicon* ("Unhappy life they
gaine / Which Love doe entertaine") as to the great sonneteers and
little or nothing to Donne. Millay wished, of course, to pay tribute
to a Renaissance master; and her sonnets imitate an earlier
Elizabethan mode known to Donne with a vitality the Elizabethans
themselves achieved when imitating Petrarch and Dante.

Fatal Interview is a vibrant, theatrical, uneven series of poems
that, like Wylie's, contemplates the "extreme disease" (5) of love.
Unlike Wylie's, however, its prevailing vision is not Christian and
Platonic but pagan and sensual. Only the second sonnet (reminiscent of Meredith's *Modern Love* 1) regrets the "sword" of adulterous
desire lodged between the speaker and her husband. The rest de-
plore whatever "moral concept" and "quavering caution" might
separate her from a scrupulous lover (22, 29). She makes no Sid-
neyesque outcry against Desire's "worthlesse ware" and, when
abandoned at the end, no conversation to "Eternal Love," as does
Sidney in a well-known sonnet. Millay's philosophy is the simple
one of the carpe diem songs whose blandishments she weaves anew:

> *All that delightful youth forebears to spend*
> *Molestful age inherits, and the ground*
> *Will have us; therefore, while we're young, my friend.*
>   [29]

Her scholarly lover, more inclined to "pale preoccupation with the dead" Cressids, Elaines, and Isolts of literature than with her "living bones" is reminded that he will shortly be "corn and roses" (6, 14) and at her mercy:

> Yet in an hour to come, disdainful dust,
> You shall be bowed and brought to bed with me.
>   . . .
> If not today, then later; if not here
> On the green grass, with sighing and delight,
> Then under it, all in good time, my dear,
> We shall be laid together in the night.
>   [8]

When at last he yields to her she dreams of "bear[ing] a son / Branded with godhead" (12) and meditates on her happiness in a group of sonnets whose classical themes and characters celebrate "the ancient tempest of desire" (13). Worshipping Venus (15), she walks the Elysian fields with her peers, women whom Jove loved (16). The sonnets' carpe diem motifs blend with Roman scenes to recall the decorative world of "Robin Herrick's" *Hesperides* but Millay's world is less placid; it is haunted by danger. Her rapture is brief. In one sonnet alone (12) is she fully content. Thirty-two sonnets present the lovers in stages of doubt or disagreement, he ever less committed, she recklessly persistent. By Sonnet 38 the love affair is ended and with courage and generosity the speaker surveys her "ruined garden" (35), survives empty days (44) and promises the lover, "I shall have only good to say of you" (47).

She speaks to him in a language whose cadences are both Elizabethan and modern. Similarly, the setting of *Fatal Interview* shifts between an Elizabethan castle with "steamy" dungeons (18) fitted with "rack and wheel" (22), the Maine countryside and seascape off Matinicus, and a surreal Art Nouveau "pavilion" in which "slow dancers dance in foam" and the speaker finds a "pink camellia-bud / On the wide step, beside a silver comb" (16). The different settings and accents express different aspects of the speaker's nature. The artificial castle in whose dungeon she is locked by her brilliant-eyed lover-"gaoler" (5) represents her frustration and yet her sexual daring; as she boasts,

> in me alone survive
> The unregenerate passions of a day
> When treacherous queens, with death upon the tread,
> Heedless and wilful, took their knights to bed.
>
> [26]

The bare Maine coast, the gardens of dahlias and marigolds describe that self "free from guile" (3) which—in an echo of Wylie's "Love Song" from *Angels and Earthly Creatures,* "To love I have been candid, / Honest, and open-handed"—offers "Love in the open hand," "apples in her skirt," "cowslips in a hat" (11). Finally, the dream pavilion suggests the scented theme of romantic desire. Millay's sonnets, like Spenser's *Amoretti,* contrive atmosphere by archaisms: "liefer," "noddle" (4), "leman" (24). Yet their Elizabethanisms live at ease with a spare rhetoric akin to what Elizabethans considered "plain style." She can attempt the embroidered antitheses of the "sugared" sonnets: "Weeping I wake; waking, I weep, I weep" (23) or confess aphoristically that it is "Time to be cold and time to sleep alone" (22).

Her most frequently anthologized poem, cunning in its simplicity and memorable for its loveliness, has dignity worthy of the Elizabethan sonnet tradition:

> Love is not all; it is not meat nor drink
> Nor slumber nor a roof against the rain
> Nor yet a floating spar to men that sink
> And rise and sink and rise and sink again;
> Love can not fill the thickened lung with breath,
> Nor clean the blood, nor set the fractured bone;
> Yet many a man is making friends with death
> Even as I speak, for lack of love alone.
> It well may be that in a difficult hour,
> Pinned down by pain and moaning for release,

Or nagged by want past resolution's power,
I might be driven to sell your love for peace,
Or trade the memory of this night for food.
It well may be. I do not think I would.

                                    [30]

This sonnet appears in *Fatal Interview* as a seemingly cynical concession to the lover's sexual indifference; really it is a defense of sensual
love, ultimately concluded as conclusions often are in Shakespeare
by the modest *volte face* of the final couplet. The sonnet builds its
argument by a catalogue of negatives. The Elizabethans who loved
arguments and catalogues sometimes strove like Petrach to define
what a woman, for instance, was by explaining what she was not.
Thus Petrarch says of Laura in *Rime* 90, "Non era l'andar suo cosa
mortale . . . e le parole / sonevan altro che pur voce umana": "her
gestures were not mortal, her words not human, she was . . ." and
he provides his own definition. In somewhat similar fashion, Millay's sonnet begins realistically by declaring what "Love is not."
Then, by mounting implication and in the last phrase of the fourteenth line, it defines by ellipsis what love is. Thus, love is not a
brute necessity to man either in daily life or in extremis. Yet without it "many" die. This general premise is established in the octave,
then particularized sharply in the sestet. Millay, who like the
Elizabethan sonneteers studies her own responses to feeling, in
Fatal Interview now scrutinizes the limitations of her fidelity to the
"god" Passion (39). Being human, she reasons, she might "be
driven" to betray her higher nature, the sensitivity of the volup-
tuary, to her lower appetite, the need to survive. Her words "sell"
and "trade" suggest her revulsion at the thought of bartering
spiritual for fleshly food. No platonist, Millay attributes divinity
not to contemplative but to sensual love and her phrase, "the memory of this night," comes as close as she cares to draw to the
Renaissance conception of love as ideal. Still, the "Energia" of style,
which Sidney thought imperative to an ardent love poem, appears in
Millay's sonnet together with devout belief in the energy of her own
passion. Ruthlessly and humbly entertaining the prospect that she

might betray love, she at last dismisses the thought with a peculiarly modern, provisional sentence: "I do not think I would".

The late Elizabethans in particular liked to debate the nature of love in its kinds: active, contemplative, practical (distinctions sifted, for instance, by the platonist Marsilio Ficino and considered afresh in the poems of Chapman, Donne, and Fletcher). Unlike Wylie, whose sensual love led at last to quasi-religious lyrics, Millay shows scant interest in love elevated beyond that of the "innocent senses" (22). Yet she would have concurred with Giles Fletcher's decision in his "Epistle Dedicatory" to the sonnets of *Licea:* "in a mind that is . . . truly amorous [passion is] an affection of the greatest virtue, and able . . . to eternize the meanest vassal." Like Sidney or Shakespeare, Millay claimed to have tasted immortality in *Fatal Interview* and like them she proposed to secure it to herself and her lover in verse. He is to remember (as sonneteers had written since Petrach and Ronsard)

> When failing powers or good opinion lost
> Have bowed your neck . . .
> How of all men I honoured you the most.
> [57]

Sonnet 30 (above), recited often by Millay on reading tours and by many readers since, has a power that characterizes her best writing and helps to justify the popularity she achieved. A more accessible poet than the reticent Wylie, Millay had a temperamental bravado, an interest in common and "progressive" causes, an appreciation of vulgarity, and a facility with sonorous language. They sometimes led her to adopt brilliantly feckless attitudes and to marshal against the lively but serene mathematics of contained forms like the sonnet, quatrain, or couplet a battery of dishevelled impulses expressed in terms calculated to shock. She was, quite unlike Wylie, a poet to whom contemporary issues mattered greatly, an eager feminist, a self-professed apostle of "free love," an enthusiast of political stances, prone to use poetry in their service. Wylie, on the other hand, was a conservative, highly literate poet-novelist whose concern was directed almost wholly to the history and stratagems of art; for her, causes, however just, were too ephemeral to express in print. And one could not know, reading her lines, that she had been pilloried for a youthful elopement and divorce, for abandoning an infant son, for a common-law marriage. Her anguish appeared in subtle if eloquent symbolic patterns and in a refined regard for what she thought permanent in the presence of chaos: the art of literature in its varied manifestations. "One Person," like her imitations of the style of Jane Austen, Oscar Wilde, Max Beerbohm, and others in her novels or her poetic tributes to Shelley in Shelleyan accents, showed how capable she was of adopting nonce forms for dramatic or ironic purposes. Like Wylie's, Millay's best work exhibits a tutored sensibility that enabled her to compose effectively within literary traditions she respected. The Petrarchan conventions to which she submitted in *Fatal Interview* served her well, moreover, disciplining her imagination yet encouraging the emotional scope her poetry instinctively sought.

After 1931, Millay continued to write sonnets in a neo-Romantic style appropriate to a votary of Keats. Elinor Wylie, even in *Angels and Earthly Creatures,* returned to composing in the neo-Aesthetic manner which was her own. The "Elizabethan" sonnets of *Fatal Interview* and "One Person" were the fruits of considered decision, ways of ennobling, universalizing, and immortalizing the love each poet knew by associating it with the great love lyrics of the language. Though both sequences are original in narrative, atmosphere, and nuances of diction, they are always conscientiously conventional. (Thus it is impossible to judge, for example, whether Millay and Wylie paid their lovers' eyes tribute because they were lustrous or because Sidney, Shakespeare, Spenser, Fulke Greville, Campion, Donne, Fletcher, and the rest celebrated *their* lovers' eyes.)

IV

In the arts, of course, the practice of imitation (often verging on or including quotation) is old and continuous. Its purposes are varied: to offer homage to an influential earlier civilization, culture, or artist; to imply connection with or ironic distance from them; to argue new directions by contrast or to insist on a perdurable artistic purpose through the incorporation of older insights and techniques in modern works. Music and the visual arts are as enriched by this practice as is literature; and in those arts, too, the imitational impulse has complex motives and different degrees of stylistic and visionary realization. Thus, to choose examples at random, Richard Strauss's inclusion of Mozartian motifs—particularly in Act II of *Der Rosenkavalier*—paid proud homage to Mozart, Strauss's *meister,* while at the same time suggesting the eighteenth-century court life Mozart knew and which Strauss was recreating in his opera. Strauss's purpose was not to assert his separation from Mozart but to invoke Mozart's world and idiom as archetypically superb while retaining his individuality. The contemporary British painter Francis Bacon, on the other hand, in his terrible and macabre *Study after Velasquez's Portrait of Pope Innocent X,* violates and challenges the heroic power of his model, Velasquez's original, to criticize a disoriented modern world divorced from the hierarchical one of the seventeenth century. In the cases of Strauss and Bacon, no perfect fusion of their styles with those of Mozart or Velasquez is intended; one recognizes the quotation in each artifact as an intellectual stratagem. On the other hand, two artists come to mind, both called "Post-Impressionist," who so absorbed and adapted the artistic attributes of other cultures that those attributes became transformed and integral to their work. They are Paul Gauguin, whose exotically colored, sensuous paintings attracted Edna Millay, and James Abbott McNeill Whistler, whose highly formalized, exquisitely fragile "nocturnes" and "symphonies" influenced Elinor Wylie's novels. In Gauguin's later paintings, Egyptian, Oriental and Javanese motifs fuse harmoniously in a unique, tapestry-like design; in Whistler's later paintings—for instance, in *Princess from the Land of Porcelain,* which Wylie probably studied as a young art student in Washington, D.C.—delicate Japanese patterns of arrangement appear reinterpreted and invigorated. The characteristic works of Gauguin and Whistler exemplify a perfect marriage of the

artist's insights and techniques with those of his models. These
seem to have been marriages prompted by inspiration and need, for
Gauguin's art was not Gauguin's until he escaped literally and
imaginatively from Paris to Tahiti while Japan freed Whistler from
the Courbet-inspired realism that inhibited his gifts.

With these thoughts in mind, one might ask: what is the
specific character of Millay's and Wylie's imitations? How deeply
felt, how realized are their modern versions of an earlier mode? I
have tried to suggest Millay's and Wylie's motives for imitating the
Elizabethans, but it is necessary to assess, at last, the nature of their
achievement.

First of all, it should be said that the imitatory patterns these
poets set up are capable of intermission both within the individual
sonnet or in the sequences as a whole. Thus Millay, for example,
will write a sonnet like 34, in which she personifies Death, Doubt,
Despair, and her (and the Elizabethans') usual enemy, Time; a
sonnet in which the setting of the Elizabethan castle "wall[ed] with
spikes" is fully limned; in which there are balanced modifiers like
"Kinsman to Death and leman of Despair," poetic inversion, and a
recondite idiom: "That he pass gutted, should again he pass." Such
characteristics contrive an enthusiastic embroidery in which to depict the Elizabethan age; but the embroidery is also shot through
with the color of newer slang. The speaker worries, for example,
"Lest Death should get his foot inside the door." The use of slang in
a formal sonnet is surely Elizabethan, but "foot inside the door" is,
as I understand it, early nineteenth-century slang, so that Millay is
either (to the cheerless mind) guilty of anachronism or imitating the
rough inclusiveness of Elizabethan rhetoric in her own way. I think
the latter. This sort of versatile imitation is constantly present in her
"Elizabethan" sonnets. Yet in a good sonnet like 36, only two
poems removed from the one I have been discussing, Millay aban-
dons Elizabethanisms altogether to write a compelling sonnet sentence in a different style:

> Hearing your words, and not a word among them
> Tuned to my liking, on a salty day
> When inland woods were pushed by winds that flung them

Hissing to leeward like a ton of spray,
I thought how off Matinicus the tide
Came pounding in, came running through the Gut,
While from the Rock the warning whistle cried,
And children whimpered, and the doors blew shut;
There in the autumn when the men go forth
With slapping skirts the island women stand
In gardens stripped and scattered, peering north,
With dahlia tubers dripping from the hand:
The wind of their endurance, driving south,
Flattened your words against your speaking mouth.

Sonnet 36 breaks with its "Elizabethan" associates to voice the anxiety and determination of the "real" Edna Millay, a woman who came from New England and who envisions conflict and loss in homely American images. The "eye" of this musical sonnet, which sees in a precise and painterly way, owes a little to Keats and something to Whitman; yet it requires no borrowed filigree to make its point cleanly. The lover has threatened departure: to the speaker, it is a threat that has the terror of natural disaster. She summons against it the bitter "endurance" of island women, isolated in their love as she is, the sibilants of "slapping," "skirts," "stripped," "scattered," "south" implying a certain natural resentment as well as tenacity. The octave and sestet of her sonnet are somewhat separate in intention, as convention requires. Here, the octave is a sort of lens providing a wider vision that is narrowed and specified in the sestet. There is a confident simplicity in this sonnet—"children whimpered . . . the doors blew shut"—which assists its dreamlike character. Sonnet 36 is a fantasy in which a remembered vision of feminine fidelity challenges the lover's desire to "go forth," and it is successful as poetry in a way that certain of the diligently embroidered sonnets of *Fatal Interview* are not.

Millay's Sonnet 30, of course, on which I have already touched, is not so much embroidered as composed in fealty to Elizabethan conventions. But if Millay is "Elizabethan" in *Fatal Interview* it is perhaps fair to say that hers is an Elizabethanism of the theatre— entered into with relish and respect, with high-minded enjoyment, with pleasure in decoration. Her "Elizabethan" sonnets are those of the actress she once was: well-mimed acts of homage. They are performed in the awareness that the passion she experienced in 1930 had once been dignified by kind and subjected to principles of order, principles to which she herself was by nature uncommitted, yet drawn.

In the case of Elinor Wylie's "One Person," however, judgments about the full feeling of the poet toward her adopted mode, or even about her success in rendering it, are more difficult to make. Wylie was all her life a scholarly chameleon, able like many greater poets to compose with faultless ease and sincerity in a style temporarily chosen. When she died at forty-three, she was—like her great contemporary, Ezra Pound—weary of the Aesthetic mode and had written many poems and essays attacking its insufficiencies. She was casting about for another way of writing; and had she lived, she might have conserved her characteristic aestheticism for certain purposes but striven to become the colleague of Donne which she sometimes imagined herself. Wylie's imitations of the Elizabethans—like her admired Whistler's incorporations of the Japanese style—are integral to her own way of seeing and writing as Millay's imitations never were.

In Sonnet 17 of "One Person," for example, Wylie pays obeisance to an imagined Elizabethan scene that includes velvet palls, graves set in churchyard walls, and bells that announce death and also to the Elizabethan rhetorical tradition with its elaborations, onomatopoeic resonances, authoritative repetitions, and instructive metaphors. She does both without hot emphasis and with graceful assimilation:

> Upon your heart, which is the heart of all
> My late discovered earth and early sky,
> Give me the dearest privilege to die;
> Your pity for the velvet of my pall;
> Your patience for my grave's inviolate wall;
> And for my passing bell, in passing by,
> Your voice itself, diminished to a sigh
> Above all other sounds made musical.
>
> Meanwhile I swear to you I am content
> To live without a sorrow to my name;

To live triumphant, and to die the same,
Upon the fringes of this continent,
This map of Paradise, this scrap of earth
Whereon you burn like flame upon a hearth.

In this sonnet there exists, I think, an understanding of the Elizabethan mode that transcends Millay's. It insists, as good imitations do, on those elements of the mode which may be summoned to modern use, vibrant there not only out of homage but due to the fusion of a modern with a paradigmatic voice. The first line of this sonnet with its doubled "hearts" is quietly elaborate; the second, with its accomplished assonance, encourages the poem's supple movement; the third and fourth lines with their suave alliteration and the fifth and sixth, both alliterative and moving towards a grander pattern of sound, establish arcane yet relevant conceits which find their fulfilment in the seventh line's encomium to the lover's voice—"diminished" momentarily like Wylie's own music. This sonnet makes one remember that the form itself was meant to glow, *sonner,* with melody; but there is no glitter here, no solicited effect. And in the sestet, Wylie employs a modernism—"without a sorrow to my name"—which is not out of place but kindles the *altitudo* of her subsequent lines. Those lines are not so remote from the Elizabethans' either, for they are, as I have said before, indebted to Shakespeare; yet Wylie transforms, tames them, even, to her own use.

Both Edna St. Vincent Millay and Elinor Wylie used Elizabethan modes and formulas with different degrees of success; neither attained the absolute fusion of inherited mode with individual insight and style exhibited in, say, the "metaphysical" poems of Emily Dickinson, a poet in whose art neither Millay nor Wylie seemed especially interested. Still, *Fatal Interview* and "One Person" are important documents. They disclose versatility and sympathetic historic insight not always suspected in these poets. Furthermore, they prove, as well as any series of poems could, just how influential the Elizabethan sonnet tradition was.

That *Fatal Interview* and "One Person" are written by women is, of course, a significant irony. For hundreds of years in hundreds of sonnets men had paid women the compliment of fascination. They had written to women (silent in riposte if not in description) of their admiration and contempt, temerity and need, veneration and lust, disenchantment and lasting desire. Wylie and Millay repaid the compliment, regarding men in Wylie's word as "danger[ous]" (2): beguiling as in the French *dangereux* and memorable. Thus Wylie commends her lord's "chivalry" (4) and wisdom (3); his appealing hands (7); the terrible "symmetry" of his face (2); his virtue, which both extinguished her pride and fed her love. Millay, more combative, more carnal, struggles against her lover's "oblivious[ness]" (5), his "stormy" eyes that "lance [her] through" (9), his "Doubt[s]" (34). But once they are united, she explores the sexual experience with feminine candor. She notes "the desirous body's heat and sweat" (8), calls the lover a "sweet thorn" by whose "thrust" she is "slain" (17) and, long after the affair is ended, remembers masculine tenderness and

> Taking your love and all your loveliness
> Into a listening body hushed of sighs.
> [35]

In one way neither Wylie nor Millay had illusions about the permanence either of love or art. In a remarkable introductory sonnet to "One Person," Wylie declares that all her protestations of love and faith to follow will in a sense be "false," the words of an artificial and ephemeral legend. And Millay, realizing "it is folly to be sunk in love" (19), regards herself and her efforts to immortalize "one who love[d] me little if at all" (17) with scornful bravery: she sees herself the mere inhabitant of a ruined town, "beg[ging] from spectres by a broken arch" (37). Nevertheless, Wylie concludes her sonnet emphatically, echoing St. Paul to imply the endurance of love and language:

> Even the betrayer and the fond deceived,
> Having put off the body of this death,
> Shall testify with one remaining breath,
> From sepulchres demand to be believed:
> These words are true.

Millay, perhaps echoing Wylie, also declares

let the fortunate breathers of the air,
When we lie speechless in the muffling mound,
Tease not our ghosts with slander, pause not there
To say that love is false and soon grows cold,
But pass in silence the mute grave of two
Who lived and died believing love was true.

[31]

To write in the style of a particular period is temporarily to
assume its convictions. The Elizabethans were aware that individual
loves might die. The sonnet tradition, however, they surmised
would survive. Prompted by the cadences of the "Elizabethan" sonnets they composed, Edna St. Vincent Millay and Elinor Wylie
shared—and proclaimed—that conviction.

NOTE

1. All quotations from the poetry of Millay and Wylie are taken from
Collected Poems of Edna St. Vincent Millay, ed. Norma Millay (New York:
Harper and Row, 1956) and *Collected Poems* of Elinor Wylie, intro. by
William Rose Benét (New York: Knopf, 1932).

Bibliography of Writings and Editions by Louis L. Martz

BOOKS

The Later Career of Tobias Smollett (New Haven: Yale University Press, 1942). Reprinted by Archon Books, 1967.

The Poetry of Meditation: A Study in English Religious Literature of the Seventeenth Century (New Haven: Yale University Press, 1954). Second edition, revised, 1962. Ninth printing, 1978.

The Paradise Within: Studies in Vaughan, Traherne, and Milton (New Haven: Yale University Press, 1964).

The Poem of the Mind: Essays on Poetry, English and American (New York: Oxford University Press, 1966). Paperbound edition, slightly revised, 1969.

The Wit of Love: Donne, Carew, Crashaw, Marvell (University of Notre Dame Press, 1969). (The Ward-Phillips Lectures for 1968.)

Poet of Exile: A Study of Milton's Poetry (New Haven: Yale University Press, 1980).

ESSAYS ON SIXTEENTH- AND SEVENTEENTH-CENTURY LITERATURE

"John Donne in Meditation; *The Anniversaries*," *ELH* 14 (1947), 247–73.

"Donne and the Meditative Tradition," *Thought* 34 (1959), 269–78.

Foreword [on Edward Taylor's *Preparatory Meditations*] to *The Poems of Edward Taylor*, ed. Donald E. Stanford (New Haven: Yale University Press, 1960), pp. xiii–xxxvii.

"*Paradise Regained:* The Meditative Combat," *ELH* 27 (1960), 223–47.

"John Donne: The Meditative Voice," *Massachusetts Review* 1 (1960), 326–42.

"The *Amoretti:* Most Goodly Temperature," in *Form and Convention in the*

Poetry of Edmund Spenser, ed. William Nelson, English Institute Essays (New York: Columbia University Press, 1961), pp. 146–68.

"Henry Vaughan: The Man Within," *PMLA* 78 (1963), 40–49.

"The Rising Poet, 1645," in *The Lyric and Dramatic Milton,* ed. Joseph H. Summers, English Institute Essays (New York: Columbia University Press, 1965), pp. 3–33.

"The Design of More's *Dialogue of Comfort,*" *Moreana,* No. 15 (1967), 331–46.

"Chorus and Character in *Samson Agonistes,*" *Milton Studies* 1 (1969), 115–34.

"*Paradise Lost:* Princes of Exile," *ELH* 36 (1969), 232–49.

"*Paradise Lost:* The Power of Choice," *Ventures* 10 (1970), 37–47.

"The Action of the Self: Devotional Poetry in the Seventeenth Century," in *Stratford Upon Avon Studies, II: Metaphysical Poetry,* ed. Malcolm Bradbury and D. J. Palmer (London: Edward Arnold, 1970), pp. 101–21.

"*Paradise Lost:* The Realms of Light," *ELR* 1 (1971), 71–88.

"Camoens and Milton," *Ocidente* (Lisbon) 35 (1972), 45–58.

"Who is Lycidas?" *Yale French Studies,* No. 47 (1972), 170–88.

"Thomas More: The Tower Works," in *St. Thomas More: Action and Contemplation,* ed. R. S. Sylvester (New Haven: Yale University Press, 1972), pp. 59–83.

"Donne's *Anniversaries* Revisited," in *That Subtile Wreath: Lectures Presented at the Quatercentenary Celebration of the Birth of John Donne* (Agnes Scott College, 1973), pp. 29–55.

"Thomas More: the Sacramental Life," *Thought* 52 (1977), 300–18.

"*Paradise Lost:* the Solitary Way," in *The Author in his Work,* 1978 (see below), pp. 71–84.

"Marvell and Herrick: The Masks of Mannerism," in *Approaches to Marvell,* ed. C. A. Patrides (London: Routledge, 1978), pp. 194–215.

"More as Author: the Virtues of Digression," *Moreana* 16 (1979), 105–19.

"Shakespeare's Humanist Enterprise: *The Winter's Tale,*" in *English Renaissance Studies Presented to Dame Helen Gardner* (Oxford: Oxford University Press, Clarendon Press, 1980), pp. 114–31.

STUDIES IN EIGHTEENTH-CENTURY LITERATURE

"Smollett and the Expedition to Carthagena," *PMLA* 56 (1941), 428–46.

"Tobias Smollett and the *Universal History,*" *Modern Language Notes* 56 (1941), 1–14.

"Notes on Some Manuscripts Relating to David Garrick," *RES* 19 (1943), 186–200 (with E. M. Martz).

"Fanny Burney's *Evelina,*" in *The Age of Johnson: Essays Presented to Chauncey Brewster Tinker* (New Haven: Yale University Press, 1949), pp. 171–81 (with E. M. Martz).

Section on "Literature" in *Bibliography of British History: the Eighteenth Century, 1714–1789*, ed. Stanley Pargellis and D. J. Medley (Oxford: Oxford University Press, Clarendon Press, 1951), pp. 275–306 (with E. M. Martz).

ESSAYS ON TWENTIETH-CENTURY LITERATURE

"Wallace Stevens: The Romance of the Precise," *Yale Poetry Review*, No. 5 (1946), 13–20.

"The Wheel and the Point: Aspects of Imagery and Theme in Eliot's Later Poetry," *Sewanee Review* 55 (1947), 126–47. Revised for inclusion in *T. S. Eliot: A Selected Critique*, ed. Leonard Unger (New York: Rinehart, 1948), pp. 444–62.

"The World of Wallace Stevens," in *Modern American Poetry, Focus Five*, ed. B. Rajan (London: Dobson, 1950), pp. 94–109.

"William Carlos Williams: On the Road to *Paterson,*" *Poetry New York*, No. 4 (1951), 18–32.

"The Saint as Tragic Hero: *Saint Joan* and *Murder in the Cathedral,*" in *Tragic Themes in Western Literature*, ed. Cleanth Brooks (New Haven: Yale University Press, 1955), pp. 150–78.

"Wallace Stevens: The World as Meditation," *Yale Review* 47 (1958), 517–36; and in *Literature and Belief*, ed. M. H. Abrams, English Institute Essays (New York: Columbia University Press, 1958), pp. 139–65.

"The Unicorn in *Paterson:* William Carlos Williams," *Thought* 35 (1960), 537–54.

"A Greenhouse Eden," in *Theodore Roethke: Essays on the Poetry*, ed. Arnold Stein (Seattle: University of Washington Press, 1965), pp. 14–35.

"Portrait of Miriam: A Study in the Design of *Sons and Lovers,*" in *Imagined Worlds: Essays On Some English Novels and Novelists in Honour of John Butt*, ed. Maynard Mack and Ian Gregor (London: Methuen, 1968), pp. 343–69.

"Iris Murdoch: The London Novels," in *Harvard English Studies* 2: *Twentieth-Century Literature in Retrospect*, ed. Reuben A. Brower (Cambridge: Harvard University Press, 1971), pp. 65–86.

Introduction to the *Collected Early Poems of Ezra Pound* (New York: New Directions, 1976), pp. vii–xxii.

"Manuscripts of Wallace Stevens," *Yale University Library Gazette* 54
   (1979), 51–67.
"'From the Journal of Crispin': an Early Version of 'The Comedian as the
   Letter C,'" in *Wallace Stevens: A Celebration,* ed. Frank Doggett and
   Robert Buttel (Princeton: Princeton University Press, 1980), pp.
   3–29; with annotated edition of the "Journal," pp. 30–45.
Review essays on current poetry for the *Yale Review,* 1947–76: 37 (1947),
   333–41; 38 (1948), 144–51; 44 (1954), 301–309; 50 (1961), 141–47;
   54 (1964), 285–98; 54 (1965), 605–20; 55 (1966), 458–69; 56 (1966),
   275–84; 56 (1967), 593–603; 58 (1969), 592–605; 59 (1969), 252–67;
   59 (1970), 551–69; 60 (1971), 403–17; 61 (1972), 410–22; 66 (1976),
   114–29.

EDITED VOLUMES

The Pilgrim's Progress, by John Bunyan (New York: Rinehart, 1949).
The Meditative Poem: An Anthology of Seventeenth-Century Verse (New York:
   Doubleday-Anchor, 1963, paperback edition; New York University
   Press, 1963, hard cover edition); with introduction, notes, and com-
   mentary. Heavily revised and expanded as *The Anchor Anthology of
   Seventeenth-Century Verse,* vol. 1 (New York: Doubleday, 1969; re-
   printed by Norton, 1973).
Shakespeare's Poems . . . A Facsimile of the Earliest Editions (New Haven: Yale
   University Press, 1964); coedited with J. M. Osborn and E. M.
   Waith.
Milton: A Collection of Critical Essays [by various hands] (Englewood Cliffs:
   Prentice-Hall, 1966); with introduction on the "Milton controversy."
Thomas More's Prayer Book: A Facsimile Reproduction of the Annotated Pages
   (New Haven: Yale University Press, 1969); coedited with Richard
   Sylvester.
Hero and Leander, by Christopher Marlowe (Washington: Folger Shake-
   speare Library, 1972); a facsimile of the first edition, with introduction
   and textual commentary.
A Dialogue of Comfort against Tribulation, by Thomas More; the Yale
   Edition of the Complete Works of St. Thomas More, vol. 12 (New
   Haven: Yale University Press, 1976); coedited with Frank Manley.
   LLM was responsible for the text, textual notes, and 70 pages of the
   introduction.
The Author in his Work: Essays on a Problem in Criticism [in honor of
   Maynard Mack] (New Haven: Yale University Press, 1978); coedited
   with Aubrey Williams.

Index

The Elizabethan Club of Yale University has provided financial assistance for the preparation of this index.